Oral Histories of the Internet and the Web

The internet and the web are among the largest human-made technological artefacts ever created. Many facets of how these inventions came into being have been depicted in books and journal articles about the histories of the internet and the web. But the voices of those who took part in the creation and development of these technologies that have changed our culture and societies profoundly have only occasionally found a home.

Oral Histories of the Internet and the Web brings together a number of interviews with people who in various ways have affected the establishing and evolution of the internet and the web, and in contrast to the historical accounts these interviews give a sense of lived and living history. The interviews were originally published in the interdisciplinary journal *Internet Histories: Digital Technology, Culture and Society* between 2017 and 2022.

Niels Brügger is a professor of media studies at the School of Communication and Culture, Aarhus University, Denmark.

Gerard Goggin is the Wee Kim Wee Professor in the Department of Media and Communications, University of Sydney, Australia.

Oral Histories of the Internet and the Web

Edited by
Niels Brügger and Gerard Goggin

Routledge
Taylor & Francis Group

LONDON AND NEW YORK

First published 2023
by Routledge
4 Park Square, Milton Park, Abingdon, Oxon OX14 4RN

and by Routledge
605 Third Avenue, New York, NY 10158

Routledge is an imprint of the Taylor & Francis Group, an informa business

Introduction © Niels Brügger and Gerard Goggin
Chapters 1–13 and 15 © 2023 Taylor & Francis
Chapter 14 © 2020 Michael Stevenson and Anne Helmond. Originally published as Open Access.

British Library Cataloguing in Publication Data
A catalogue record for this book is available from the British Library

ISBN13: 978-1-032-33338-0 (hbk)
ISBN13: 978-1-032-33339-7 (pbk)
ISBN13: 978-1-003-31919-1 (ebk)

DOI: 10.4324/9781003319191

Typeset in Myriad Pro
by Newgen Publishing UK

Publisher's Note
The publisher accepts responsibility for any inconsistencies that may have arisen during the conversion of this book from journal articles to book chapters, namely the inclusion of journal terminology.

Disclaimer
Every effort has been made to contact copyright holders for their permission to reprint material in this book. The publishers would be grateful to hear from any copyright holder who is not here acknowledged and will undertake to rectify any errors or omissions in future editions of this book.

Contents

Section III: The web and digital cultures

Section IV: Methods

Citation Information

The following chapters were originally published in various issues of the journal *Internet Histories*. When citing this material, please use the original page numbering for each article, as follows:

Chapter 1
Tell us about...
Valérie Schafer
Internet Histories, volume 1, issue 1–2 (2017), pp. 188–196

Chapter 2
Conversations with a pioneer: Paul Baran in his own words
Morten Bay
Internet Histories, volume 1, issue 3 (2017), pp. 273–282

Chapter 3
Conversation with a pioneer: Leonard Kleinrock on the early days of networking, the ARPANET...and winning in Las Vegas
Morten Bay
Internet Histories, volume 2, issue 1–2 (2018), pp. 140–152

Chapter 4
Conversation with a pioneer: Larry Roberts on how he led the design and construction of the ARPANET
Morten Bay
Internet Histories, volume 3, issue 1 (2019), pp. 68–80

Chapter 5
French memories about the ARPANET: a conversation with Michel Élie and Gérard Le Lann
Camille Paloque-Bergès and Valérie Schafer
Internet Histories, volume 3, issue 1 (2018), pp. 81–97

Chapter 14

The historical trajectories of algorithmic techniques: an interview with Bernhard Rieder
Michael Stevenson and Anne Helmond
Internet Histories, volume 4, issue 1 (2020), pp. 105–114

Chapter 15

Internet histories and computational methods: a "round-doc" discussion
Niels Brügger, Ian Milligan, Anat Ben-David, Sophie Gebeil, Federico Nanni, Richard Rogers, William J. Turkel, Matthew S. Weber and Peter Webster
Internet Histories, volume 3, issue 3–4 (2019), pp. 202–222

For any permission-related enquiries please visit:
www.tandfonline.com/page/help/permissions

Notes on Contributors

Morten Bay, Annenberg School of Communication, Center for the Digital Future, University of California, Los Angeles, CA, USA.

Anat Ben-David, The Department of Sociology, Political Science and Communication, the Open University of Israel, Ra'anana, Israel.

Niels Brügger, School of Communication and Culture, Aarhus University, Denmark.

Elena Danescu, Centre for Contemporary and Digital History (C2DH) at the University of Luxembourg, Esch-sur-Alzette, Luxembourg.

Maria Eriksson, Humlab, Umea Universitet, Umeå, Sweden.

Andreas Fickers, Centre for Contemporary and Digital History (C²DH), University of Luxembourg, Esch-sur-Alzette, Luxembourg.

Sophie Gebeil, History, Aix-Marseille University, Marseille, France.

Gerard Goggin, Department of Media and Communications, University of Sydney, Australia.

Anne Helmond, Media Studies, University of Amsterdam, Amsterdam, Netherlands.

Guillaume Heuguet, GRIPIC, Sorbonne University, Paris, France.

David Howarth, Department of Social Sciences, University of Luxembourg, Esch, Luxembourg.

Ian Milligan, Department of History, University of Waterloo, Waterloo, Canada.

Julie Momméja, Institut de la Communication (ELICO), Université Lumière Lyon 2: Lyon, Auvergne-Rhône-Alpes, France.

Francesca Musiani, Centre National de la Recherche Scientifique (CNRS), Paris, France.

Federico Nanni, Data and Web Science Group, University of Mannheim, Mannheim, Germany.

Camille Paloque-Bergès, HT2S, Conservatoire National des Arts et Metiers, Paris, France.

Victoria Peuvrelle, Business Ananlyst, Barcelona, Catalonia, Spain.

Julia Pohlee, Wissenschaftszentrum Berlin fur Sozialforschung gGmbH, Berlin, Germany.

Richard Rogers, Department of Media Studies, University of Amsterdam, Amsterdam, the Netherlands.

Valérie Schafer, Contemporary European History (C²DH), University of Luxembourg, Esch-sur-Alzette, Luxembourg.

Ignacio Siles, School of Communication, Universidad de Costa Rica, San Jose, Costa Rica.

Michael Stevenson, Media Studies, University of Amsterdam, Amsterdam, Netherlands.

William J. Turkel, Department of History, The University of Western Ontario, London, Ontario, Canada.

Matthew S. Weber, Hubbard School of Journalism and Mass Communication, University of Minnesota, Minneapolis, MN, United States.

Peter Webster, School of Communication and Information, Rutgers University, USA.

Dwayne Winseck, Professor, School of Journalism and Communication, Carleton University, Ottawa, Canada.

Oral Histories of the Internet and the Web: An Introduction

Niels Brügger and Gerard Goggin

Oral histories in Internet Histories

Many facets of how the internet and the web came into being have been depicted in books and journal articles. But the voices of those who took part in the creation, adoption, and development of these technologies that have changed our culture and societies profoundly have only occasionally found a home.

The following pages bring together a number of interviews with people who in various ways have affected and have been affected by the establishment and evolution of the Internet and the web, and in contrast to the historical accounts these interviews give a sense of lived and living history. In addition, the voices of some of the academics who have discussed how the histories of the Internet and the web can be studied are included. The interviews have been published in the interdisciplinary journal *Internet Histories: Digital Technology, Culture and Society* between 2017 and 2022. Since its 2017 founding, one of the hallmarks of the journal has been its interviews with people who have played a role in the history of the Internet and the web. With this edited volume we are marking the journal's fifth anniversary by publishing all the interviews that have been published in the first 5 years of the journal's lifetime.

Oral histories as a source genre

The Internet, and in particular the web are young media artefacts, but they are coming of age and they have both crossed the 30-year line that is often used as a criterion for considering a topic relevant to study in a contemporary historical perspective (Winters, 2017, p. 239).

When writing contemporary history it can be challenging to get the needed distance to the events of the past because they may still impact the present in very direct ways which can blur the interpretation. But contemporary historiography also comes with an advantage, namely that well-known source types can be supplemented with oral accounts from the people who took part in or witnessed events and activities in the recent past.

In his critical review of developments in the international history of oral history, Alistair Thomson (2007) identifies four paradigmatic revolutions in the theory and practice of oral history since the field's emergence after World War II:

> the postwar renaissance of memory as a source for "people's history"; the development, from the late 1970s, of "post-positivist" approaches to memory and subjectivity; a transformation in perceptions about the role of the oral historian as interviewer and analyst from the late 1980s; and the digital revolution of the late 1990s and early 2000s.
>
> (Thomson, 2007, p. 50)

One of the recurring topics of discussion within all four phases of oral historiography iden-tified by Thomson is that of the possible unreliability of memory. There may be several reasons why memory is potentially an unreliable historical source. At a minimum, the following four interconnected issues are relevant to have in mind when doing and reading oral history. First, it is very likely that the interviewee does not remember all aspects of what happened in the past, and therefore to some extent the oral history is a reconstruction of past events. The oral history also is created in a kind of singularity, with the interviewer and interview coming together. Further, memory is often influenced by the broader 'cultural memory' of an institution, so this kind of interplay is involved in the reconstruction also. Second, when doing this reconstruction the interviewee – and partly also the interviewer – on the one hand has to forget what happened after the event in question, with a view to remembering the openness of possible actions or roads to be taken in the past, of which only some became "the future" (now part of today's past), while, on the other hand, still remembering what actually came later because what followed after the event may pro-vide an interpretative lense on the past. Third, interviewees may have stakes in interpreting the past, including their own role, and in that sense the reconstruction based on memory may be guided by an agenda of putting one's own actions or ideas in a positive light while downplaying those of others. Fourth, the fact that the interviewee is being asked to par-ticipate in an interview may also play a role as to what is remembered. The interviewee is offered a platform, and the interview relationship entails that the interviewee is expected to remember something, just as the concrete questions and topics of the conversation will also (partly) determine what is remembered.

However, despite these reservations oral histories also constitute a rich source type that can be used on a par with other source types. As a historical method oral history comes with some advantages that should not be overlooked. It is possible to have stories told that otherwise would remain untold, in many cases because the interviewee's actions in the past have not left material traces. Also, oral histories provide insights into how the past is consciously and unconsciously remembered and interpreted in the interviewee's subjective ways of seeing the past in the present, including what is not remembered, and in that sense oral histories constitute a privileged window into how meaning is added to the past. Finally, oral histories enable the direct conversation with and about a source, as pointed out by Paul Thompson:

> Every historical source derived from human perception is subjective, but only the oral source allows us to challenge that subjectivity : to unpick the layers of memory, dig back into its darknesses, hoping to reach the hidden trouth.
>
> (Thompson, 2000, p. 173)

In summary, oral histories should be approached in the same reflexive and cautious way as any other historical source and method, and they should be evaluated with the same source critical yardstick as any other narrated source type: Who are talking? With whom? Why? With what aim? In what context? And when read or used in historical studies its con-tent should be cross-checked with other sources to evaluate the consistency and credibility of its message.

The partiality and diversity of Internet oral histories

The collection of these interviews that appeared across the foundational years of the *Internet Histories* journal provides an opportunity to reflect on who, what topics, and what kind of framing features in these texts. In relation to the "pioneers", there are distinct absences and biases that go deep and have been the subject of significant scholarship in the field (Abbate, 1999, 2012). This is despite the ways in which the journal seeks to aim to register, promote, and advance research, analysis, and theory on the ways in which Internet, web, and digital cultures are constituted internationally, across categories and relations of difference, geographies, and power.

It is evident, for instance, a number of the interviews include celebrated figures from the period of the Internet in which North America played a leading role. Due especially to the historiographical leadership of co-editor Valérie Schafer and her European colleagues, such as Camille Paloque-Berges (who has also contributed interviews here), we hear from key figures from elsewhere in the world and gain a clearer sense of the interplay among technical, infrastructure, economic, and cultural developments of the Internet around the world. There are accounts included from South Korea and Costa Rica that underscore the specificity and regionality of Internet histories as much as their translocal, cross-regional, and transnational character. Accordingly, we are keen to greatly expand the range of locations, perspectives, and perhaps most fundamentally, characterization of Internet pioneers that feature in future oral histories and interviews (Goggin & McLelland, 2018).

One particular absence is flagged by Schafer in her interview to the first oral history text carried in the journal, based on responses from various pioneers: "One can certainly note the absences in this mixture of perspectives, among which the notable absence of women — not because we have neglected to contact them, but because they did not reply" (Schafter, 2017, p. 188). The imbalance in gender is evident in the interviews with pioneers generally in this collection, perhaps reflecting the early shaping of the Internet. However, in both the interviewees and interviewers across the full set of pieces collected here, we see greater diversity across gender in tandem with broadening and great mixity of conceptions of the Internet as documented in much research (among many others, see: Nakamura, 2005, 2008; Noble & Tynes, 2016; Paasonen, 2005; Ramos & Mowlabocus, 2020; White, 2015, 2019). Indeed it is an emerging priority of the journal to centre these voices that have been missing.

A quality of this volume may well be that the conceptual and historical yield of oral histories alongside the need for care and reflexivity is brought to the fore because of the mix of kinds of historical conversations that are collected. As noted, there are interviews conducted seeking to elicit, explore, and record the perspectives of Internet pioneers; there are also interviews with researchers and theorists which aim to trace and bring to light the interplay between histories of Internet, web, and digital cultures, on the one hand, and the concepts, methods, practices, values, and contexts of those studying them (and the settings, movements, and institutions in which such investigators are embedded). In the roundtables on markets, policy and governance, and technology, or digital and computational methods, or interviews with intellectuals and theorists that bring into play art, culture, social movements, and politics, or underpinning concepts such as authentication – the sum total may well be to enlarge the charmed circle of what counts as a pioneering contribution, by which actors, where, and in what kind of orchestrations. After all, a thread in the interviews among the garlanded early Internet pioneers of the 1960s and 1970s is who received credit, and did it make sense, given the collaborative nature of much of the technology developments.

One feature of contemporary interviews shaped by the very same digital technologies that are at stake is the capacity for interviews to be approached as a co-production or collaboration between interviewer/s and their interlocutors. After all, conversation and dialogue is always relational and collaborative by nature. Networked digital technology makes it easier for interviews to be updated, reworked, and amended prior to publication. The appropriation of digital technology for interviewing involved experimentation over many years. One obvious example can be found in the temporality and terms of engagement of an interview, which can also be recast: hence the rise of asynchronous interviewing by email. One of the interviewees in this anthology, Geert Lovink pioneered this form conducting interviews online over weeks and months that were collected in his book *Uncanny Networks* (Lovink, 2002). Lovink makes a case for the multi-faceted nature of interviews as well as their role in creating connections:

> Interviews are all about creating contexts, together with chats and debates, reviews, links, and other reference systems … Interviews are one of the many sorts of imaginative text one can use in creating common, networked discourses.
>
> (Lovink, 2002, p. 5)

Especially since the COVID pandemic, interviews will be conducted using many other Internet technologies as well as audio, visual, textual, computational, and other media.

In this volume what further expands the repertoire and reach of the interview for oral histories is the addition of the roundtable including in the guise of what is dubbed, in the age of software as conversational architecture, the "round-doc". The roundtables collected here have the advantage of including multiple voices. They also can more easily include speakers who do not have the burden of being under the "spotlight" of pioneer, expert, and so on. The loss of space, focus, and development of responses, due to turn-taking of participants and simply less time, as the diminished expectation that the listener may concentrate less on the one exceptional individual, is offset by the production of a more comprehensive and diverse set of resources – a fuller indication of the historical threads to be disentangled and followed through.

Structure of the book

The interviews of this book are structured in four main sections, each focusing on a specific theme in Internet histories (numbers and years in parenthesis after each title below refer to the volume and issue of *Internet Histories* where the interview was first published, followed by year).

The first section entitled "The Internet" brings together conversations with people who took part in the early development of the ARPANET and the Internet, and who constitute a relatively small international network community, which is also why the same actors, groups, and organisations appear in several of the conversations. The interviews of this and the following section thus constitute elements of a transnational Internet history. In "Tell us about..." (1(1–2), 2017) Vinton Cerf, Steve Crocker, Abhaya Induruwa, Dennis Jennings, John Klensin, Gerard Le Lann, Paul Mockapetris, and Ted Nelson testify to the early Internet "spirit" as they perceived and lived it, and they contribute with thoughts on protocols and technical architectures, the applications and uses of the Internet, its evolving governance, the complex and collective processes, genealogies and trajectories of innovation, as well as national and transnational issues across continents and countries, from the United States and France to Sri Lanka.

Then follows three "Conversations with a pioneer" that were all made by Morten Bay from a series he conducted. In "Conversations with a pioneer: Paul Baran in his own words" (1(3), 2017) Paul Baran talks about the histories of networking and the Internet, including his version of the history of one of the core ideas behind the Internet, packet switching. Also, Baran shares his views on technological development and determinism and his hopes for the future of the Internet.

"Conversation with a pioneer: Leonard Kleinrock on the early days of networking, the ARPANET...and winning in Las Vegas" (2(1–2), 2018) address a vast array of issues and topics related to establishing a well-functioning large scale computer network, the ARPANET. Additionally, this interview highlights the pivotal approach of breaking messages into "blocks of data" is pivotal, and the reader can also learn more about the development and implementation of the first switch, the Interface Message Processor (IMP).

The construction, expansion, and spread of the ARPANET network is also the central theme in "Conversation with a pioneer: Larry Roberts on how he led the design and construction of the ARPANET" (3(1), 2019). In addition, the conversation tells the story of early pre-network connecting of two computers through a telephone line, just as it adds new facets to the history of the development and spread of email.

In the second section – "Global perspectives" – the view is broadened to include the voices of the mediators between the development of the Internet in the United States and elsewhere, including histories of computer networks outside of the United States. The section opens with "French memories about the ARPANET: a conversation with Michel Élie and Gérard Le Lann" (3(1), 2019) where focus is on the US experience of the two French interviewees and how they participated in and linked the development environments in the United States to those of Europe. Topics discussed include the need for standardisation as well as when the first nodes came into activity and how the TCP/IP protocol was developed.

The second interview of this section, "25 Years of the Internet in Central America: an interview with Guy de Téramond" (1(4), 2017) tells the story about how Costa Rica was connected to BITNET and later to the Internet in the early 1990s, and how the spread of the Internet in Central America in the 1990s and 2000s was pushed forward. This includes accounts of the political and technical challenges related to introducing and expanding the Internet in the different national contexts.

The section's third interview takes us to Asia. The interview "The real 'poor man's Arpanet'? A conversation about Unix networks with Kilnam Chon, godfather of the Asian Internet" (5(3–4), 2021) tells a story about how the international distributed UUCP network based on machines running on the Unix system was introduced and expanded in South Korea, a development that ran in parallel with becoming connected to the Internet. In continuation of this the interview also focuses on the UUCP network's role in the spreading of early digital networks in Asia.

"The internet and the European market" from a multidisciplinary perspective: a "round-doc" discussion" (4(2), 2020) is an interdisciplinary round table discussion that takes place in written form, hence the term "round-doc" discussion. The conversation adopts a Europe-wide and political/economic perspective when discussing Europe in global histories of the Internet,

European integration, and governance issues. The participants David Howarth, Francesca Musiani, Julia Pohle, and Dwayne Winseck touch upon a wide range of topics, including privacy, data protection, copyright, and net neutrality, and the conversation is rounded off with reflections on possible avenues for future research about the Internet and the EU market.

Europe and the EU is also the focus of the last conversation in this section, but now from the perspective of someone who has been deeply involved in policy debates and decisions in the EU. In the interview "Viviane Reding on her action in the field of the information society and media (2004–2010)" (4(2), 2020) Viviane Reding, a former Member of the European Parliament, and of the European Commission, introduces the reader to key elements of the political context in which digital media like the Internet is embedded in Europe. The conversation highlights how the decision-making process was carried out in relation to important regulations of digital media and the Internet, including the General Data Protection Regulation (GDPR), contract law, e-government, e-learning, e-health, and public–private partnerships.

When reading the interviews in the first two sections about the establishing of the Internet in different national or regional settings one recurring theme stands out: the negative or ambiguous role of telecommunication operators. According to many of the interviewees in the early days of computer networks telecommunication operators constantly questioned the feasability of networking, and they did so in different ways, from being reluctant and delaying development in various ways, to working against or directly obstructing the establishing of computer networks, including the Internet. If these oral histories can be accepted at face value the Internet was created in spite of everything. From a historiographical point of view these oral histories call for further cross-national studies to understand the nexus between, on the one hand, telecommunication operators' delaying of the development of the networks, and, on the other hand, the stubbornness and staying power of the network enthusiasts, not to say 'evangelists', the term used by Guy de Téramond in the interview with him.

In the third section – "The web and digital cultures" – the World Wide Web, and the digital cultures that developed with the advent of the web are brought into focus. In the interview "Behind the scenes: an interview with Pierre Beyssac" (2(3–4), 2018) French web specialist Pierre Beyssac tells the story of his itinerary as a "digital native", from the 1980s to the beginning of the 2000s. His path illustrates a general trend from being an amateur in the computer network area (including email and newsgroups) to becoming first a "pro-am", a professional amateur to finally establishing himself as a true professional. An important part of the story is the introduction of the web in France and the co-founding of Gandi, a French company that was involved in the country's growing market of domain names.

The establishing and development of digital cultures is at the heart of "Interfacing counterculture and digital cultures: an interview with Geert Lovink" (2(3–4), 2018). The interview tells the story about the many actors who in the mid-1990s were part of the digital cultures scene in the Netherlands, from media activists, media artists, and programmers to designers, cultural producers, and researchers. Also, the establishing of some of the venues for this development are unpacked, including the *Mediamatic Magazine*, the community access network De Digitale Stad Amsterdam (DDS), the Internet art space desk.nl, and the Nettime discussion forum and network.

Creating communities with digital networks is the topic of "'I am an engineer and therefore a radical': an interview with Lee Felsenstein, from Free Speech Movement technician to Homebrew Computer Club moderator" (5(2), 2021). We learn about the story of the first public semi-virtual community "Community Memory" that was established in the San Francisco Bay Area, as well as of the Homebrew Computer Club (founded in 1975), out of which 23 companies originated (Apple being one of them). A common thread in the interview is the focus on supporting the exchange of information among people by digital means with a view to creating communities of interest.

The "Interview with Aleksandra Kaminska" (5(1), 2021) takes up a specific theme related to digital cultures at large, namely how authenticity and identity of things is ensured in a digital world. This topic is addressed by focusing on the material side of "authentication devices", and by adopting a historical perspective that highlights the continuities between the analogue (e.g. secure printing used for banknotes and passports) and the digital realm, as well as the hybrid forms of analogue-digital.

Section 4 – "Methods" – presents two chapters where focus is on the methodological challenges related to studying different aspects of computer networks and of their histories. "The historical trajectories of algorithmic techniques: an interview with Bernhard Rieder" (4(1), 2020) revolves around a broad discussion of historiography as a method to understand our digital present. It demonstrates that continuity and discontinuity emerge and are combined in complicated ways, and therefore historical work is important with a view to identifying and mapping these lineages. Finally, a call is made for historiographical work being attentive to technology, whereby it can serve as an example and as a vehicle for technical culture.

The book is rounded off with another "round-doc" conversation that brings together leading experts within the field of computational methods and historiography. In "Internet histories and computational methods: a 'round-doc' discussion" (3(3–4), 2019) Anat Ben-David, Sophie Gebeil, Federico Nanni, Richard Rogers, William J. Turkel, Matthew S. Weber and Peter Webster contribute to the discussion of how digitally based methods can be used when writing history in general, and Internet and web histories in particular. Topics discussed include questions such as why scholars of Internet histories should consider using computational methods, what scholars should be looking out for when they use these methods, how the process of collecting influences computational research, what impedes the use of computational methods, to what an extent Internet historians should learn to code (or conversely, if developers should learn about historical methods), what are the most defining moments in the history of computational methods, and, finally, the future of using computational methods for historical studies of the Internet.

Acknowledgements

We wish to thank everyone involved in creating these interviews and this book.

Our thanks first to the interviewers and interviewees, as well as the participants in the roundtable and round-doc. We are grateful for their efforts, conversations, and contribution in the first place, and support for their publication in this form.

We thank Taylor & Francis for accepting the proposal for bringing together the interviews as an edited volume, and especially our editor Robinson Raju for his exemplary work.

Finally, our thanks to the rest of the *Internet Histories* editorship collective for reviewing, editing, and publishing these interviews, and for their feedback for this project. In particular, we thank and acknowledge Valérie Schafer for her clear insistence on the importance of making interviews a foundational element of the journal, and for her outstanding practice in the genre.

References

Abbate, J. (1999). *Inventing the Internet*. MIT Press.

Abbate, J. (2012). *Recoding computing: Women's changing participation in computing*. MIT Press.

Goggin, G., & McLelland, M. (Eds.). (2018). *Routledge companion to global Internet histories*. Routledge.

Lovink, G. (2002). *Uncanny networks: Dialogues with the virtual intelligentsia*. MIT Press.

Nakamura, L. (2005). *Cybertypes: Race, ethnicity, and identity on the Internet*. Routledge.

Nakamura, L. (2008). *Digitizing race: Visual cultures of the Internet*. University of Minnesota Press.

Noble, S., & Tynes, B. M. (Eds.). (2016). *The intersectional Internet: race, sex, class, and culture online*. Peter Lang.

Paasonen, S. (2005). *Figures of fantasy: Internet, women, and cyberdiscourse*. Peter Lang.

Ramos, R., & Mowlabocus, S. (Eds.). (2020). *Queer sites in global contexts: Technologies, spaces, and otherness*. Routledge.

Schafer, V. (2017). Tell us about … *Internet Histories*, *1*(1–2), 188–196. https://doi.org/10.1080/24701 475.2017.1301132

Thompson, P. (2000). *The voice of the past: Oral history*. Oxford University Press.

Thomson, A. (2007). Four paradigm transformations in oral history. *The Oral History Review*, *34*(1), 49–70, DOI: 10.1525/ohr.2007.34.1.49

White, M. (2015). *Producing woman: The Internet, traditional feminity, queerness, and creativity*. Routledge.

White, M. (2019). *Producing masculinity: The Internet, gender, and sexuality*. Routledge.

Winters, J. (2017). Coda: Web archives for humanities research—some reflections. In N. Brügger & R. Schroeder (Eds.), *The Web as History: Using Web Archives to Understand the Past and the Present* (pp. 238–248). UCL Press.

Section I
The internet

Tell us about... (Vinton Cerf, Steve Crocker, Abhaya Induruwa, Dennis Jennings, John Klensin, Gerard Le Lann, Paul Mockapetris and Ted Nelson)

Valérie Schafer

Notwithstanding Andrew Russell's warnings within this first issue to refrain from adopting a hagiographic relationship to Internet pioneers and core actors – and definitely keeping them in mind – we could not resist the opportunity to share their viewpoint with you. So, after the perspectives of historians on Internet history and its actors, it is their turn to give us a little bit of theirs...

By means of open and sometimes slightly "shifted" questions (for example, on their enthusiasm as Internet users rather than developers – in fact in the early days of the Internet, they are usually "user-developers" –, or what they would change or relive in the history of the Internet), well-known pioneering actors Vinton Cerf, Steve Crocker, Abhaya Induruwa, Dennis Jennings, John Klensin, Gérard Le Lann, Paul Mockapetris and Ted Nelson address a vast array of issues and topics which fully align with those of our journal: protocols and technical architectures, the applications and uses of the Internet, its evolving governance, the complex and collective processes, genealogies and trajectories of innovation, as well as national and transnational issues across continents and countries, from the United States and France to Sri Lanka.

Although our approach is different from the full-fledged academic interviews that will then fill this section, in these short and crossed interviews we have tried to capture a bit of the early Internet "spirit" as these actors perceived and lived it. One can certainly note the absences in this mixture of perspectives, among which the notable absence of women – not because we have neglected to contact them, but because they did not reply. However, a number of original viewpoints come out of the following pages, telling us a great deal about collectives, communities, a *Zeitgeist* where ideas, innovations and actors circulated. These pioneers unveil an effervescent, nascent world, the memories of which include technical issues as well as human, political and societal ones.

It is now time to leave the stage to Vinton Cerf, Steve Crocker, Abhaya Induruwa, Dennis Jennings, John Klensin, Gérard Le Lann, Paul Mockapetris and Ted Nelson, but not before thanking them warmly for having indulged in this short exercise with benevolence and generosity.

Valérie Schafer for the Editors

Tell us about … one of your best memories as a pioneer/key actor in Internet and/or Web history…

Ted Nelson, who launched the Xanadu project, which, according to Pierre Lévy was the "absolute horizon of hypertext", opens the list of these souvenirs by going back to the mid-1960s.

> In 1965, shortly after my presentation at the ACM national conference, I got a direct call from the director of information processing research for the Central Intelligence Agency. He came to my house and said they would fund my work. I was excited - I thought I would get a great setup, and that I would give my government a system they badly needed, thus improving our nation's understanding and policy.

Steve Crocker, whose pivotal role in ARPANET and the RFCs is readily acknowledged, goes back to the end of the 1960s.

> I was one of the graduate students at UCLA that put the first node on the Arpanet. I helped develop the initial suite of protocols for the Arpanet, created the RFCs and formed and led the Network Working Group, the forerunner of today's IETF. I also spent three years at DARPA. I've watched network technology and use take off from the initial four nodes in the western part of the U.S. to become an intimate part of lives around the globe.

> In 1973, the Arpanet was in full bloom. The Internet, i.e. interconnection of multiple independent networks, was envisioned but not yet underway. Nonetheless it was already evident how the net was changing the lives of the people who were connected to it. As a program manager at DARPA, I interacted with a number of different parts of the U.S. military. One day at a meeting I introduced two Air Force captains to each other that I had been working with separately. After I introduced them to each other, I stepped back and they continued to talk. When they finished, they asked each other for their email addresses instead of their military system phone numbers (Autovon) I knew each of them had. I knew then network connectivity would become universal.

From ARPANET to the Internet, three key dates have persisted in **Vinton Cerf**'s memory within a path he has largely contributed to trace. Two of them are particularly well known by historians, and considered as fundamental steps in Internet history:

> November 22, 1977 – First demonstration of a three-network Internet using the Defense Advanced Research Projects Agency networks: ARPANET, Packet Radio Net and Packet Satellite Net.

> May 1974 – Publication of the first paper describing TCP and the architecture of the Internet in IEEE Transactions on Communications, May 1974

> January 1, 1983 – the day we officially declared the Internet operational.

The Seventies are indeed an effervescent period – French pioneer **Gérard Le Lann**, at the time working within the Cyclades project, launched at the *Institut de recherche en informatique et automatique* in 1971, remembers it well…

> Between October 1972 and April 1973, I had built a large simulation program (in Simula-67) for studying the dynamic behaviours of the Arpanet NCP protocol and the early versions of the Cyclades protocols. They suffered from unexplained erratic dysfunctions (e.g. blocking, losses, memory overflows). Causes and remedies were found, notably how to reliably open and close end-to-end connections despite losses or excessively long delays, and the sliding

window mechanism for end-to-end error and flow control (elimination of reassembly lock-ups). My Cyclades colleagues were the first to know, Hubert Zimmermann in particular. Updated versions of the Cyclades protocols were implemented end of 1973. I visited Vint Cerf at Stanford (Digital Systems Lab.) in April 1973, showing him my simulation results. Vint invited me to join his Arpanet team, which I did until summer 1974.

I vividly recall the numerous brainstorming meetings with Vint, at his house in Palo Alto, sitting on the ground for examining the large print outputs of the Simula-67 programs, and combining my findings with the on-going revisions of NCP undertaken by the Arpanet community (Robert Kahn, BBN, etc.). These novel schemes became essential constituents of the original TCP protocol. Great times in what was not yet named Silicon Valley!

The official launch of the Internet in the early eighties, and its distinction from ARPA-NET, opens up the way to the network of networks' steady rise within civil society, led by the scientific and academic world and the development of local and regional networks – as reminded by **Dennis Jennings**, the first Program Director for Networking at the National Science Foundation in 1985–1986 …

One of my best memories is the trip that I made to Cornell University to talk about the NSFnet plans.

The first thing I remember about that trip is that the weather was exceedingly hot (July or August 1985, I think) and I travelled in shorts and a short sleeved shirt - and the airline lost my luggage! So I had to go into Cornell and meet the people there the following day in the clothes that I had travelled in! Not my style at all.

More importantly, after my talk about the emerging plans for NSFnet, the Cornell people gave me a presentation on their ideas for NYSERNet, the New York State Education and Research network. At the end of the presentation they asked me whether the NSF would be interested in assisting with funding. I was very enthusiastic, because I realised that the development of State and Regional networks would greatly leverage my limited NSF budget, and, more importantly, would expand the community of teams of networking experts working on the vision of a US national research and education network of networks - or internet. I confirmed my enthusiastic personal support (with, as usual, the caveat that I could not speak for the NSF, and that the NSFnet programme had its own procedures to follow). This meeting stimulated me to publish the NSF Solicitation for Proposals for Regional Networks as part of the NSFnet programme.

Since the eighties, the interest in networks is evident in several countries and progressively extends to all continents. **Abhaya Induruwa**, who developed a Local Area Networking strategy in 1986–1987, funded by a Japanese government grant and implemented within the Department of Computer Science and Engineering which he founded in 1985 at the University of Moratuwa (Sri Lanka), and who then proposed to set-up Lanka Experimental Academic and Research Network (LEARN) in April 1989 to the Sri Lankan government, notes that one of his best memories is

… meeting great Internet pioneers like Vint Cerf, George Sadowsky, Ben Segal, Randy Bush, etc., in the early nineties and getting inspiration to make the seemingly impossible possible. In the late eighties I started building an Internet in Sri Lanka literally with no money. My struggles bore fruit in 1995. Never in my wildest dreams did I imagine that, two decades later, I would be fortunate to share space on the Internet Hall of Fame with such Internet greats!

Tell us about one of your best memories as an Internet or Web user ...

Email, Mosaic, medical applications: those who have contributed to the Internet's first steps – oftentimes among the first in their countries – are, in the early days, designers-users. Asking them what impressed and enthused them, and not just what they contributed to, led us to discover...

... the enthusiasm of one of the Internet's founding fathers, **Vinton Cerf**, in front of the Web and of Mosaic:

> Seeing the avalanche of content arrive on the Internet via the WWW after the introduction of the MOSAIC Browser by Marc Andreessen and Eric Bina at the National Center for Supercomputer Applications at the University of Illinois at Urbana-Champagne.

That of **Steve Crocker**, faced with the power of a governance he contributed to build himself, by organising the Network Working Group and initiating the Request for Comments (RFCs):

> In September 1994 I gave a talk at the Indian Institute of Science in Bangalore, India. Afterwards I was introduced to a graduate student who had built an impressive system that combined several pieces of technology. I asked him how he had learned how to do all of this. He said he downloaded and read the RFCs and put all the pieces together. I was struck by the power of system of protocols, documents, and open access we had set in motion 25 years earlier.

Gérard Le Lann's, for the open, networked communication the Internet made possible:

> As a user, I have two best memories. The first one (chronological order) may seem incredibly naïve to contemporary readers: my first email from the West Coast to the East Coast. That was in 1973. The second one is my first experience in distributed co-writing. In 1982, from Rocquencourt, France (IRIA premises), I had to write a few chapters for a book (Distributed Systems - Architecture and Implementation, An Advanced Course, D.W. Davies and B.W. Lampson Editors), to be shipped to Maynard (MA), USA (B. Lampson was with Digital Equipment Corp.), and corrected interactively on-line. At that time, IRIA had access to the Internet via the MIT (MA). It worked very smoothly.

And the same taste for "real-time", but in another field, retraced by **Abhaya Induruwa**...

> ... organising a workshop in Colombo, Sri Lanka in September 1995 on the « Use of Internet for Medical Practitioners » and demonstrating data from Visible Human Project in real-time. For those who had previously seen and used WAIS and Gopher, accessing and displaying images in full colour, and in real-time, was a sensational experience.

Or the plurality of uses allowed, as reminded by **Dennis Jennings**, by performance improvements:

> In summer 1985 I had dial-up access to the ARPANET. One of the frustrations of using the ARPANET at that time was that the IMPs (routers) could only hold a cache of a small number of addresses (64 I was told!) and increasingly often the address of the site one wanted to access was not in the cache and there would be a long delay before connectivity could be established (the DNS was being designed at around that time by Paul Mockapetris). One day that summer the cache and software was upgraded to support double the number of addresses. Performance was suddenly greatly improved!

Should you choose one date/event in Internet history that you would like to live again, and one that you would like to change, what would they be?

Speaking of happiness and regrets with pioneers, technology is never very far away, as testified by **Steve Crocker**:

> We made a major mistake in the design of some of the early protocols when we allowed addresses to be communicated as ordinary data. The File Transfer Protocol (FTP), for example, passes the address of one of the parties to another as part of the data instead of the control. We should have used a bit of encapsulation and indirection to treat addresses as objects. If we had done so, the transition from IPv4 to IPv6 would have been manageable and nearly seamless. I remember feeling queasy when FTP was designed, and I had tried to do something different within the underlying Host-Host protocol. (The Host-Host protocol, later called the Network Control Protocol, was the predecessor to TCP). My particular proposal was not accepted by the community and there wasn't clear recognition of the importance of treating addresses as a special object. I wish we had been able to articulate the importance of treating addresses as objects.

and **Vinton Cerf** ...

> I think it would not work but I would have chosen a larger IP address space than 32 bits if I had realized that we would have hand-held smart phones and the Internet of Things. As it is we have to move to IPv6 and its 128 bit address space as quickly as we can. I also wish it had been feasible to introduce public key cryptography sooner into the system.

Notwithstanding the moments of "grace", as **Abhaya Induruwa** recollects:

> What would be a date/event in Internet History that I would like to live again ... the day in 1986 when we connected a Radio Shack TRS80 running Xenix at the University of Moratuwa to a similar computer at the University of Colombo using UUCP over a 300 baud modem connected to a telephone line. The moment we saw the login prompt from the remote computer on our screen at Moratuwa ... Little did we realize that this moment marked the beginning of the computer networking era in Sri Lanka. Some important milestones followed such as the first Ethernet LAN in a Sri Lankan University (at the University of Moratuwa) in 1987; first Internet based email (LEARNmail) in 1990; first IP WAN (LEARN) in 1994 and finally, after less than a decade from this moment, connecting LEARN to the Internet in 1995.

or **Gérard Le Lann**:

> The inception of one of the very first distributed algorithms, published in 1977 - IFIP Congress 1977[1], is one of the most exciting moments in my scientific carrier.

> The discovery of synchronization problems in networks where two distant processes (end-to-end connections) shall interact correctly through time varying and lossy channels prompted me to look at the general problems arising in systems where n (n > 2) processes need to coordinate their behaviours, despite differing individual views of "current system state" and no central locus of control. The Distributed Computing discipline emerged from Computer Networking in 1976. I could "sense" that this terra incognita was a mine of fascinating problems. This is the reason why my research interests bifurcated from network protocols to distributed algorithms at that time. It turns out that those algorithms devised in the late 70's and the 80's are at the origin of numerous system solutions implemented nowadays in the Web, in large databases, in search engines or in clouds.

> A date/event I would like to change: the overlooking of anonymity requirements in Arpanet/Internet communication protocols, requirements, which are now so much essential with mobile networking. Voluntary (e.g. beaconing as suggested for autonomous/automated

vehicles) or unintended disclosure of – and reliance on – IP addresses or MAC addresses is a risk-prone feature, especially when enriched with time-dependent geolocations. It would have been wise to offer at least two options with TCP/IP-based communications, public (well known) naming and anonymous naming. Privacy rests on the ability for every process to compute names that are unique, in a certain geographical zone or/and during a certain time interval, no third-party involved.

That was a terribly hard-to-solve problem in the 70's, with static processes in wired/managed networks. Nowadays, with mobile processes forming ad-hoc short-lived or long-lived open networks, that problem is even more difficult.

Beyond these moments of technical doubt or clear success, there are human adventures too, as **Ted Nelson,** who coined the term hypertext in 1965, testimonies:

In 1988, when our Xanadu Project got major funding, a programmer threatened to quit because my partner Roger Gregory, who was in charge of development, had become tyrannical. I did not ask Roger his side of the story, and acted swiftly to reduce his authority. If I had not done this, Xanadu might have been the international hypertext system, instead of the World Wide Web.

That is the day I would like to live again, and change.

However, there was the feeling to contribute to an adventure, either grasped at the right time or with some delay. **Paul Mockapetris,** who created and developed the Domain Name System (DNS) since 1983, recalls:

One of my happiest moments was when RFC 974, the specification for email routing over DNS was published.[2] This was the first application of my invention, DNS, which I didn't do myself, and proved that others were on the way to adoption.

I'd like to relive the transition from ARPAnet to TCP/IP protocols that happened January 1983. This culminated years of work and thought that essentially replaced all of the network architecture.

If I could change one decision, I probably should have joined the start of Internet commercialization when I finished my tour at ARPA.

It was also about slightly modify one's path, or changing temporalities and mindsets, **Abhaya Induruwa** reminds us:

What would be one that I would like to change … the date we finally connected Sri Lanka to the global Internet … it would have been better if we were able to do this earlier than 1995. In the eighties I was influenced by the trends in the UK and Europe and their efforts in trying to steer ahead with ISO-OSI so my first proposal in 1989 for a country-wide network for Sri Lanka was obviously based on X.25 technology. By the early nineties it was clear that X.25 was disappearing and TCP/IP was here to stay. In January 1992 I reformulated the proposal encompassing TCP/IP technology and resubmitted it to the Sri Lankan government. I now feel that I should have gone with TCP/IP from the beginning notwithstanding the push in Europe towards X.25. Would that have brought Internet to Sri Lanka sooner? That is something I can't tell and it is a hypothesis that we'll never be able to test.

… as well as **Dennis Jennings:**

I returned from the US, after my 15 months at the NSF and 4 months at the Consortium for Scientific Computing in Princeton, in the summer of 1986. Back in Europe I found the period from 1986 to 1991 to be pretty miserable for those of us who were interested in providing networking services for research and education. Networking in Europe was controlled by the technologists on the one hand, and by the PTTs/Governments/European Commission on the other. This combination of experts focussed on technology and officials willing to provide funding only for ISO/OSI protocols and for the use of low speed public packet switched (volume charged!) networks, was an absolute disaster - and ultimately doomed to failure since the approach could not address the end-to-end, workstation to workstation, environment actually used by researchers. While the USA stormed ahead with an increasingly high speed, high functionality, pervasive Internet for research and education, Europe stagnated.

I tried my best to change that, but I was unable to penetrate the closed minds of the technical experts and the funders. I wouldn't like to live that period again, but if I had to live that miserable period again, I would like to be successful in changing the minds of those involved.

Internet history is ...

What are the actors' perspectives on the field of Internet history? Often summarised by an optimist and ecumenical vision, a relationship between past and present that may enlighten the current issues, they warn us that it may also lead to a "presentist" look, rewritings, oblivion...

Fascinating, tells us **Abhaya Induruwa** ...

... fascinating. It is short but its impact on mankind is unparalleled. During a short period of time it has touched the lives of every human being on this planet in one way or another ... and it is just the beginning! From a humble beginning connecting four university computer centres who would have thought the Internet will grow to connect billions of people and tens of billions of things ... signalling the beginning of a new wave: the Internet of Things that is transforming the Internet to a whole new ball game.

A fascinating history for **Gérard Le Lann,** as well, but not without its pitfalls...

A fascinating topic. We have not seen yet all the implications of the advent of the Internet. Given the very deep consequences of what is and has been a fantastic journey in human history, it is no surprise that the Internet history is being written and re-written over and over. Trustable accounts have been provided by most actors of the Arpanet/Internet revolution. Unfortunately, the Internet history is also tainted by mistaken articles and biased interviews produced by improvised "experts."

... and shadows, as noted by **Ted Nelson**:

Internet history, like all history, is a fading tangle of misunderstandings that becomes more and more inaccurate.

While **Dennis Jennings** points out the risks of oblivion, memory biases, of the writing of history itself...

Internet history is a collection of the memories of all the participants. It varies from person to person, and the history remembered varies depending on the point in time and space at which one started to participate in the development or use of the Internet. For example, there were many precursor networks and technologies that are now forgotten, not just the ARPA-NET, and the ARPANET network wasn't the Internet, or even part of the Internet, until 1 January 1983.

... **John Klensin** underlines the forgotten trajectories, the paths that were left unquestioned, and the variety of genealogies and contributions to a history that cannot be constrained within narrow perimeters. In particular, he goes back to the messaging applications, the history of which he knows well – before serving on the Internet Architecture Board from 1996 to 2002 and 2009 to 2011 and being its Chair from 2000 to 2002, he was involved in the design and implementation of some key email systems and gateways, contributed to the design of contemporary email protocols, and served as working group chair or document editor for IETF Working Groups focused on messaging and email extensions to support a broader range of writing systems.

> For email specifically, there are a number of under-reported covered areas that are not going to be covered by anecdotes about specifically Internet history. Craig Partridge's IEEE piece[3] covers the Internet-specific history rather well, but there were many other email, forum, and discussion systems that grew up in parallel. The mail systems were ultimately integrated via gateways and the like, but, in the process, their design ideas and that of Internet email, evolved. As far as I know, there has been no careful look at the impact of Minitel on modern e-mail and messaging. I think most historians, especially outside Sweden, have vastly underestimated the importance of Jacob Palme's work on COM and its descendants, but simply dismiss them as a path not taken. The bulletin board systems and netnews were important too. While there were mailing lists on the ARPANET and Internet rather early, most of the important developments in list management and distribution derive from the work of Hank Nussbacher and, later, Eric Thomas on BITNET and EARN. Similarly, there was what we would now call instant messaging capability in the Unix "talk" protocols and, even earlier, in the SEND (and SAML and SOML) capabilities of early SMTP. Those never really took off but a good history and analysis of why not would be interesting.

> Even X.400 and the work leading up to it are relevant in that regard. While the protocol itself died a painful and probably well-deserved death, the influence of many of its design ideas have been underreported, partially because they are not considered "Internet" and we might be better off had we picked up one or two more of them.

John Klensin notes the dangers of the "unique and only inventor" figure, very familiar to historians ... in particular when it comes to the recent controversies concerning the paternity of email:

> Part of what makes all of this difficult for trying to reconstruct the history is that, with rare exceptions, almost any "who invented that" question asked in the 60s or 70s would have gotten an answer along the lines of "collaborative effort, lots of ideas in the wind, and everyone building on the ideas of everyone else." It has only been in recent years that (sadly from my point of view) there has been a scramble to figure out who invented what or to claim individual credit for particular developments.

This (hi)story, that has become for many a matter of recognition, is a collective one – as reminded by **Vinton Cerf**...

> ... a story of a grand global collaboration to create an information access and communication resource intended to benefit every person on the planet.

... and turned towards the future, for **Paul Mockapetris**,

> dedicated to recording what happened, but more importantly pointing out principles which we can apply again and again in the future.

It is time to leave the last word to **Steve Crocker**:

Internet history has progressed from a history of the technology to a history of modern communication. It is now intimately entwined in all aspects of our lives, so "Internet history" will shortly be indistinguishable from "human history."

... a gargantuan program and "construction site", indeed, for historians of today and tomorrow. We invite you to share it with us, and this journal, as issue after issue unfold.

Notes

1. https://www.rocq.inria.fr/novaltis/publications/IFIP%20Congress%201977.pdf
2. https://tools.ietf.org/html/rfc974
3. Partridge, C. (2008). The technical development of Internet email. *IEEE Annals of the History of Computing, 30*(2), 3–29.

Disclosure statement

No potential conflict of interest was reported by the author.

Conversations with a pioneer: Paul Baran in his own words

Morten Bay (iD)

ABSTRACT
This interview is based on two conversations the author had with Paul Baran in 2004 and 2010. The 2010 conversation represents one of last times Baran participated in an interview before his death in March 2011. Topics discussed include how Baran drew upon inspiration from Warren McCulloch's work on neural networks to bring distributedness to communication networks and how this led to Hot Potato Routing, which later became known as packet switching. The latter, being an foundational part of Internet technology, has placed Paul Baran firmly in the histories of networking and the Internet, even if the origins of packet switching are hotly contested – a topic that is also discussed in the conversations. Finally, Baran also shares his views on technological development and determinism and what the future for the Internet holds.

Introduction

The first time I met Paul Baran, it was just a few days before the US presidential election in November 2004. I pulled my rental car into his driveway in the Silicon Valley town of Atherton, which at the time had the highest real estate prices in the entire United States. Baran was waiting outside his front door with a big smile on his face, wearing a classic sport coat and slacks. He looked every bit like the "retirement failure" he described himself as; an elderly gentleman whose immense cognitive abilities were overshadowed only by his modesty.

As we spent a couple of hours having lunch at a nearby restaurant, he told me his version of how he went from working on one of the first proto-networks, the SAGE system, to being inspired by Warren McCulloch when writing his classic papers on distributed communication networks at the RAND Corporation between 1960 and 1964. This work described what would later become known as packet switching and would, through a rather serendipitous route, find its way to Larry Roberts, who was in the process of designing the ARPANET in 1967. Consequently, most digital communication relies on some variant of distributed networking and packet switching today.

But Baran was never one to take any credit. At the time of our first conversation, awards were being given out left and right to people claiming to have "fathered" or "invented" the Internet. Paul Baran felt that we should all honour the concepts instead of the people.

He inhabited a deep, almost spiritual version of technological determinism, in which he believed that technology would appear when it becomes "ripe", created by our collective consciousness. And for that specific reason, only small amounts of credit could be taken by those involved in the early days of the Internet. He talked about "taking the blame" for the Internet, which he – presciently – predicted would be cursed as much as celebrated in the years to come.

Still, in 2004, Baran hoped that the Internet could potentially be a peacemaker. We were, after all, discussing the matter as America was deeply mired in two wars in Iraq and Afghanistan, and was only days away from re-electing George W. Bush. He hoped the Internet could achieve this by making all the world's information available to everyone. Post-colonial studies and social critiques have since shown us that it is not that simple. And Baran knew this. He was well aware that the Internet could only be used for peace through a deliberate strategy.

The second time I interviewed Paul Baran, he was no longer living in Atherton. In late 2010, his new home was an assisted living facility in Palo Alto, right by Stanford University. He had his own apartment in this large, swanky facility for elderly Silicon Valley residents. As I was interviewing him for a documentary, I arrived with a camera crew, and the then 84-year-old Baran sat through three hours of interviews under hot lights with only a single break. His speech was a bit slower and his voice slightly raspier, but otherwise, he was as sharp and energetic as when I had met him six years prior. After the interview, he even excused himself to go read newly arrived e-mails about some startups he was involved with.

Baran repeated much of the history he had relayed to me in 2004, but also talked at length about how the networking that humans produce in both social contexts and technological infrastructures really comes from the fact that we are part of nature, which in itself has a myriad of similar network structures to observe. It was as if Baran had reached a new level of contentment and comfort with the way things had unfolded. He was gracious, gentle, funny and brilliant.

Only a few months later would I realise why his demeanor was so forgiving and why his voice was raspier. Paul Baran had terminal lung cancer when we interviewed him, which was also why he had moved to an assisted living facility. He died on March 26, only about four months after we had visited him in Palo Alto. Despite the lung cancer, Baran still sat under those lights for three hours. Still managed to be funny. Still managed to be brilliant. And still went to check on his startups after the interview. It was hard not to be inspired by him.

Both interviews have been edited for readability, and as there was much overlap, only a few, but very profound lines from the 2004 interview have been included.

Interview conducted November 2010

You graduated with a B.S. degree from Drexel Institute of Technology in 1949. How did you get into computers?

Well, I did a couple things at the back. After Drexel, my first job was working at Eckert-Mauchly, a computer company. A couple of crazies had this idea that they could build a computer, and I worked there for a short time and convinced myself that this didn't have any future (laughs).

I went on to a company called Raymond Rosen Engineering Products and we designed equipment that was used to... the first equipment that formed Cape Canaveral. We took equipment out of the laboratory and brought it down there. That was first telemeter equipment over there. I was there for several years and did a few other things along the way. In 1955, I married a Californian who was working in New York at the time. And Californians don't transplant well, so it was just a matter of time until we moved back to California.

Where did you end up?

We moved to Los Angeles. I went to Hughes Aircraft and was there for about four or five years, then over to the RAND Corporation. At Hughes, I would work on two different things. The first was in the Systems Group, building a "vest pocket" version of SAGE, as we called it. It was a lot of the capability of the larger SAGE air defense system, but transistorised and squashed down into a small army vehicle. The services were competitive. The Air Force built their thing, and the Army duplicated this smaller version. The SAGE system was a system that combined radar plus computers, and the idea was that you had your expected enemy bombers coming in and you had to track them and know where they were, in order to send interceptors who were to fire missiles at them. So it was the predecessor of missile age defense.

And that was centralised?

Yeah, everything was centralised in those days. There was some alternative routing, but there was very little of that, and all these systems were vulnerable. I ended up working in the vulnerability analysis group of Hughes and that's where I got interested in the general subject of survivability.

How did you get to RAND?

I walked. (Laughs) Or in car.

What was the motivation for you to move to RAND and for the work you did there?

Well, the work arose out of a realization that we were moving into a very dangerous age. We underestimated the Soviet capability and we were overreacting to it. They seemed 10 feet tall and we were concerned about the arms race. Now at that time – between 1959 and 1962 was the time I did most of the work - both the U.S. and Russia were building weapons. And the characteristic of the weapons looking forward was that they were getting more lethal and the accuracy was improving. We reached a point where no single spot could ever be safe. And this was in that crazy period where whichever country fired first would destroy the retaliatory capability of the other side.

So that meant for a very dangerous situation, a crazy situation where people's fingers were on the trigger for fear of being second. To cool things down, a concept was created, a survivable command and control system that would be able to take the first strike and then return the favor in kind, should the war break out. Now, this was more easily said than done, because at the time, our communications systems were highly centralised and would fall apart just on collateral damage. This meant that we could not have a defense capability that could withstand attack, so that you could keep things cool until you were certain that it was for real. And the whole thing is unreal, you know. That you can use nuclear weapons, in retrospect, is absolutely crazy. But nevertheless, that was the feeling at the time.

The world was on edge and it was not so much the concern about the intentional attack, but the accidents and the stupidity that could be caused by somebody miscalculating, panicking, something going wrong. So that was a very dangerous situation, and the whole thing hinged upon the survivability of communication. I got interested in that, and in saying: "Is it possible to build a communications system like a fishnet, where, if you break certain links, the rest of the system can survive and route traffic around the damaged areas?"

Well, if you take a pencil to paper, you can show that. With a computer, you can show that you can build pretty survivable networks. But we didn't know how to send traffic from one point to another point, and then to another, and how to make it go around and find its way through the network. So that took a little work. But with that in place, it became theoretically possible to build a network that could withstand an attack and the parts that survived physically could then be in communication with the other nodes. Now, the only way we knew how to do that was with digital communications, which really didn't exist in those days. So, it was a matter of having the technology and putting together a system to do this.

How did you go about conveying this theoretical network to the right people?

I took the briefing charts around the various places and I got all sorts of objections. My first briefing was back in the days when you just wanted to pass the word that the president had declared war or that missiles had arrived. I called it "minimum essential communication." We only needed a very limited number of bits to transmit such messages, and then we needed to figure out how to build such a network using radio stations and ground wave transmission.

The first one was just using a broadcast stations-to-relay system and the concept of "minimum essential communication." That's one of these great concepts, but if you look at it carefully, everybody found that they needed more communication than just the minimum of knowing whether you're at war or not. When we took this around the government, we found that everybody had a long list of things that they needed to communicate.

And so I went back to the drawing board to see whether it was possible to build a network with so much capacity that it would not be an issue. And then the next question came up: How much capacity do we need? We didn't know. Because it was open-ended, I would say: "Let's build something that has limitless capacity." Knowing how things were improving over time, we didn't want any hard limit on the capacity. That's how we got there. It was just saying: Is it possible to build a network that could survive a nuclear attack? Theoretically, we programmed behavior of what happens to the nodes when there's damage, is there a path, does a path exist? We didn't know how to route packets at that time, but just theoretically, would there be a path?

We found that it's a function of the number of links you have and that you have this magical property. When you hit about three links, three times as many links as the minimum network, then it took on this property. And that work was done at RAND in the period about late '59–'60.

In other words, your solution is what was described in the reports P-1995, B-265 and P-2626 from 1960 to 1962?

If you're going to go through the literature, I suggest the first one that you read is P-1995, which I think is August 27, 1960 or something like that. That is the discovery that a network of a certain redundancy can be made very robust. How we do that is another matter. And then there were some reports on the use of the broadcast stations. I don't remember what their numbers were.

The next one, B-265, was the classified one.[1] Originally all the work was unclassified. Then when it got interesting, it got classified because of specifics. Later, the major work was unclassified, I'd say about 80-90 percent of the work was unclassified. In about 1964 I had everything all done.

I had to write a lot of papers by the way, and the reason is that I'd give a briefing, there'd be somebody in the audience, saying "It won't work because…", and I listened to him, maybe he was right. I'd go away and study that issue and say, no, that's not the reason. But I'd put together some paper describing the rationale and then another person would say: "You haven't defined how to do so-and-so right." And that sort of cluttered up the literature with piles of reports at the time, on the subject. By about 1964 it was pretty much all together.

RAND had a formal recommendation to the Air Force to proceed to build the network. But then at that time, the Defense Communications Agency was being formed and that combined the communications capability of each of these competing military services that now had to work together. At that time, it was headed by an admiral or a general from one service and a general from another service who had no understanding of digital. We knew that if they attempted to build a digital network at the time, there was no way it would work, and it would probably be years before we could get back to it. We then suggested that the network not be built at the time, but rather that we wait until we had a more competent group that was able to take it on.

From a totally different direction came the work Bob Taylor was doing over at ARPA. He was interested in the problem of supporting computer research and connecting computers remotely. He had three different terminals in his office that each spoke to a different computer. His question was: "Why can't I just have one terminal that could speak to all these other computers?" Along the way, the two concepts merged and we ended up with the ARPANET and it later morphed into other things, including the Internet.

In the P-1995 paper, you made an illustration of a centralised, decentralised and distributed network that has since become staple of network science, textbooks and Internet histories?

It's obvious that a decentralised network is very vulnerable, a single point. The telephone company had some decentralization and a few backup routes. The idea was obviously something like a fishnet… In P-1995, we did a computer simulation of a network of nodes and what happens if you throw random raids against it and destroy, say, half the nodes. What survives and can communicate? The theoretical basis for it was done very early. It was all out of the way by 1960. This was work I'd done with the help of a programmer who really did the work, I just told her what to do.

The thing that took time was coming up with a system that was real, that would work beyond just the theoretical survivability. That was a very interesting number of years, as the phone company fought it tooth and nail. It was just very difficult for them to understand how anybody who wasn't in the telephone business could possibly have the nerve to talk about doing something differently. It was "no, it won't work because…", one reason after another. It was a matter of salesmanship, which I'm obviously not very good at. It took years.

You've told me in a prior interview that the idea for the structure of the network was inspired by conversations with Warren McCulloch?

Yeah, Warren McCulloch, this was back at Hughes, he was a consultant there on a project. He was the guy responsible for the first... They had an electrical imagination of what a neuron would do and be like, and they had something called the McCulloch-Pitts model. This was the early, early days when people were looking for similarities between computers and brains. His experience covered both, he had worked in the medical end as well as electrical engineering. And he described how, when you cut a part of your brain that carries certain information, the learning comes back in an adjacent area. It somehow moves over. That's very interesting, because that's saying that there is some self-learning, self-adaption and there's a higher chance that we would be able to have that sort of performance in a network of the same type.

So how did you meet him?

This was at Hughes when I was working on the vulnerability analysis there. He was there as a consultant from MIT and was a very interesting character. Very interesting. He had a long beard, he loved wine, would drink it profusely and recite long poems that went on endlessly. He was coming out to Los Angeles for a couple days to do some consulting work on this issue. Hughes was bidding on the Minuteman missile program and that was a program that all of us were very concerned about because it was missiles that would be fired very quickly and be very dangerous. Hughes was going to bid on the contract to build the command and control system for it.

We were all concerned about a number of issues, and survivability was the issue where McCulloch was. His advice was used on how to select the people who had to push the button. I had a lot of thoughts on that subject. In the discussions with him at the time, we were all interested in the question of: "How does the brain work?" I was a guy who had been thinking about that, so I had the opportunity to chat a bit with him.

Did you have a moment, or a light bulb going off when you were working with the network structures where you sort of said, "Well, this is what McCulloch was talking about?"

Yeah, you know, looking backwards, that was when we simulated the performance of packets moving around the network. We started off with half the network destroyed and the other part very quickly, within about a second of real world time, working intelligently, rerouting the traffic and the light went on. I said, "My God, this very simple algorithm called Hot Potato Routing exhibited intelligence!" A very simple thing, every node doing the exact same thing. It gave you the effect, if you look at it from a distance, of remarkable intelligence. Then the thought came back of McCulloch talking about how the function moves when there's damage – aha!

How did you think of Hot Potato Routing?

I found that if you had about three times as many links as the absolute minimum you need to connect networks, then an interesting phenomenon took place: The network became very robust. There's sort of a flipping point. With Hot Potato Routing, we said, well how do we do this? What rules do we have to have at each link of these nodes so that they pass the packet along?

They had to do two things. They had to learn the route and then forget the route when there was damage and relearn the new route. So how do you describe this? Hot Potato Routing became a pretty interesting way of phrasing it. It treated the packet as if it was a hot potato and you had to get rid of it very quickly. If the best route wasn't available, you'd send it over to the next-best. If that wasn't available, you'd send it over to the next-best.

One of my colleagues suggested that we think of it in terms of a little postman at each node. That way, by looking at the cancellation date of the message or how long it's been in the network, you can use the return address to know which is the best way to send traffic. So that's all it was. It was a very simple algorithm.

How did you figure out that setting a specific size for the packets is essential?

Well we knew that the system I was designing had to be used for everything, including voice. If you had voice, you had to get the messages very quickly. You also knew that if you made a mistake, you had to repeat the packet you sent. That meant that you had to run at milliseconds. So, it was because of the need for being able to send voice that you had to have short packets, which aren't as efficient as long packets, because you have the same overhead. But I came up with a number of about a thousand bits, 1024 bits to be exact. It seemed to be a good compromise between efficiency and delay time. So that's why it's a packet of that size.

The packets do a bunch of different things. One is, if we have a network like a fishnet, you can break it up into pieces and the traffic has to route itself. So, whatever you do, the traffic has to find its own way through the network and along the way, it'll hit noise and other problems. And if you have a problem, you repeat the last packet. Now you're waiting for an acknowledgement, a receipt. If you don't get that right away, then you resend it. The receiving end now has the task of sorting out the packets that arrive out of order and make sure there are no missing packets…and that's it. Everything that you want to send can be expressed as bits, whether it's telephone or facsimile or anything in those days, now TV. All communication can be carried as bits. We now build devices that process bits very well, like computers. So that turned out to be a good way to build networks.

You had distributed networking in P-1995 from 1960, and packet switching, which you called Hot Potato Routing, in P-2626 from 1962. But even with that in mind, there still seems to be a little bit of disagreement on how packet switching emerged from your work, opposed to Donald Davies' and Leonard Kleinrock's work?

Yes, there is. The guy that was probably most sensitive on this was Donald Davies. Don Davies did his work totally independently and later came up with the exact same idea - which shows there really is no great intellectual content to the idea because, it's just a matter of time for somebody to look at it and say: "Of course!"

Davies came up with this as well, just focused on data communication, and tried to do it cleverly. He later said he was thoroughly embarrassed to find that it already been done, but it's a very fine piece of work. He didn't feel that Len Kleinrock's work was really packet switching. But Len is a hell of a nice guy. A friend. And if he's convinced that what he came up with was packet switching…God bless! I'm not about to say what anybody…

… But which one came first?

... Well I think the dates on the papers is the easiest way to solve that one. Kleinrock's stuff was around 1962. He wrote a very interesting Ph.D. thesis around 1962 that was later turned into a book on queueing theory. Excellent piece of work. I approached it from a totally different point of view. Later, around the late 60s, I was also on a Department of Defense Committee. We would meet every other week in Washington. All of these things overlap, criss-cross and... I couldn't be less concerned.

So, it was just a question of time before somebody came up with packet switching?

I'm saying that that's indicative of the nature of the concept. It's such an obvious thing. If I didn't do it or Davies didn't do it or somebody else didn't do it, it would just be a matter of time before somebody else did. When technology moves along, it gets ripe and certain things will happen. I don't view that as being a great insight or that things would have been that much different if I never existed.

What do you say to the current research that is finding network structures in biology and nature that are very similar to the network structures you introduced?

Well I didn't introduce them... slime mold forms perfect distributed networks. Slime mold has been around a lot longer than I have (laughs)! All I did stumble into this type of view of the network. These networks have been around a long time.

But you could say that no-one had articulated it as well as you did?

Well, I articulated it...I don't know how well I did! (laughs). It's a realization that this has been going on for a long time and we're just catching up a little bit, understanding how nature works.

It's not just a question of technology becoming ripe, it's really nature... ?

Yeah. Yeah. Hey, we have some awfully damn clever systems and stuff running around and communications... we think of an idea, but it's already been used in the body somewhere. Again, take slime mold. It looks horrible on a pond as pond scum, but if you look at the movies of how this network grows, it's all... it looks just like a distributed network. You say, well, here's old pond scum at work that has been around probably 500 million years.

And the neural networks in the brain?

And in the brain... you start seeing things that tells you it's probably how things are connected. You can draw these parallels, it's the same mechanism. The communication processes are the same. You can have highly centralised human communication networks with a certain behavior, you have a king and information just flows from there. That's one type of social structure.

And then you can give everybody access to all the world's information, and that's a different type of social structure, with different characteristics and different degrees of robustness. Now, one can be very efficient, but fragile. And the other could be more chaotic, but stable and large. So yeah, there are a lot of parallelisms there. It is a very useful way of understanding how this very complicated world works. It's obvious now, but that's one of those little mechanisms that give you a little insight.

You said it's obvious now - how was it before?

We didn't think about it! If you didn't think about it, it didn't exist.

Interview conducted November 2004

What is you biggest wish for the application of your work in the future?

That it be used for universal education. That it be used to reduce of the disparity between the rich and the backward countries. You won't have peace unless you do.

Is that the contribution you want people to remember?

My contribution was just a little bit added to everybody else's. I don't want to take the blame for the whole thing (laughs). The major thing about it, I think, is that for the first time, you allow a poor kid in any part of the world to have access to the whole world's information.

That'll mean a lot of help in terms of economic development in a part of the world that's so far behind. If you notice, the countries that get into wars are always the poor countries. The wealthy countries will get into wars, but not initially. The Thomas Friedman model says that two countries who have a McDonald's never go to war with each other.

I've heard that you prefer not to be called a "founding father" of the Internet?

One thing that we should be doing a little differently is that instead of giving awards to people for this invention or this idea or that idea, we should honour the concept. To hell with the people! And if you take the Internet, it's a wonderful concept, but there were probably 50 guys involved. Instead of taking two or three who claim to be the fathers, you really should say: "Look, it's a great idea, there's a bunch of graduate students who really made that thing possible." Bolt, Beranek and Newman really did the engineering work, and we shouldn't be hung up on picking one person. So, you can see my discomfort in getting more blame...

I love the way you use the word "blame" in this context...

Oh, I think "blame" is a good word, because one day, we're going to view the Internet as being the most horrible thing ever done. I think so. No good deed ever goes unpunished. It's going to be so distorted, it'll cause so much damage, people will be cursing it and wish it never existed.

Note

1. B-265 was in fact not classified, but designated "For Official Use Only", which meant it was only available to RAND employees and employees Department of Defense. It has since been made publicly available.

ORCID

Morten Bay (iD) http://orcid.org/0000-0003-1431-3297

Further reading and viewing about Paul Baran

Baran, P. (1960). *P-1995: Reliable digital communications systems using unreliable network repeater nodes*. Santa Monica, CA: RAND. Retrieved from https://www.rand.org/pubs/papers/P1995.html

Baran, P. (1962). *P2626: On distributed communication networks*. Santa Monica, CA: RAND. Retrieved from https://www.rand.org/pubs/papers/P2626.html

Baran, P. (1964). *On distributed communications*. Santa Monica, CA: RAND.

Computer History Museum (2011). *An evening with Paul Paran*. Retrieved from https://www.youtube.com/watch?v=SZey878-Mp4

Internet Hall of Fame (2017). *Paul Baran|Internet hall of fame. Internethalloffame.org*. Retrieved June 17, 2017, from http://internethalloffame.org/inductees/paul-baran

Mayo, K., & Newcomb, P. (2008). *The birth of the world wide web: An oral history of the internet. Vanity fair*. Retrieved June 17, 2017, from http://www.vanityfair.com/news/2008/07/internet200807

Nordin, H. (2011). *Hi-tech heroes #32: Paul Baran*. Retrieved from https://www.youtube.com/watch?v=CoeHrKB5Fa4

O'Neill, J. (1990). *Oral history interview with Paul Baran. Conservancy.umn.edu*. Retrieved June 17, 2017, from http://conservancy.umn.edu/handle/11299/107101

RAND (2017). *Paul Baran and the origins of the internet. Rand.org*. Retrieved June 17, 2017, from https://www.rand.org/about/history/baran.html

Conversation with a pioneer: Leonard Kleinrock on the early days of networking, the ARPANET…and winning in Las Vegas

Morten Bay

Introduction

In December of 2010, I visited Professor Leonard Kleinrock in his office at UCLA. It was not the first time I had done so. I had already completed a round of interviews in 2004 with several ARPANET and Internet pioneers, Kleinrock among them. The 2004 interview took place on the day of that year's presidential election, only days after the 35th anniversary of the launch of the ARPANET, so Kleinrock was busy, and our meeting was brief.

But in 2010, Kleinrock had much more time and was generous with it. In a friendly and relaxed manner, we talked for almost three hours about how he began his career at MIT with two other friends who would later become legendary pioneers in computer history in their own right, Larry Roberts and Ivan Sutherland.

Professor Kleinrock took us all the way up to the present time and touched upon some entertaining and unexpected stories. He has given many interviews over the years and participated in in-depth oral histories like the invaluable one recorded by Judy O'Neill for the Charles Babbage Institute as early as 1990, months before Tim Berners-Lee released the World Wide Web documentation. The interview below has been edited for length and for any redundancies with these prior interviews, unless they were deemed necessary for context.

Kleinrock also talked about being right in the middle of a small group of people who would change networked communication forever. Not just through the emergence of the Internet, but also through mobile communications and the development of personal computing devices. Before the interview was over, however, Kleinrock had dished out stories of the mad capers he and Larry Roberts were involved in while they were working on the development of the ARPANET. They included being thrown out of Las Vegas casinos for counting cards and collecting silver quarter coins for future melting, because these tech wizards had found out that the silver content in the coins was worth more than the coin itself.

Two years later, I would enroll at UCLA myself, where I would have many more enlightening and fun interactions with Professor Kleinrock. But back then in 2010, I was just a willing listener. Because even though Leonard Kleinrock is just one of the many, many key people who brought the ARPANET and the Internet to life, he might just be the most entertaining storyteller of them all.

Interview conducted December 2010

So, take us back to the late 1950s. You were at MIT. What were you doing?

So, I got to MIT in 1957 to do my master's thesis on a wonderful program that MIT Lincoln Laboratory had provided, whereby they pay for your education if you work as a research assistant. I worked there in the summer. At Lincoln Laboratory, I worked for Ken Olsen, the gentleman from Digital Equipment Corporation. In fact, the first summer I worked for him, he formed DEC, and he asked me if I want to join him in his company. I said, "No, no, I've got better things to do. I've got a graduate degree".

I got my Master's degree on schedule towards the end of 1958 and I was supposed to stop and work at the laboratory. But one of my professors said, "You really got to do a PhD". And I said, "I don't want to. I'm married, I've got a child on the way, scheduled when this degree was supposed to finish". But they kept saying, "You really got to do it". So, I thought "If I'm going to continue on for the PhD, I'm going to do something important that I get gratification out of, not just an ordinary dissertation". And one of the things I wanted to do was to work for the absolute best professor at MIT and at the time that was Claude Shannon. An icon of information theory. When I began working for him, I started working on a chess playing program we had. All of his PhD students were working on information – no surprise – and coding, and I looked around and I saw that the problems they were working on were really hard and they probably would have very little significance, because Shannon had already done the great work. He'd settled the field. So, being surrounded by computers, I recognised that sooner or later, these things would have to talk to each other and there was no way they could do it at the time. Nobody was working on it, it was a new field, an exciting field with lots of applications. I could foresee this was for me. So, I started to develop a theory of how these machines could talk to each other, what technology would work. And the only existing technology at the time was the way the telephone network functioned using something called circuit-switching. And circuit-switching was woefully inadequate to handle data transmission. In fact, the way the telephone system worked, it would take basically 35 seconds for you to dial up the call, you'd get a minimum charge of three minutes and the computer just exchanged one tenth of a second of data. So, a new technology was needed and I decided to develop what was needed then, and that's what my PhD dissertation was about.

I looked into ways in which computers which burst information – now and then, only occasionally, and very quickly - could use the communication lines efficiently, and this led to a concept like what we now call packet-switching. The idea of packet-switching is to use a communications link only when something needs to be sent and don't tie it up while you're waiting for the next bit of information to be sent. In the telephone network when you and I talk, if it's a dedicated communication link from me to you and if I decide to pause in my conversation and I get a cup of coffee, that link is being wasted with no conversation. Now in telephone conversations, that happens about one-third of the time and you can withstand that kind of inefficiency. But in data communications, when machines talk to each other, it would be idle 99.99 percent of the time. Therefore, I had to find a way to share resources among many data streams.

Tell me how you employed queuing theory in your dissertation work?

Well, queueing theory was the tool that I used in order to evaluate the performance and do some design for these computer networks, these data networks. You needed some mathematical tool and the reason queueing theory was so effective is that it talked about exactly the quantities of interest, like throughput, response time, delay, storage, buffering; just the metrics you would use for deciding how well data was being moved through a network.

It wasn't called packet-switching, then, though?

No, we just called it "blocks of data" at the time. But there were various efforts talking about packet-switching. My work at MIT, Paul Baran's work at the RAND Corporation,[1] and a few years later, Donald Davies at National Physical Laboratory. Basically, we were all talking about the same kind of thing.

And that was when?

1962. April '62 was when my first paper appeared on the concept of breaking messages into packets. I started doing work in the area in '61. Claude Shannon had a great influence on me. When I decided to look into the design and evaluation of data networks, I thought about designing large networks influenced by Shannon's thinking there. In fact, the title of my original thesis proposal was "Information Flow in Large Communication Nets". Now if you're going to build a large network, you can't put all the control in one location for a lot of reasons. It gets overloaded, it's vulnerable, it just doesn't scale. If you want to scale, you must distribute the functionality. So, in the idea of the network that I was thinking and writing a theory about, everybody has a part of the control. Nobody controls it at all, we all share the control. In addition, you need parallel paths, adaptive paths, alternate paths, to get through this network. If any one breaks, there are plenty other ways around. The robustness depends upon the distributed nature of the control and the topology, and so, in my design, I put that into the idea that everybody has a little bit of control.

You met Larry Roberts and Ivan Sutherland at Lincoln Lab, right? Later, both became directors of the IPTO at ARPA, with Larry beginning as chief scientist in charge of designing the ARPANET?

Larry Roberts and I were classmates on this MIT Lincoln laboratory program to support us through our graduate degrees. In fact, he wrote the compiler for the computer system I was using to test my theory, on a computer called the TX-2 at Lincoln Laboratory. He was intimately familiar with the work I had done. He even suggested that I apply that theory to automobile road traffic because the same ideas made sense. And yes, the next IPTO director after Licklider was Ivan Sutherland, another classmate of mine. In fact, Larry, Ivan and I were all working together under a collective group of supervisors. We shared faculty members on our thesis committees. Shannon was on all of them for example, Marvin Minsky was on one of them, a few others. We took our final thesis defense together. We all had to present our dissertations at the same time because all three of us were using the TX-2 computer to demonstrate our capability and our technology, and our theory. So, we all went out to Lincoln laboratory, we're sitting around a table with the faculty there and we're demonstrating on the TX-2 what we were doing. Ivan had a really wonderful program called Sketchpad, where you could draw some shapes on the tube screen and try to make it satisfy certain constraints. So, after he made his wonderful presentation, he began to talk to one of the faculty, and Marvin Minsky wandered over to the computer console and put in his own constraints. Ivan's program couldn't handle the set of constraints he put in, and so on the screen you saw these bubbles of explosions as the system was trying to stabilise, and it didn't. Ivan had no idea what was going on, and we were all hysterically laughing. But we all passed.

How did you use the TX-2?

My focus was on putting together a mathematical theory. Once I had developed that theory using queueing theory as the underlying tool, I was able to show how it would perform, I could show that the packets wouldn't fall on the floor. Distributed routing was a very important element. I even discovered that the larger you make network, the more efficient it is, something that was unknown at the time. Queueing theorists were amazed that this was the case when you think about the right way of analyzing it. Having done that, I had to make some assumptions in the mathematical theory. In order to test those assumptions, I had to simulate the network with and without the assumptions, and so I ran these things running packets and messages through this network extensively. I was running it for four months on the TX-2 computer at Lincoln Laboratory. I spent four months debugging and running the simulation program of my data networks, and I would get the machine assigned to me for seven hours of the night, from midnight to 7 AM, four nights a week. They were not contiguous nights, so my sleep schedule was awful. I could be there late at night working really hard with his million-dollar machine all to myself. You get tired, and you get worried because you don't want to break this machine so you learned what every sound meant: the little whisper, the whistle, the whirring. What all the parts look like. This was an experimental computer, and every so often there were parts of it that were missing that were being modified.

One night I'm there, and I'm working, and I'm tired. I need a shave, and my mouth tastes bad, and I suddenly hear a sound that sounds wrong. Kind of like [whistles], and I said, "Uh-oh, something's going to break". So, I looked around. I was looking over the control panel and where one of the missing pieces of the computer was supposed to be, where one of the empty slots was, I saw a pair of eyes looking at me. It scared the hell out of me! And son-of-a-gun – it was Larry Roberts. He'd snuck into the room. He scared the hell out of me that night. I could have killed him, I almost did.

I've heard that you and Larry pulled some pretty crazy stunts back then?

Larry and I had more relaxing things we did occasionally. For example, he and I liked to gamble and we put together a gambling system for Blackjack. We've been to Vegas many times in the 70s, and we been thrown out of many clubs. We had a system similar to Edward Thorp's system, which was from "Beat the Dealer", and we could win anytime we wanted. One time we tried to put together a machine for a roulette. Casino roulette is a very simple game. The wheel goes one direction, the ball goes the other, and Newtonian mechanics tells you when the ball is going to fall in, and if you can predict which half of the wheel it's going to fall on, you have 100% advantage over the house. So, we tried to make some measurements. Larry took a microphone, put in his palm and wrapped it up as if he had a broken arm, ran the wire through his jacket into the recorder in his pocket because he wanted to measure the speed of the wheel, and the whirl of the ball. When the ball comes around it goes, "Humm... humm". So, the two of us walk over to the roulette table and I'm the decoy. I start betting and Larry is there sort of resting his hand where he needs to. Well the hell of it was, I started winning! I started hitting the numbers, only by luck. Now you got to picture this: The pit boss is there, watching this. He sees us working together, cleaning up the table and Larry's got his hand awfully close to that wheel. So the pit boss grabs Larry's hands and says, "Let me see your hand". And he pulls this broken arm allegedly and at that point, Larry and I looked at each other and we were out of there in seconds. We could have ended up in the desert, you know how. That's just one experience but we had a great time doing the Blackjack.

Have you never been caught?

Ohh! Many times, I mean, if you're counting cards... I remember one time I was there by myself playing, and I'm just head-on with the dealer, and the dealer says, "You count pretty well, don't you, Sonny?" And I said, "Count? What are you talking about? I can't even add up the cards". I said, "You mean some people count these cards?"

But there was another caper that Larry and I got involved with in 1968, prior to the Internet being formed. Larry and I were very close at that point. Larry pointed out that the silver content in silver quarter coin was worth more than the 25 cents it represented. Now, they stopped making silver quarters in 1964, and this is four years later. So, there were the copper ones and the silver ones in circulation. The trick was to take the pure silver coins out of circulation and store them until the United States would make it legal to melt them down, which was illegal at that time. We decided to collect some. How do you separate this silver from the non-silver? I invented a machine which was based on something called an Eddy current. Silver is a better conductor than copper, and if you run it past a magnetic field, the silver coin will go this way and the copper coin will go that way. So, I made a machine that I fed coins into, mixed silver and copper. They would come down a chute with a big magnet and they'd separate. I had a World War I bayonet to separate them. It could handle $10,000 an hour, but the trouble was, we couldn't get our hands on enough mixed coins. The banks wouldn't give it to us. I went to the slot machine companies, I went to the washing machine companies, but I just couldn't get enough. We put ads in the paper. I got calls at 3AM, from the racetrack. "I've got a hundred dollars worth of quarters now" That's not enough, we need more. Finally, we ended up having somebody pick them up in Mexico. Then the price of silver went down and they made it legal to melt. I still have bags of silver coins in my vault. They're not quarters anymore because I originally had the quarters stored in the bank. I went to collect them one day and they were gone. So, they had to replace them, and they replaced them with silver dollars and silver half dollars, numismatically extremely valuable. I'm sitting on a little silver mine there one day to be exploited.

How did you get to Los Angeles and UCLA?

I graduated from MIT and I was scheduled to work at Lincoln laboratory. For some reason, UCLA thought I wanted a faculty position. They invited me out, they offered me a position and now I had a dilemma. Stay and do this wonderful work of research at MIT Lincoln laboratory, well-paid job, an environment I knew, on the East Coast where my family was, or go out to this place called California all the way across the country for half the pay to try something I really didn't know if I would like or not. So, I decided to try it. And the reason I did by the way is because Lincoln Laboratory was extremely generous about this. They said, "Look, try it. If you don't like it, come on back". You can't miss an opportunity like that. Well, I came here in 1963 and I've been here ever since.

You fell in love with California?

It's is not so much California as the teaching that I love.

Okay, so you are in California in 1963 and you get a call from Larry Roberts?

Well, it wasn't the call from Larry Roberts that got this started. What happened was that from the time I came out here, I started trying to push networking companies to accept this technology that was now clearly in their best interest to develop, and AT&T wanted nothing to do with it. In fact, I remember at the conferences, the Spring Joint Computer Conference, Fall Joint Computer Conference, there'd be 10,000 people at a plenary session, and on this panel, there'd be the telephone guys and the computer guys, and we'd say to the telephone guys, "Please give us good data networks. Make a network we can use". And their answer was, "What are you talking about? The United States is a copper mine. It's full of telephone wires, use the telephone networks". And we said, "No, no, you don't understand… your network just won't handle efficiently what we want to do". And they turned around and said, "Little boy, go away". So, little boy went away and collectively, we developed this technology.

When did you first get involved with ARPA, then?

I'm going to step back a bit. In 1957, Sputnik went up. Caused a great distress for this country. We were now behind the Soviets in space technology. So, to his benefit, President Eisenhower created the Advanced Research Projects Agency, and decided to fund research in all areas of science including electrical engineering and computer science etc. In 1963, Licklider basically became the head of the computer side of this research effort. Now Lick was at MIT at the same time I was. He had a vision as to what a network might do in terms of human man-computer symbiosis. Give people connectivity and they'll do some wonderful things. He had no idea how to do it. Meanwhile, at MIT, I had already begun laying out the technology. Ivan [Sutherland] became the second IPTO director. The third director was Robert Taylor, and by this time, ARPA had been supporting a large number of research groups around the country, and each research group was given a computer to do computer research on and develop unique technology. University of Utah, excellent computer graphics. UCLA did simulation. Stanford Research Institute did databases. University of Illinois, high-performance computing. And every time ARPA took on a new researcher, the researcher would say, "Want me to do a research? Fine, buy me a computer". ARPA would say, "Fine, I'll buy you a computer". The researcher would say, "And also, I want everything everybody else has: the graphics, the high-performance simulation database etc. And ARPA would say, "We can't afford to do that. But what if we put you in a network and you want to do graphics, you log onto Utah and run their machine? You want high-performance? Log onto Illinois and run their machine". So, the idea of a network bubbled up. Meanwhile, Larry had run an experiment to try to send data across United States on a dial-up connection. He succeeded, but with great, great difficulty. There were no protocols, no error control, no standards, so he recognised that this was not a good way to doit. Bob Taylor now said, "We need a network". He brought Larry in to make this network happen, and manage it, and fund it, and supervise it. And Larry came to me and he said, "Len, we need to develop this network. Help me put together the specification".

Can you tell me more about your interactions with Licklider?

Well, we tangentially worked with each other, since he was directing ARPA at the time, and I was visiting ARPA because Ivan was there, and I was very close to Ivan. I wasn't familiar with what Licklider had in mind until I began to read the early paper that he had written about man-computer symbiosis. I told him about the technology that I had, but there was no nothing to do with that information. There was no plan, no goal, until Bob Taylor said: "We have to make a network to connect our researchers together". So, when Larry contacted me and said he's basically been given the responsibility for creating this network, we decided that we had to write a specification, so we could let this contract out to some vendor to implement the technology that we were describing. Larry called together a number of researchers in 1967, got us all in the room, and we began to write the specification. For example, one of the things that was specified is that this network has to have no more than half a second response time. If we're going to give the same impression as people using time-sharing terminals, it has to feel real-time. We said: "Let's make sure that it has reliability, so that if one thing breaks, everything else will keep working". We decided to have what's called a two-connected topology, which means there's two ways to get from any node to any other note in this multi-node network. So, if one node breaks, you can route around it. We also decided that it had to have some measurement technology. This was intended to be an experimental network. You need some tools, you need to be able to generate artificial traffic, you need to be able to measure response times, to store them, to send probes through the network, to follow paths through the network, and so I said: "We have to have the software which will do measurement and storage of information".

Wes Clark was there, and Wes Clark is brilliant. Wes Clark was the fella who supervised my work at MIT Lincoln laboratory, and Larry's work, and Ivan's work. He was in charge of the group running the TX-2. And he said, "Look, if you guys are going to create a network and with all this communications overhead where you're breaking messages into packets, putting them together, doing error correction, routing, sensing what's happening on the network...don't load up the computers with that effort. Create special computers that sit alongside the main machines and let all the communications work run on that switch, that communications processor". And so we decided that's what we were going to do. The specification called for what that processor would do, and we described the response time to spot the packets, described how big it should be, and a request for proposal was created which went out to industry in 1968. Many, many people submitted proposals. IBM was going to and didn't. AT&T did not, unsurprisingly. So, these proposals came in, they were evaluated by the folks at ARPA and the award was given to a company called Bolt, Beranek and Newman, a Cambridge, Massachusetts vendor. It was their job to take the specification and select the computer to be that communications computer. And they selected a minicomputer, no surprise. They would take that minicomputer, change the software to match the spec, change the hardware to provide the functions, deploy them around the country, lease communication lines from AT&T to connect those switches together and deploy the network. The plan was to deploy a 19-node network. They were given this contract around Christmas time of 1968 and were to deliver the first switch to right here to UCLA in September 1969, over the Labor Day weekend. Now the funny thing is that I had seen this particular minicomputer a year earlier at one of the computer shows. It was a military hardened version of this minicomputer and at the show they had this machine hung up on hooks swinging in the show, running. They had a huge big guy, a brute of a guy, stripped to the waist, with oil on his skin and a sledgehammer, and he was going "Whack! Whack! Whack!" Whacking on this machine and it kept running. So, we knew that this machine was in fact hardy, and so we all got military hardened machines. Because this machine was supposed to be able to be a standalone machine, unattended, with no rotating parts, no discs, no tapes, no paper tape etc. The very first machine, the one we got, was loaded with the paper tape to get the software. From then onwards, the software was loaded through the network to the other switches.

So, BBN was scheduled to deliver this thing in September. Meanwhile here at UCLA, we were very busy trying to get interface between our timeshared computer, the host computer that was going to connect through the network to other host computers, to be able to talk to this funny thing called a switch. The name associated with the switch is an Interface Message Processor, otherwise known as an IMP. The machine is a size of a telephone booth. So, the machine was scheduled to arrive, we had to work on the interface, and BBN - Bolt, Beranek and Newman - had not released the specification for that IMP-host interface yet. So, we had to work with them to develop it. We were frantically developing our piece, BBN was frantically developing their piece. Then we heard from BBN that they were running two weeks late, and we breathed the sigh of relief because we needed that time, and then they fooled us. They put the damn thing on airfreight and delivered it to our door on the Labor Day weekend. The damn thing wouldn't fit in the elevator! We had to hoist it up the side of the building! It got into the building over the Labor Day weekend, and on the Tuesday following the Monday of Labor Day, we were going to have the big opening. We were going to connect that switch to our host and try to run bits back and forth. You can imagine, there were a lot of people attending that ceremony. There were the folks from UCLA Computer Science, from the Engineering school, from Bolt, Beranek and Newman, from ARPA, from AT&T, as we're going to use their long lines, from Honeywell who had manufactured of that minicomputer, etc. And everybody was ready to point the finger to everybody else if it didn't work. Happily, we connected it and bits began to flow. They began to flow back and forth, and it was a big success. That happened on September 2, 1969. We didn't have a camera, we didn't have an audio recording, we didn't have any record of that day except the people that were there.

And then you put out a press release?

Ah yes. Two months before that instance of the IMP talking to the host, in preparation for this, UCLA put out a press release, it came out on July 3, 1969, in which I'm quoted as discussing what this network might become. I talk about some applications, some machine-sharing, and toward the end of that two-page press release, there's a quote there where I talk about the visions of where this network might evolve to. I talked about the fact that we would be able to access it from any place, your home or office, it'll be as invisible as electricity and as simple to use, you'll be able to reach out to computing utilities out there in the network. So, if you look at those words I just said, the computing utilities were almost there with web-based IP services, but the invisibility is something we've not yet achieved. The Internet is not an easy thing to use and the interfaces are ugly in many cases. Most people have features on their applications they've never learned to use. But the fact that it's available everywhere and as ubiquitous as electricity, and you can access to it from everywhere you go, in fact was correct, and that was two months before the Internet "came to life", if you will.

Tell me about that moment.

Well, after our IMP was delivered in September, the schedule was to deliver a second IMP up at Stanford Research Institute 400 miles to the north in Palo Alto in October, and a month after to UC Santa Barbara, and a month after that in December, University of Utah.

We had a four-node plan. We were going to pause for three months and then begin to deploy again while we tested our four-node network. So, by the time October came around, the second IMP was delivered to SRI (Stanford Research Institute), and they connected their IMP to their host computer there, an STS 940 computer. Now, it felt natural to provide the high-speed communications line from our switch to their switch and try to connect. So, one night, my programmer Charlie Klein and I were in the computer room, and we had a programmer up at Stanford Research Institute, Bill Duvall, and the point was to try to make a connection. So here, we're approaching the day when the first message on the Internet is going to occur and nobody's there to listen to it! There were two of us down here, one of them up there, so nobody was present. And what was the first message? You know, most people don't know what the first message ever on the Internet was. We all know what the first message was for the telegraph network, "What hath God wrought". The telephone network, "Come here, Watson, I need you". First man on the moon, "A giant leap for mankind". We weren't that smart - but those guys were smart. They had the press available, the media, and a great message. All we wanted to do was to login from our host computer through the first switch, over that long-haul line, to the second switch and the SRI host. So, Host-to-Host login. All you need to do the login is type "LOG" and the remote machine is smart enough to type the "IN" for you. So, we're ready to do this and we had a telephone connection from Charlie to Bill. So we typed the L, and then said "Did you get the L?" Bill said he got the L. "Did you get the O?" Got the O. Typed the G. "Get the G?" Crash! The network went down. So, the first message ever on the Internet was "Lo" as in, lo and behold. We couldn't have asked for a shorter, more prophetic message than that. I think it beats all the other messages, like "What hath God wrought", by miles. Short and prophetic. [Laughs]. No record of it, no photograph, no tape recording, except for an entry in a log called the IMP log, in which we did record that we connected to SRI host to host, and the date of that was 29 October 1969, 10:30 at night. I like to refer to that as the instant when the infant Internet uttered its first words. Now you might wonder what crashed. It wasn't our host, it wasn't our switch, it wasn't the high-speed line, it wasn't the switch at the other end, it was the SRI host so it was their fault. [Laughs]. The first link connecting the first two switches on the Internet on the line from UCLA to SRI was running at a blazing speed of 50,000 bits per second. Today that's slower than the slowest DSL you can get. But in those days, it was fast. We were used to 10 characters per second, 30 characters per second, much lower speeds. This was fast.

What went through your head as you were walking home, after you had made the connection?

So, after that successful login, it was already getting pretty late, when I began to think about what we just did. And to be honest with you, it was not a momentous occasion. It's not something that was a "Eureka!" moment. It wasn't even the other kind of moment, when people discover things which is like "Hmmm... that's funny". It was a sense of gratification. We succeeded in getting these two machines to talk to each other, we knew we could expand it, but didn't quite foresee where it would lead. We knew that we could make machines talk to each other, which was the original purpose of the ARPANET. Let machines talk, let people talk to machines. But what I missed was that my 99-year-old mother, just before her death, would be on the Internet. I missed the fact that it was human to human communication. It was communities forming, people to people, not machine to machine, or people to machine.

Did you read Bob Taylor and J.C.R. Licklider's 1968 paper where they basically said the same thing?

That paper was published in 1968, but it wasn't popular till much later. Lick's "Man–Computer Symbiosis" I certainly did read. Lick was talking about those kinds of applications. He foresaw that. But that vision sort of quieted down, and we were busy with the engineering task of putting this network together. It really was an engineering task. Originally, the plan was to have at most 64 hosts on that ARPANET, the original network. But it continued to grow. What's interesting is that in the period from 1963 to 1969, after the technology was developed and the Internet basically came to life, we kept approaching AT&T to get involved and their typical response was that the technology wouldn't work. AT&T dismissed the idea that this technology would work, and in fact they even said "If it does work, we want nothing to do with it". That was before the ARPANET.

What came next?

We had this four-node network, we decided to test it, and we found that parts of it worked properly and parts of it didn't. UCLA was designated to be the network measurement center, which means it was our job to try to break the network. There were many, many deadlocks, degradations, failures and slowdowns that came about because the protocols were very slow in being developed. We had interesting names for these deadlocks, things like "piggyback lockup", "Christmas lockup", "store-and-forward lockup" and a number of others. Every time we found the fault, we would contact Bolt, Beranek and Newman and ask them to fix it, because only they could repair it. The response usually was "it'll take us six months to fix it", and we said, "no, no there's something wrong with that, we think we know what the trouble is". But they wouldn't let us see the code, they kept it private, until one day, ARPA forced them to release the code and open it up. Now we had the code, and every time we found a failure we'd tell BBN exactly how to fix it. It still took six months to fix it, though. And you know, we can smile about that. But you have to understand what it means to be in production, to run a system, keep it up and maintained; and so, I can understand that it was slow for them because they had a protocol to follow, but was terribly frustrating for us. You know, we were the young hotshots finding the things, fixing it is obvious.

So, the network began to grow. We crossed the United States all the way to Cambridge in summer of 1970. We grew and grew and began to continue to test it and implement it, and for five years out, through 1975, UCLA was the network measurement center. We measured the heck out of this network. Constantly finding things to fix, and improving, and understand the underlying behavior. That was our goal, what was going on, why was it behaving this way. In 1975, the Defense Communications Agency was given the role of measuring the network. As far as I know, that's when the entire measurement capability dropped almost to 0, and they stopped making measurements and understanding what was happening to the network. More and more hosts were attached, in fact at one point there was a danger that too many of the machines coming on as host machines onto the network were PDP-10s, and we wanted a heterogeneous network. So, we had to force some of the other manufacturer's machines on the network. In the very early days, by the way, we had to convince the sites that were attached to come onto the network. You'd go to University X and say, "Join this ARPA network, you're a part of the ARPA community".

And they'd say, "I don't want to join the ARPA network because if I do, the network is going to steal cycles from my machine and deploy them out in the network". And we said, "Yes, that's likely to happen and you'd be able to use the other machines". And they resisted dramatically, until we basically forced them to do it. ARPA came to them and said, "You're receiving your funds from ARPA. You're going to join the network". As soon as they joined, they loved it of course.

In 1972, email was introduced by Ray Tomlinson at BBN. As soon as it was attached to the network, within a few weeks, it began to dominate the traffic on the network; and that's when I realised : This is about people talking to each other, not about machines talking to each other. It was a great great ad hoc add-on to the Internet, and it grew over those many years.

When was it that you and Larry first engaged in what some people jokingly have called the first illegal use of the Internet and at the same time, the first online chat session?

1973. There was a major computer communications network conference in Brighton, England, at the University of Sussex. It was a great conference, in fact that's the conference where Bob Kahn and Vint Cef first started talking about this thing called TCP. I had to leave a day early, I came home, I'm unpacking, and I realise that I left my electric razor in Brighton. Now at that meeting, we had taken a high-speed line from London, which was an ARPANET node, down to University of Sussex to make an ARPANET node there during the conference. So, when I was unpacking my clothes, it was at night in LA. It was a crazy hour in the morning, like four in the morning, in Brighton. I said: "What crazy person will be on the network at four in the morning? Maybe Larry Roberts would!" I got onto my computer terminal and there was a very nice program there called "Resource Sharing Executive". You could type in the name of anybody and say, "Where Roberts", and this piece of program would log onto every computer on the ARPANET- and there weren't that many in those days- and see who was logged on along with them. Finally, five minutes later, it came back and said, "Roberts logged on teletype 13". We had the ability to communicate. There was no formal chat session, it was an ad hoc kind of chat session. People were able to communicate by typing things out on the other person's terminal. I could type on his and he could type on mine. It was a kind of rudimentary chat session. I basically started to talk to him and I said, "Larry, I left my razor there, I'd like it back". The next day, Danny Cohen came back with my razor, and so in fact, I admit that was the first illegal use of the Internet, because it was a personal use and not devoted to science and technology as it was supposed to be [Laughs].

So how did you experience what happened over the next decades when the Internet first emerged and then subsequently went private?

In 1975, Larry Roberts went over to Telenet to try to make a public network offering. In the late 70s, AT&T tried to make a public network. They kept stalling and stalling until 1983, when they finally came out with their premium network, Net1000. Three years later, in 1986, they closed it down at a billion-dollar loss. In 1969, we proved the technology would work, but even by 1986, AT&T still couldn't make it happen properly with that old mentality of circuit switching and large systems. Now in the early 80s, the National Science Foundation began to fund supercomputer centers around the country. In the mid-to-late 80s, they decided that they wanted the supercomputers to be able to talk to each other, and what better network to use than the Internet at that time? So, they began to beef up the backbone of the Internet and took over some of the functionality. Prior to that, computer scientists in certain government research agencies were the only people on the Internet. As soon as the National Science Foundation came in, all scientists were allowed. Physicists, chemists, physiologists, oceanographers, psychologists etc. and so, the constituency enlarged dramatically. Now, think of the chemists that were added. These chemists worked in research laboratories that were attached to the network. But these research laboratories lived in a larger organization of a chemical company. A bona fide chemical company that did business, had salesmen and marketing managers, and all the rest. What were those researchers doing? They were using email, it was the main application. Or you can imagine that the manager, the staff, all the other people in the corporation said, "Chief, that's a wonderful tool, we'd like it". So, the email began to leak out from the research group to the rest of the organization, and that's when the dot-coms began to come in, toward the end of the 80s and early 90s. At the same time, Al Gore, then Senator Al Gore, who was the greatest proponent of internetting in Washington DC, began to see what was going on. He put together a Senate committee, for which I testified, and we showed them how we could create a national research and education network. He basically promoted the idea of industry, government and academia to work together to create a very high-speed backbone network, and so Al Gore did in fact make a significant contribution at that point in the life of the Internet. So, the dot-coms appeared, the constituency enlarged, the backbone network was there, and people wanted a high-speed network. The capability was there but the interface was terrible. It was very clumsy to get onto the net. Just around that time, Tim Berners-Lee comes out with the World Wide Web, and it gets basically a good graphical user interface out of the University of Illinois, and now we had a very easy way for anyone to get onto the net. The backbone speed was there, the applications were there. Poof! It suddenly hit the public eye, and so we began to see millions and millions of people joining the network. That's when the public saw it, that's when it began to gain significant recognition across the world.

You got involved with the industry side of things alongside your UCLA even before the ARPANET?

1968 was an interesting year, not only because of the silver caper, but in fact that particular year in October, Irwin Jacobs, Andy Viterbi and I had decided we would form a company called Linkabit Corporation. I was the first president, my home was the first facility. I got the first contract, and the company grew. It went down to San Diego, I stayed here UCLA, Andrew and Irwin went down there. They sold that company, and they took the funds from that company and formed Qualcomm. In 1976, I formed a company called Technology Transfer Institute, a conference company. I did that in 1976, because I published my book on computer networks, and I wanted to get the message out there. What better way to do it than to give a three-day seminar on it? So, my wife and I formed TTI, and I did a three-day conference at three locations across the United States. Very successful. I thought, "This is a good idea. Let's bring in other aspects of technology: databases, ALOHAnet, performance evaluation, other communications aspects". I brought in the best people who'd written the best books, were most well-known, were great speakers, and I started running a number of three-day conferences. That company still exists, and it's got a wonderful history. I've recently formed a company, which is looking at the search technology for a consumer application. So, I've been involved with that business side all along, and by the way, that business side is very important. It allows me to bring the real world into academia so the students can understand why they're studying and what they're studying. I've remained in academia since 1963, but I've been able to involve myself in these external events as well. What I've done basically, I have graduated 47 PhD students who basically form a kind of small army of experts out there across the world. By sending out emissaries called PhD students I've been able to stay in touch with what's happening in the real world.

Note

1. An interview with Paul Baran appeared in *Internet Histories*, vol. 1, issue 3.

ORCID

Morten Bay ⓘ http://orcid.org/0000-0003-1431-3297

Conversation with a pioneer: Larry Roberts on how he led the design and construction of the ARPANET

Morten Bay ⓘD

ABSTRACT
In this interview, the man who first managed the ARPANET project and made the network come in to existence, Dr. Lawrence G.
Roberts, gives his account of how the ARPANET came to be. He
contributes his perspective on the many other innovations made
to computer science by ARPA in the 1960s and 1970s, and shares
his view on the contentious origin narratives surrounding the
Internet, ARPANET and packet switching. He also talks about his
life-long friendship and collaboration with another Internet/
ARPANET pioneer, Leonard Kleinrock.

Only a few days before the final deadline of this special issue of Internet Histories, Dr. Lawrence G. Roberts suddenly passed away on December 26, 2018. Although not intended as such, the interview below now stands as a memorial over the invaluable contributions he made to the emergence of heterogeneous computer networks. Dr. Roberts was 81.

Introduction

In November of 2011, I visited Lawrence G. "Larry" Roberts at his home in Redwood City, California. Roberts had agreed to do an interview about his involvement with the ARPANET, which perhaps was more significant than any other of the early ARPANET and Internet pioneers. Roberts was hired by ARPA to design and lead the construction of the ARPANET, being one of only a handful of people in the U.S. research community who had any sort of relevant experience for the task.

In 1965, while Roberts was doing postdoctoral work at MIT's Lincoln Laboratory, Thomas Marill proposed an experiment in which the Q-32 computer at Systems Development Corporation in Santa Monica, California would be connected through a telephone line to the TX-2 computer at Lincoln Labs in Massachusetts. This connection between heterogenous computers over a phone line was one of the first connections of its kind, and Roberts was asked to partner with Marill on the project, providing the necessary technical insights and capabilities. Roberts was mostly focused on graphics through his Ph.D. work, but connecting two computers diagonally across the entire United States put him on the radar in the newly-emerging computer science field of networking.

ARPA tried to recruit Roberts all through 1966, until Roberts was finally persuaded into joining ARPA's Information Processing Techniques office. Here, he directed the design of the ARPANET and brought together many of the key players in ARPANET history throughout 1967, and by 1968 he was in charge of the proposal round which eventually landed Bolt, Beranek and Newman the job of constructing the Interface Message Processor (IMP), which became the first version of what we now think of as a router. He was in charge of the ARPANET project when it came online for the first time in 1969 and when it became fully operational and demonstrated to the world at the ICCC conference in 1972 (which Roberts erroneously says was in 1971 in the interview). In 1973, Roberts left ARPA to try to make build a commercial version of the ARPANET and has since had an illustrious career as a network technology pioneer. But before then, Roberts had also contributed to wireless computer networking through his and ARPA/IPTO's involvement with ALOHAnet in Hawai'i and pre-TCP/IP internet-working, when other networks, like ALOHAnet, were connected to the ARPANET.

At the same time, he was in charge of funding and project managing early work in artificial intelligence and overall development of computer technologies from his ARPA/IPTO perch. With his central position in the development and management of the ARPANET, Roberts' perspective has very little distance to actual events that occurred. In this interview, Roberts not only shares this view of history, but also his perspective on the contentious origin narratives surrounding the Internet, ARPANET and packet switching, as well as his life-long friendship with another Internet/ARPANET pioneer, Leonard Kleinrock.

MB: Tell me about the early days at MIT. You were working on graphics, correct?

LR: Basically, the beginning of my career after my Ph.D., or during my Ph.D. at MIT, was to work on graphics, and I really had undertaken to do the first hidden-line elimination display. In fact, at the moment they claim 12 of the original facets of mov-iemaking are based on that work of creating images in 3D and displaying them. At that point, I just figured I was way beyond where anybody was going to use it for 30 years, and I was right. I met Licklider at a conference when we were both sitting around talking between meetings and Lick was talking to me about what the import-ant things in the future would be, what we needed to do, and one of them was to build a network where we'd connect all our computers together so we could share knowledge. Back then, computers were incompatible and couldn't share anything between them. I had had the same problem at MIT, I had photographs on a machine and no one else did because I had the only scanner in the environment. I had rebuilt an old fax machine to scan into a computer. So [Marvin] Minsky wanted those for his artificial intelligence work, and I had to mount a new tape drive on the machine and interface it to it, and then build a tape for him which was compatible with his machine. It was very difficult to do things, to make data transfer between machines. It would take a month to make the transfer. This was sort of like the problem I was starting to think about, which was that language let people talk or communicate in years with knowledge going from person-to-person over generations. Publishing did it in months. And we needed to do it in seconds to get knowledge around the world, to improve the growth of knowledge. So that was the original impetus in my head. Lick had left ARPA; he had been funding and transferring research into all the universities. Lick left Ivan Sutherland in charge of the program at ARPA and Ivan had worked me at Lincoln [Laboratory] before, and we knew each other. Ivan funded a project that I wanted to do, which was to try and connect two computers together, and I did that experiment between the computers at Lincoln Labs, the big TX-2 which was the whole basement, and the computer at SDC in Los Angeles. And that worked beautifully, as far as the computers were concerned. I could talk to the other computers and do a matrix multiply on this machine and then come back and use the results and do shared computing; I could use his computer, and he could use mine and so on. And that worked great, but I saw that the real problem was that we used the dial-up tele-phone network, and it was much too slow, and we were using it $1/15^{th}$ of the time, it was bursty, so we had a very high peak error rejection which held up through-times, that's the way computers are. And so, we knew it was costing us 15 times as much as we really needed, but we couldn't dial up every time, it was too slow. And dialing up was slow to begin with, it took 4–10 seconds to get connected, and on top of that, the reliability and the noise was pretty bad on the line. In the process, I designed packets so that they had a sumcheck that was related to the noise rate on top of lines, so that I had an optimal transfer data rate because I had to retransmit it if there was an error.

MB: Where did you get the idea of splitting a message up into packets from?

LR: Well, the packet splitting was necessary in order to be able to have the error rate reasonable. If you send too long a packet, you'll have an error for sure. Telephone lines have burst noise, and so we'd have a burst on some other telephone, and that would just ruin a block. We lost a block at a time, and so we made the block short enough that the transfer rate was optimal. And that was easily configured once we measured the rate.

MB: And when did you do this experiment?

LR: This was done in 1965. I met Licklider in 1964, and the experiment was done in '65, and we published it in '66. Ivan left ARPA and left his deputy in charge. Bob Taylor was his deputy and was a behavioral science major, like Licklider was. They were not really computer people to begin with, and didn't really know how to do it, but knew it should be done. And so, Bob kept on pursuing me, as Ivan had been doing before, to come run the program and build the network. I thought manage-ment was not what I wanted to be doing, but it turned out that's what I was doing at Lincoln. I took over the whole team there just by fiat because the director left and no one else was going to manage it, so I managed it. And I wound up finally getting a call from the director of Lincoln saying that Herzfeld, the director of ARPA, who Bob had talked to, had called up and said they had 51% of Lincoln's funding, and it would be good if I came down and worked with them. And the director was very good, he convinced me that it'd be worthwhile for me and he'd take me back if I didn't like it.

That was sufficient motivation to go on, at the end of 1966, to join ARPA. I did that as the Chief Scientist, so that I wasn't in the same box as Bob, basically. I worked and actually managed the IPT office, the technical aspects of the office. Bob handled a lot of the administrative things and worked with the military and interfacing with them, and he left about the time we started the network. I designed the network in that period, in 1967, when I came to the office.

MB: You came to ARPA to plan and project manage the ARPANET project. You brought an old friend on board fairly quickly, correct?

LR: Leonard Kleinrock was my office mate at Lincoln, and we worked together all through that period, then he went to UCLA. He wrote his book on network theory in 1964, and I had that book, and I had worked with him on the queuing theory parts of it. He had worked a lot on all parts of the network theory of how you might do top-ology, how you might do packets. We didn't call it packets until I met with NPL later, but we knew they were split messages. He'd run up all that very effectively and so I knew that if we could do the queueing and not lose packets, we could have a big enough buffer to manage packets in the network. The SDC/Lincoln Labs experiment didn't need switching because it was a single link. So that was where packets were designed with packet length and set headers and trailers and sum checks. And Len's work gave all the queuing theory and network theory, and when I went to ARPA, I hired Len at UCLA to do the measurement of the network once we got it going and he ran the measurement lab because we knew his theory had to be proven. It was all theory, and he now needed to go and measure what was happening and make sure the theory was correct, which it was. So, he was doing that. My job was to layout the project, which I did in 1967. I talked to all of the ARPA PIs at the annual meeting at '67 and explained to them what I wanted to do and that they all should be connected on their computers. All of them said no ... or almost all of them said no. Len said yes, SRI said yes, and Ivan, who was at the University of Utah said yes. But the others said no because they didn't want to lose computer time to everybody else. Within a year, that all changed. But it wasn't hard to convince them because I said: "I won't buy you any more computers until you connect to the network". So it was very simple because it would give you computer power all across the network and my projection was that we would save a lot of money on computing. I saved three times as much money as they would have spent on computing by having the network built - and the network was well less than a third of that cost. So we basically saved money on our computing with the network, but the network was the real success.

But so, in 1967 I then commissioned a group of people at the various locations, Elmer Shapiro was the lead on that project, and they wrote up the RFP for me to, under my direction, in how to build the network equipment, a switch. And the network consisted of lots of pieces. For one, it had telephone lines that were all over the country, and we had to choose the right kind of lines. Luckily, in '67, I also gave a speech on the network at Gatlinburg, Tennessee and met with a colleague of Donald Davies at that meeting. He gave a paper on what they were thinking of as packet networking in their lab, they couldn't get funding for a nationwide or a wide area network, but they were doing an experiment locally. He pointed out that there were higher speed lines than I had known about, that we could get 50 kilobit lines. They used nine telephone lines and a huge modem that was the size of a great big box, but it was feasible and being a top actor in the government, I could get that economically. So I then changed my plans from going with lower speed lines to the 50-kilobit lines. That made it much more economical and much faster. And I also changed the name to use 'packet', because they used 'packet' in England, because in England, mail was packets, and that was a nice word to use. So that all changed during that period, we got the RFP out and BBN won that RFP to build the switch. We had written up the RFP with help from the contractors to lay out what kind of switching equipment we needed so that we could have a little computer, a minicomputer, that would do the switching and use the main computer just for the connection. That was Wes Clarke's idea. I had originally done it in the main computer between SDC and Lincoln. And that was okay, but it was a special job at every machine, so it would be better to have a separate switching machine and we did that. It was difficult at the time because there weren't many minicomputers or small enough computers. Both IBM and SDC said this is impossible, no good. AT&T of course and the Western Union people thought this was hopeless as well. DCA, the Defense Communication Agency, told me I was crazy. Luckily ARPA was strong enough, so that wasn't an issue, what other people said. And in fact, much of the Congress supported the program that I put forward. It was only a $15 million project to begin with. It got bigger over time, but to build the network up to where it was started, it was 15 million. So it wasn't a major undertaking in terms of expense. The job of laying out the network is a topology design job which wound up optimizing the cost, because you can have lines in different connections between all of the switches and the cost is very different. I did a huge amount of work on that myself and laid that out. Later in that program, I hired a contractor who was going to help me out with the program. But I just gave all of the papers on that to the museum they're starting at UCLA on the network, showing how the network was designed. I then ordered all the lines because I was within the DoD. I ordered all the lines, and I chose the universities and got them involved and had them do their work too. Each one of them connected to the network.

MB: But why did you do that? Why involve the universities? What was the motivation for that?

LR: We needed it to be anything but a defense network like SAGE, which sort of connected computers, but in a very specific way, for very specific purposes, so it wasn't a general purpose concept. The only way to take a new concept like a network and have it be general purpose and find out all the things you could do with it, you needed people to experiment and do what they wanted to do between computers. And so, one of the things I encouraged was people to use other computers at night on the other side of the country and that sort of thing. That gave them computer power somewhere else, where it was available. If a student needed additional computer power at, say, ISI in California, they'd built up a big collection of computers. And if they needed parallel computing, I'd send them to the ILLIAC IV when it came up … It was started in Illinois, we put it at NASA Ames. Similar, special capabilities … but also, people who were just working in a similar field, like Minsky at MIT and McCarthy at Stanford, who were both doing artificial intelligence and worked together on papers and things like that. People used the network for many, many different things throughout the country, and that got all the concepts going. In 1971 we had a whole collection of things that worked over the network, and I hired Bob Kahn out of BBN where he had been working on the design of the switch, into ARPA, so he could help. He ran and built up a big conference in Washington in 1971 where we showed the world what this could really do. And there were experiments, all sorts of experiments in there that showed things being remotely controlled throughout the network from other computers around it, including robots that ran around the room and things like that.

MB: Which conference was that?

LR: Well, that was the ICCC in 1971. It was part of the conference, a standard large communications conference. It was a huge success because nobody ever thought about this before and nobody, hardly anybody in the world had noticed it until 1971. We had put it in papers and presented it previously; I'd written a number of papers and continued to do that. But, that was that. Then it became clear that it was successful and effective. We knew what the cost-efficiency was. It was still the 15 to 1 [cost-efficiency] that I had figured out, so we knew that it was tremendously less expensive than what we were doing. Even less expensive than voice, which is 3 to 1. In other words, you talk a third of the time, I talk a third of the time, and the other third is silence. So my way is I use only a third, so I knew voice would be cost effective as well, even though it turns out the packet switching is now much less expensive because you can use very high-speed lines and share them completely without fixed-rate audio or you can have variable, different size transmissions, and it's not fixed to 64 kilobits. So, voice over IP had a net gain, and I proposed that by 1981 in the speech I gave at the conference in Stockholm ... Len and I were given the first award, which was the same as the Nobel award except that it was done by Ericsson because Nobel didn't allow an award in mathematics or computer science.

MB: Can you tell me the reason for that?

LR: Well, the story that they told me was that Nobel's wife ran off and married a mathematician, and that's true. The fact that he wrote it out of his will so the guy could never win the award is unclear, but that was the total reason. But he probably didn't believe it was worth it. It wasn't a real science like physics and chemistry. In any case, we got that award, and my speech was that voice would happen in 20 years because it would take that long for the telephone industry to change even though it was much cheaper.

MB: Hmm ... And that's exactly what happened.

LR: That's exactly the year that it started.

MB: That's interesting. So going back to 1969 when the first IMP arrived at UCLA. Where were you at the time?

LR: Well, I was in Washington because I needed to do many other things and I actually came out afterward and met with SRI and UCLA, but I was organizing the next nodes and organizing the overall program, which was a large program in computer science. I mean, I was running a $15mn project in computer science, and so, actually, that grew to $50 million while I was there. I was running a lot of different activities, and I knew that they would succeed in what they what doing. BBN was there to install it and Len and UCLA and SRI connected up the computers in October 1969. And we kept on installing, In Santa Barbara and Utah for the first four and then on through the country, back to the east coast pretty quickly because we wanted to get BBN and MIT connected.

MB: Tell me about how the network grew from there?

LR: Well, it kept on growing, we added new machines continuously as fast as we could get lines and machines installed. By '71 when the network became really functional, in the period between 1969 and 1971 it was experimental, and people were trying things and doing things, but I would say that real work and real, savings in computer activity work of many types were serious in 1971. In 1971, we also started email because [Ray] Tomlinson had built a program that did read mail and send mail. It would send a message that came out like a teletext stream, and I tried that. Steve Lukasik, who was then the head guy at ARPA, the director of ARPA, tried it, and it was hopeless. He couldn't read it and use it because it was just sort of like a teletext stream of messages and you had to try and then reenter all the addresses and so on. So, in my spare time, I wrote a program in an editor that would do email in system like e-mail programs today and send and receive.

MB: Okay, so you actually wrote that? Because the general consensus is that Ray Tomlinson did email.

LR: Ray Tomlinson did the initial work of having a program in the computer that would send a message with an address being something@something. So the @-sign came from Ray. But those programs were rather dysfunctional in terms of being able to use them very well. So I wrote the program that was just done in a text editor that looked at all that, put it in a file, sorted them out and just gave me the headers and then I could read when I wanted, and I could forward it, and I could save it to files, and I could reply, that sort of thing. And that made it much more usable and then, at that point, Steve Lukasik decided it was so functional that he demanded everybody at ARPA, all of the agencies, all of the officers, to use it because ARPA was all over the world. Keeping people together in time zones on phone calls was impossible. So this helped tremendously in managing a worldwide organization, and it was … from then on, it was just hundreds of messages a day for me and the people involved. And each one of the locations got involved and then we added more locations including Xerox PARC and IBM and other commercial sites where they were doing research and could help with research.

MB: So could you tell me a little bit about what happened after?

LR: NSFNET was after this, but in '71, the ARPANET was then connected into lots of places and added ALOHA and the radio network in Hawai'i, and we added the English network. We had a line, a seismic line to Norway that we were paying for in ARPA and Steve figured that we could squeeze that in as just another process on a switch in Norway. So we ran a line from Norway to the UK and connected them end to end. He basically then connected all of the UK computers in by a separate translator and gateway between the ARPANET and sort of a UK network. And we had also planned the packet radio network that we were going to build with spread-spectrum. Something like WiFi, very much like it. WiFi didn't use spread-spectrum, but it used Slotted ALOHA, which I designed in '71. That was the way to send, how to get a slot. And we had all of these things going on, and so I thought that it was pretty well sta- bilised and I talked to AT&T and Western Union about taking over the network. Could we get somebody to run it as an operation because ARPA did research and not opera- tions? Well, they wouldn't. AT&T spent a good bit of time looking at it. They had a huge group from the labs and the management, and they said that it was incompat- ible with their network. They didn't want it even though I was offering it to them free and they could charge for it. So they basically turned it down. I went to Bernie Strassburg at the FCC, and I said, "What can I do?" And he said, "start a company, we're open for new companies, like MCI. So I told BBN about that, and they worked on that, and they put together the concept of a company and planned to do it. Because I knew the next step had to make it commercially viable. It was viable as long as the government paid for it. Everybody now argued that it wasn't viable com- mercially. So, my next proof was to make it commercially viable and starting Telenet, which BBN originally funded, and I worked hard to find somebody to replace me in '73 at ARPA and Lick came back for a little while to do that. Eventually, Bob [Kahn] took over; Bob was there. And Bob hired Vint [Cerf] to come in and work with him. So Bob and Vint basically continued the network activity. Bob Kahn and Vint worked in the office and continued that theory and found that there were tons of things to do so they did some and they turned over to DCA, in part, to do the military part. They turned the other part over to NSF and NSF took that over. And then NSF eventually put their own switches in and switched to T1 lines and not the BBN equipment. That was a transition that happened and then they let it go commercial in the early 90 s, but it was ... it was a process of getting it out of ARPA into both NSF and DCA, and then NSF wanted to get it out and just let it go commercial.

MB: When did you go into the private sector?

LR: Well, I went to Telenet in '73, and in October I'd helped write the prospectus for the FCC, and we filed that when I left ARPA in October of '73. That got approved pretty quickly, even though AT&T argued against it. But we got approved, and I had the right because of the government rights to free software, we used the ARPA soft- ware. We bought similar machines and started the network using that software, but modified to have a new interface, because I knew you couldn't use this old connection we used. We had to build a network connection which was the X.75. And I planned and designed the X.75 and took it to the CCITT, which is now the ITU in Geneva, to approve our standard to the world. And that standard was done within three years. It was approved by '75, and we could then use it about when we were ready with the network. We had an interface built for the PDP-10 and I bought a small company that built it for the IBM machine. We had interfaces for two machines and people could build other ones, so it worked out pretty well.

MB: Working at the DoD, how did the Cold War sentiments of the 1960s and early 1970s influence your work to push computer networking forward?

LR: Well, let me just talk about what ARPA, what we told Congress, as far as the world's interest was. The military certainly needed communications that were effective and pervasive and could talk between all the locations and could handle video and voice and data and move information quickly around for them. But so did the entire world. So this was pushed to the Congress as basically something that would help both of them equally. It wasn't just military. It was not for nuclear defense; that was a concept that Paul Baran had in his work. We knew that reliability was critical in any network, just because we didn't want it failing a lot, and in fact, at that time, we had computers that failed fairly often, and we had network lines that failed fairly often. So we had much less reliable parts than we have today. Today, networks are pretty stable and far better, and therefore the packets can be longer. That hasn't changed as much as it should, because we designed the packets, back when I started, for telephone lines, and now we have fiber and it could be much different. But in any case, that's something that the military was interested in. They clearly thought it was valuable for them and the government thought it was also valuable for the civilians, and it was. I was interested because this would let knowledge be shared and let research move at a much higher rate, allowing people to communicate at a much faster rate between each other and handle problems faster. Management, research, everything.

MB: When did it dawn on you that the network had to be distributed rather than centralised?

LR: Well, Len and I talked about this quite a bit when we were at MIT in the early 60s and the question of it being centralised we both hated, because the reliability is ridiculous. You can't build a reliable system. The concept in my mind was always that it was distributed, absolutely. In fact, one of my problems with the open flow concept that people are putting forward today is it's going more to centralisation, which is very dangerous. We've seen that problem in networks throughout the world. There was a failure in Japan which was extremely serious. Electricity failed in a whole section of Japan, all of the voice telephones came back up at once and tried to call in to get their SIP number, couldn't get it because they all hit at once and the computer overloaded and crashed. Then they all came back as soon as the computer came up and it crashed again. What they had to do was turn off the power in all of the city, except section by section. This is the only way they could get the network back up, and this problem is really severe, and we've seen it happen to our cloud networks as well. You have too many things that are connected in too seriously complex a way, and coming back up, they can't do it. You have to have that problem solved from the beginning.

So, every network I've designed has been one where there is no single component and no component that can be overloaded.

MB: Was that just something that you discovered during your early studies or did it come out of a science fiction interest, such as the one Leonard Kleinrock says he was inspired by?

LR: Oh, I have read a lot of science fiction and that may have had something to do with it. But it was more just thinking about the reliability of what we were working with at that time, and working with Len on what the network topology needed to be, and he was working on it from 1960 on, and we were sharing an office during that whole period.

MB: Okay, one anecdote I'd like to get in there is the razor story, Kleinrock's electric razor?

LR: Well, one of the things that we undertook to do in the program was to have meetings periodically with all of the people to talk about what was going on in the programs. We did that in England because [Peter] Kirstein could arrange a location at the university for us, and so we were in Brighton, England. We were staying in dorm rooms and had our meeting and Len left his razor in the room, in his room, his electric razor, and went off to home early. And basically he found me on the network. Well, at that time … you see, we think that instant mail or [iMessage] that we use today is new. It was going on *then*. What we did then was to say, "Where is this person?", and it looked at all the computers and found the person, if they were online, and then he found me online, I was actually on the ISI machine. But he found me online and could connect to me and send text and everything he typed, I could see, and vice versa. So he then asked me to bring his razor back. It turned out that Danny Cohen was going to California, so I gave it to him to take to Len. But we got it to him. And he now points out that was the first illegal use of the network. We had claimed it shouldn't be used for personal use. We didn't push that very hard, though, because people all over the network were using it for whatever they wanted … who were on it legitimately, but they used it for all reasons. We found out, in fact, that it was a lot of people in Hawai'i who were getting all of their news through the network because somebody had connected the news feed to the network and they didn't have any newspapers that weren't local in Hawai'i. They couldn't find out what the price of gold or anything was. So, they had to use the news feed to get it to him.

MB: How did you react when Tim Berners-Lee built the World Wide Web as an application on top of the Internet that got it out to a much broader audience?

LR: Well, I thought it was fantastic, but we knew that was going to happen. Ted Nelson had been talking about it for years. Ted was a friend and colleague during that period, and he had this idea about that, and somehow, he had built that within their data center that we used straight from the beginning, to do all the documentation, but it was only within the building. It wasn't used over the net, and so I knew how it worked, and I knew that it would work. But nobody built it. Tim got frustrated with the world and had the capability at CERN to go do it, and he did it. It was really the people here that helped turn it into Netscape and made it commercial that made it happen, widespread. But Tim pushed it very hard and really got the thing going and had the first program, and he's continued to maintain it, to maintain the concept.

MB: What would you want your legacy to be?

LR: Well, what I really wanted to do since then … when I started the network, was to work with flows and packets because packets needed to be there … chop up flows into packets. And a flow is a telephone call or video stream, or a data file transfer, that's a flow. It may be huge, it may be short, but we have to break it up into packets to move it effectively. The problems the network still has have been there since we started. That is the fact that by only managing packets and sending them to the destination, even if we keep them in order, even if we do everything we can, by queueing them and discarding random packets and adding delay in the queueing, we're seriously hurting the quality of service we can deliver and the response time that people get. A web page should come up in a fraction of a second. There's no reason why it shouldn't. But it takes seconds because of the congestion at the local access link, and that's due to delay and packet loss in the local link where the main congestion control occurs and queueing. And we started with queues because it was the only thing we could do. The memory on a computer in 1969 was so small, 4K words or so, it was extremely small, we couldn't store all the flows, there was no way to keep track of them. Today, memory has gotten cheaper much faster than broadband. So now we can store all the flows and make the system much cheaper, five times less expensive than doing it with queueing by keeping track of all the flows. As soon as we route the first packet of flow and keep track of where it's going, we can stream it at the right rate, and we can manage it without having to use queueing and dropping packets randomly and delaying them. By getting rid of that, we can dramatically improve what the network looks like, and dramatically reduce the cost. But I haven't been able to get that completed in startups because startups are very hard to run to the point of widespread deliveries and it really needs to happen within a larger company, which I've been trying to get going as well. The network needs to change; it's just got too much … we don't have to change the protocol; we don't need to change what TCP looks like, we need to change how the network works, so it doesn't destroy the traffic.

MB: But, that's kind of what you're working on now. How do you want to be remembered?

LR: Well, I'm sure I'll be remembered for starting it. But what I knew at that time was that I was doing it wrong. And I want to get that fixed. Because it needs the quality that we could have, so we can do surge rates and can do other things that we can't do today. Even voice works substantially poorly over the wireless. Moving on to voice over IP over wireless, everybody will find that there are serious problems over WiFi or wireless. Today, you have your phone, but it's cellular voice, it's not wireless voice, it's not voice over IP, and that has too much data. We need to fix that. That can be fixed pretty easily. When it's not easy to fix wireless, wireless is the worst media because you're competing to send.

MB: Bob Taylor had a note in The New York Times around the time of one of the Internet anniversaries where he basically diminishes the role you and Leonard Kleinrock played in this. Do you have a reaction to that or have you seen what he said?

LR: Oh, I have seen Bob, not recently, but at the point where he was very mixed-up about this. He just is mixed-up at this point. I don't know what his problem is and I'm not willing to argue with him anymore about it, because he just wants to believe that his place in the process isn't properly accounted for. And in reality, what he did was to get me hired. That's all he did. That was important, but that wasn't what invented the network. It didn't design the network, it didn't help... the network really was designed at MIT before we left. By the time Len and I had finished our work, and I went to ARPA, I knew how to build it, that wasn't the problem. The problem was to get the funding and get the organization behind it. And so it really is sad that Bob is going off like this. Of course, Vint and Bob [Kahn] would like to believe that the Internet started when TCP started, but that's not viable either because the Internet was really there since we started, and packet switching was there since we started, which is really the primary change. TCP... IP will change, I mean, IPv6 will replace it shortly. TCP will be there, TCP is actually very effective, but I've got a new standard now at the ITU that I'd just completed that will dramatically improve that. That will make it stream smoothly through the network at the maximum rate you can send without any delays.

MB: Bob Taylor also once said that the four of you "breathe your own exhaust", and that in the case of TCP/IP, he had the PUP protocol running at Xerox PARC which basically was the beginning of the Internet. Vint Cerf reacted very strongly to that when I interviewed him. Can I get your reaction to that?

LR: There clearly were many different protocols that people worked on over time, and the thing that was critical about TCP/IP is that it became the worldwide standard and that was joint function of Bob and Vint. Bob was probably the strongest in that respect. I mean Vint did all of the design and a lot of people had to argue with him over certain parts of it and he took their advice and added IP, because originally, he didn't want IP. Eventually, in 1986 it had to be improved because it was collapsing due to not enough congestion control. But TCP has been overall... it's a very strong protocol. The reason why it's important is because it was a standard that got used worldwide. That happened because Bob made it a standard required for selling to the government. And made the program that received it free. So, you could just use the program and if you sold to the government, you had to have it. But that really locks in the standard in a way. As far as Bob [Taylor] goes, his arguments against people, all of us, not just me, in fact I don't know how much of it is against me or how much is against Len, is really, mostly noise as far as I can see. Because he wants to believe that there were many more people involved in the work, and there were, but none of them contributed critically to the core. What happened was, when the National Academy of Engineering met and tried to decide who really were the key people, they decided on the four of us, and that was a critical decision. Of course, that was early in the path and the World Wide Web hadn't become serious yet.

MB: The four of you being?

LR: Bob Kahn, Vint Cerf, Leonard Kleinrock and myself, who are called the "Four Fathers" because of the National Academy of Engineering decision … which is the only really serious decision and exploration of who was critically involved. They interviewed hundreds of people. And Bob was involved because he got me involved and got the office involved. The money was actually only authorised even though he got Herzfeld to say something or do something early, I had to get the money approved totally independently after that, and that money was like $15 million at that point, not $1 million. But the issue with Bob is one of … I wish that he would just calm down and take what credit is due to him rather than trying to argue about everything else. The Internet was a critical change in the society, we know that, and it started with packet switching and got improved with TCP and got improved with the World Wide Web. That was a major change. In fact, the second most important award in my career, besides the one from the National Academy, was the one that occurred in Spain where they have a similar ceremony that's like the Nobel ceremony. Big parades on the street and everything else, and they had myself and Bob Kahn and Vint Cerf and Berners-Lee. Len was the research part. They weren't looking at the development part.

MB: What is your take on the origins of packet switching?

LR: Paul [Baran] was one of the first people to write about it. He wrote about it and published it mainly in '64, but he did some earlier things. Len published his thesis proposal much earlier and had the first known papers and certainly the first book. It was published in '64 as well. But Paul never tried to claim he was involved in it. He just wanted to keep on moving the technology forward and believed in it. So he did many other companies and Paul was an amazing person. I think that it was other people who mixed it up and he actually tried to correct them all the time.

MB: Finally, there are some crazy stories about your adventures Leonard Kleinrock in Las Vegas before all of this happened?

LR: Yeah … We spent a lot of time developing a counting system is now used in Vegas for BlackJack, the Hi-Lo system. I don't know how it spread, but I developed it early on, and Len and I converted to that. Len was using the Thorpe system, and that was impossible to use. But we won quite a bit at that time. Can't do that anymore.

ORCID

Morten Bay (iD) http://orcid.org/0000-0003-1431-3297

Section II
Global perspectives

French memories about the ARPANET: a conversation with Michel Élie and Gérard Le Lann

Camille Paloque-Bergès and Valérie Schafer

ABSTRACT
Although the ARPANET was a United States-funded project that was deeply rooted in US post-war science and technology policies, it had an international dimension from its very early days. The memories of Michel Élie and Gérard Le Lann are oriented towards their US experience. They testify to an early French presence in the ARPANET project at two stages of its history: in 1969–1970, when the first nodes came into activity, and in 1973–1974, when TCP, which evolved into TCP/IP and became the Internet's flagship protocol, was defined, replacing NCP, which was at the heart of the ARPANET. They thus highlight crucial but different sides of the ARPANET's genesis.

Although the ARPANET was a United States-funded project that was deeply rooted in US post-war science and technology policies, it had an international dimension from its earliest days. This can be attributed not only to a geopolitical configuration that saw new interest in computer-related innovation in the context of the Space Race and the Cold War, but also to the allure of the research topic, which attracted the interest of several other institutions and countries. This meant that the influence and participation of scientists from abroad was palpable, with some making the trip from Europe and Asia in order to keep abreast of the latest developments in computer technologies. Moreover, an appreciation of the need for standardisation as an integral feature of communication networks was clear in the definition of ARPANET's protocols from the start – although this appreciation was less normative than experimental, as historian Andrew Russell (2014) has shown.

The early transformation of the Network Working Group (NWG), set up in 1969 at the University of California, Los Angeles (UCLA), into the International Network Working Group (INWG) in 1972 demonstrated an international openness. But this openness was relative, and debates on Internet development and governance have pointed to the strong American biases in the ARPANET's genesis.[1] In parallel with the development of the ARPANET, a number of initiatives were also being launched across the Atlantic, both in the United Kingdom, at the National Physical Laboratory,[2] and in France.

The accounts by Michel Élie and Gérard Le Lann are oriented towards their US experience. They testify to an early French presence in the ARPANET project at two stages of its history: in 1969–1970, when the first nodes came into activity, and in 1973–1974, when TCP, which evolved into TCP/IP and became the Internet's flagship protocol, was defined, replacing NCP which was at the heart of the ARPANET. They thus highlight crucial but different sides of the ARPANET's genesis. It is notable that they both remember a particular way of working together (a tangible "spirit") based on horizontal collaboration and personal initiative, which appeared to be more supported and encouraged in the United States than in the French context.

Nevertheless, on returning to France, they found people who were interested in these issues and a dynamic and complex national and European context, which we will trace in broad terms to enable the reader to contextualise the two accounts.

Michel Élie and Gérard Le Lann benefited both from the strong boost given to computer science and technologies by the French government programme *Plan Calcul* (Griset, 1998), launched by President Charles de Gaulle in 1966, which aimed to develop the national computer industry as well as to strengthen education and research in the field (Mounier-Kuhn, 1998); and from funding for transatlantic research trips, which was granted because the USA was considered a pioneer in this area.

Michel Élie studied engineering in the 1960s, starting in electronics, which served as a suitable grounding for a career in the emerging field of computer technology. He subsequently gained experience in pioneering manufacturing companies supported by the French government, including SEA (Société d'Électronique appliquée à l'Automatisme – Company for Electronics applied to Automatics) and CII (Compagnie Internationale d'Informatique – International Informatics Company). Indeed, electronics sustained one of the three main strands underpinning the French computing industry at that time: alongside science- and management-oriented strands, computing was machine-oriented, rooted in the expertise of engineers and incorporating an experimental side that would pave the way for the field of computer science, which was formalised in the 1970s (Neumann, Petitgirard, & Paloque-Bergès, 2016). Élie's first steps were therefore among telecommunication engineers, who applied radio techniques and electronics to information processing to help manage networks. He contributed to early experiments on interactions between computers and telecommunications, real-time computing and remote processing, and his involvement in the industry also meant that he was confronted with issues related to machine-assisted tools and accountability management. As soon as punched-card systems allowed remote processing, decentralised transactional networks brought about the modernisation of data input, transmission and processing in large companies. With computerisation, the development of transnational networks, most of them supported by telecommunication infrastructures, accelerated in the civilian sector throughout the 1960s, especially in transport, energy and banking. By 1967 there were about 400 transmission terminals (Mounier-Kuhn, 2002).

Gérard Le Lann's scientific career began in applied mathematics, initially at CERN (the European Organization for Nuclear Research), then at IRIA (the French Institute for Research in Computer Science and Automation) (Beltran & Griset, 2007). Although networks were not an immediate focus of the research programme pursued by IRIA, which was set up in 1966 as a result of the *Plan Calcul*, the scientific community had begun developing an interest in networks in the mid-1960s. The first area to attract attention was real time and time-sharing, as reflected by a symposium on the topic held by the society AFIRO[3] in 1966. INRIA (known as IRIA until 1979, until an "n" for "national" was added) tackled the topic with projects on operating systems such as ESOPE, which contributed to computer science being recognised as a legitimate research discipline in France (Paloque-Bergès & Petitgirard, 2017). From 1969 onwards, after a major conference on teleinformatics called for the computerisation of telecommunication technologies, computer systems became inextricably associated with remote computing (Mounier-Kuhn, 2002). In 1972, at the instigation of the "Délégation à l'informatique," set up to stimulate French computer research, the famous Cyclades project, which aimed to develop a data network, was hosted by IRIA. Led by Louis Pouzin, this packet-switching network was initially inspired by ARPANET and its first official demonstration took place in November 1973. Although it was operational, the Cyclades network was then cancelled in 1979 after struggles with the telecommunications people, who distrusted datagrams.[4] This temporarily sidelined a technical solution that would later influence packet-switching networks and the ARPANET protocols (Schafer, 2012; Russell, 2014). Indeed, the datagram model was later adopted in TCP/IP. Pouzin himself had visited the United States to find out about Project MAC (Project on Mathematics and Computation) at MIT in the mid-1960s and would cross the Atlantic again several times in the 1970s (Salus, 1995), also sending Gérard Le Lann, who had joined his team, to the USA.

At the same time, the powerful French telecommunications administration was also interested in networks. Indeed, networks were at the confluence of computing and telecommunications: possessing the necessary infrastructures to develop networks, telecommunications specialists also conducted research on packet switching in the early 1970s; this led in 1976 to the Transpac network, which would go on to support French Minitel traffic. Although we will not go into detail about the divergent paths in packet switching adopted by the French computing and telecommunications industries (see Russell & Schafer, 2014), the tensions between the two approaches were also apparent in other countries such as the United Kingdom. However, European countries were also willing to set up transnational networks.

In the early 1970s, alongside the first public demonstration of the ARPANET in 1972 and the development of the TCP protocol by Robert Kahn and Vinton Cerf in 1974, packet-switching networks were also being studied at European level, resulting in the EIN (European Informatics Network) and Euronet. The EIN drew on ideas similar to those of the ARPANET or Cyclades for its packet-switching network, while Euronet, launched a few years later, fell more within the realm of the work being carried out by telecommunications operators; its choices were similar to those adopted in 1976 at CCITT (Consultative Committee for International Telephony and Telegraphy) with the recommendation X25 (*Avis X25*), which became a credible alternative to TCP/IP and was adopted for a lengthy period in France (within the Transpac network, which supported the Minitel traffic until 2012; see Schafer & Thierry, 2012; Mailland & Driscoll, 2017) and also in Costa Rica (Siles, 2017).

The interviews with Michel Élie and Gérard Le Lann indeed emphasise the major issue of standardisation and the "protocol wars"[5] that arose in the 1970s and continued into the 1980s and 1990s. These battles were not limited to the choice between TCP/IP and X25. Although the tense relationships between French computer scientists and the telecom sector shaped the development of data networks in the 1970s and 1980s—with the telecom model winning a first match with the Transpac network, which famously hosted the Minitel terminals from 1984 onwards—it is also important to bear in mind the OSI (Open Systems Interconnection) model.[6]

Finally, Michel Élie and Gérard Le Lann look back, while also keeping an eye on the present and the future, highlighting why these innovations are still relevant and continue to merit our full attention 50 years on.

Camille Paloque-Bergès and Valérie Schafer (Itw): Let's start from the beginning ... How did you get involved in networks? What was the situation in France at the time, in terms of computer networks research and developments?

Michel Élie: I studied the engineering of strong currents at Supélec[7] in 1961 and then I learnt about weak currents and transmissions at Sup Aero, the National School of Aeronautics. Then I did my civil service in 1964–1965 in Algeria. I was working on hydroelectric plants and dams.

In 1965 I returned to France and worked at the CAE (Compagnie d'Automatisme d'Électronique – Electronics Automation Company), which at the time of the Plan Calcul,[8] in 1966, merged with the SEA (Society of Electronics and Automation) and other companies, in order to create the CII (International Computer Company). The CII would become the leading French computer manufacturer.

At the CAE I worked on transmission issues for EDF (Électricité de France, the French national electricity company), on automating the French electric dispatching system. Real-time and resilient systems were involved, and we installed one of the first high-speed links between Paris dispatching and the CDC 6600 Control Data supercomputer of the EDF research department in Clamart.[9] I was somewhat of a system engineer, working on architecture.

We developed transactional networks based on pre-processing data locally through what we called "*concentrateur-diffuseur*" systems. This approach consisted in concentrating data from terminals, thanks to an end-user dialogue for data pre-processing. There were also other networking developments in big companies, usually in the shape of dedicated, specialised networks, such as networks for processing airline reservations or meteorological data. Telecommunication networks, such as message switching and telex were also emerging.

At the time, computing power was, in France, in the hands of computer centres, which were very much centralised, and imposed their conditions on users and even on companies. They were able to "hold up" the entire computing world. Machine centres were quite an investment: they hosted workshops of tabulating machines (called *mécanographie* in French) for punching cards. Transmissions were very slow, and data communication costs very high.

Itw: What led you to leave for the USA in 1968? What was the state of the computing world in the social context of that year?

Michel Élie: In 1968 I decided to get some fresh air. In France, 1968 was an eventful period ... and equally so at the CII in that respect. There was a lot of innovation in this company, in particular in the field of programming, led by François-Henri Raymond.[10]

He was keen to involve engineers in the company decisions, and took the opportunity of an annual general meeting at the Louveciennes headquarters[11] during the May '68 events to make proposals in this direction. This did not help him afterwards …

I did not get formal training in computing. I was keen to study in order to increase my basic knowledge. I thought it was a good idea to go to the USA. At SICOB,[12] we had demonstrated a piece of remote transaction management software called GESTRA. This demonstration had been prepared with Gérard Deloche, who left for UCLA just afterwards. I stayed in touch with him and applied for a scholarship. As part of the "Plan Calcul," there were incentives available to send young engineers to the USA. Several types of scholarship were available. I got one from the CRI (Computing Research Center). I could choose between several universities, including UCLA, Utah and Yale, and Gerard Deloche convinced me to go to UCLA and work on the ARPA network project. I arrived in the summer of 1969 and I left in the autumn of 1970.

I enrolled in a Master's degree and discovered the US university system, of which I became very appreciative, especially for its openness. We could study in one main area, computer science, but at the same time take courses in others. Thus, I chose to attend courses in business administration and linguistics. Above all, I realised that if I had ideas, I was encouraged to implement them, while in France we had no freedom of action at all.

The computer science department was self-administered by its staff. Every 2 years the department head switched; classes were redefined. The teachers punched their cards and ran their programs themselves. Their availability and familiarity with students impressed me: they organised seminars with doctoral students, where everybody could share their ideas.

In parallel I was hired as a Research Assistant working on the ARPANET project, and I was a member of the NWG (Network Working Group) led by Steve Crocker. So I joined the ARPANET project, where I could contribute my experience with data transmission. My first reading was the "RFC 11," written by Gérard Deloche. I was the second European to get involved in ARPANET.

The NWG had been formed a short time before. A paper by Steve Crocker entitled "Initiating the ARPANET,"[13] published in the March 2000 issue of *Matrix News*, clearly recounts what the NWG was. Indeed, this article describes the project pretty well, although it does use some anachronistic terms, for example when Steve Crocker mentions "layers."

The team consisted of doctoral and master students. And you have to keep the context of the Vietnam War in mind. There were recruitment posters on the campus. Students dreaded the Vietnam draft. Angela Davies was a professor at UCLA. There were activists on campus. I believe that a convergence of several of these influences defined the network itself. On one side, there were requirements with somewhat military origins, which consisted in answering reliability needs and a desire to create consistency in DoD (Department of Defense) research programs. On the other hand, the libertarian movement made claims for openness and sharing.

Specification of the ARPANET was achieved through open publication of "Requests For Comments" (RFCs). In RFC 3,[14] in April 1969, Steve Crocker first described the RFC

format and stated its objectives as follows in somewhat unusual terms for technical documents:

"

First, there is a tendency to view a written statement as ipso facto authoritative, and we
hope to promote the exchange and discussion of considerably less than
authoritative ideas.

Second, there is a natural hesitancy to publish something unpolished, and we hope to
ease this

inhibition

."

RFCs are open documents available to everybody. This contradicts the opinion that
the ARPANET was a military project. Although ARPA (Advanced Research Projects
Agency), thanks to credits from the DoD, funded the network, I worked on the project
without signing a confidentiality agreement. These specifications were more open
than those of most civilian projects were at that time. After more than fifty years and
more than 8000 documents published regarding ARPANET and Internet, this support
for technical exchange is alive, still using the same primitive format.

**Itw: Within the ARPANET project, which tasks were you entrusted with? What
was the working environment and atmosphere like? Did you witness the first
actual ARPANET connections?**

Michel Élie: The system used by BBN (Bolt, Beranek and Newman) within the
ARPANET project had been developed by DEC (Digital Equipment Corporation) and
was selected by Bob Kahn and Franck Heart. BBN was in charge of the development
of packet-switching IMPs. The NWG specified the protocols between emitting and
receiving computers (host-to-host, host-to-IMP, IMP-to-IMP). UCLA was to become the
NCC (Network Control Center) of the ARPANET. My work as a research assistant was
mainly concerned with the Host-to-Host protocol and the definition of a Network
Interface Language (NIL). The transmission procedures currently used in the industry
by computer manufacturers were between a master station and several slave stations.
ARPANET introduced the notion of peer-to-peer (P2P) and transparency of the data
stream, which was in line with the libertarians' philosophy. Packet switching, proposed
earlier by Paul Baran from the Rand Labs, was something new to me.

My first adviser was Professor Gerald Estrin, who was very friendly and had
previously got along very well with Gerard Deloche.[15] My second adviser, Professor
Leonard Kleinrock, was younger, but very brilliant. He had recently joined UCLA and

was a specialist in queuing theory. They both were Contract Officers for the ARPANET contract with ARPA.

There were internal meetings at UCLA and once every quarter there was a whole-sale meeting outside. The atmosphere was good but there was a lot of work too; we worked days and nights. Campus libraries were actually open all night.

The computing department at UCLA had a Sigma 7 Xerox machine. CAE and the CII had marketed this computer in France. So I already knew this machine, which was running a time-sharing system (called SEX!) developed at UCLA. Time-sharing was key at the time and provided context for most of the work on computers. It had started at MIT in 1966 in a project in which Louis Pouzin (initiator of Cyclades in 1972 in France) had taken part.

On my arrival, I was asked to develop a printer driver. It did not have much to do with the network itself, but little by little I got accustomed to the ARPANET specifica-tions and had ideas, which I discussed within the NWG, some of which were published ultimately in RFCs. This was collective work, and that is why I am a little reluctant when one seeks to assign individual paternities in the history of the ARPANET and Internet.

Itw: You worked in the Network Working Group (NWG), which was to become the International Network Working Group (INWG) in 1972. Before that, were there discussions about taking into account non-American perspectives when designing the protocols and software?

Michel Élie: Back then the NWG was composed of a dozen people. UCLA was set to become the Network Control Center (NCC). I shared an office with Jon Postel, who would go on to play a very important international part in ARPANET and Internet as the manager of IANA.[16] The network started in October 1969. I stayed one more year. Some adjustments were needed.

The project was to develop a network between heterogeneous computers, as a blank page where one could interact. For ARPA, the main goal was to promote sharing of data, software and hardware between researchers working on ARPA projects throughout the USA. It was at the start a US-confined project. Once I ques-tioned character encoding. The network was transparent to character encoding but later, the Unix operating system, which provided the most popular vehicle for Internet diffusion, happened to support only ASCII characters. Even later, Internet domain names were also restricted to ASCII characters. The actual internationalisation of the network took a long time, with many hurdles.

Our work was to plant a seed; we did not know how it would grow. We felt, how-ever, that this work was important and we suspected we were working on a baobab seed, but could not imagine how invasive it would come to be.

Itw: You drafted the RFC 51[17] on Network Interchange Language. Did you feel that you were participating in something historic? What followed this experience?

Michel Élie: The most skilled person suggested the network specifications, then we had to reach a group consensus to be able to actually write an RFC: this was not a solitary achievement. RFC 51 suggested having a network control language rather than programs written in assembler. But it collapsed after I left. Often things weren't getting done. Years later, Jon Postel told me that this RFC was an early intuition for Java! It is an amusing idea, but I cannot really defend that position.

The project had a follow-up in France: Michel Monpetit from INRIA (French Institute for Research in Computer Science and Automation) and Alain Profit, who represented the telecommunications side, came to visit us during my stay, and because they expressed interest, we discussed the project. Great Britain was also interested, especially the NPL (National Physical Laboratory).

When I came back to France and the CII, the fact that I had worked on the ARPANET was of no interest to anyone! I did a presentation at INRIA[18] attended by Louis Pouzin, who had been commissioned by Maurice Allègre[19] to develop a similar project in France. In this way, I ended up cooperating in the Cyclades network, launched by Pouzin and his team, as a CII member. François Sallé, technical director and deputy director of the Computers and Systems Division, and myself had agreed that the CII would provide the Cyclades project with equipment for development. I spent a good part of my time participating in the definition of Cyclades architecture with Hubert Zimmermann. I could rely on my previous experience in ARPANET, where we did the groundwork on the notion of layers (Élie, 1972). We published some papers around 1972–1973 (Élie & Zimmermann, 1973) and Vinton Cerf referred to our contribution on transport protocol (Zimmermann & Élie, 1974) in his first version of TCP. The idea of extended layers was key to the later part of the Cyclades project. By the end of Cyclades in 1978 Zimmermann had become invested in the work of the International Organization for Standardization (ISO) with the definition of the OSI (Open Systems Interconnection), which was accepted internationally in 1984.

Within CII, the idea was to promote a Cyclades-compatible network architecture, which we called NNA (New Network Architecture) and to develop products derived from the Cyclades implementations in order to support telecommunications and computer networks into operating systems. An NNA front-end was developed: a sort of IMP including the transport host-to-host protocol. It was a follow-up to the ARPANET experience. But the end of Cyclades forced us to adapt our architecture. The NNA front-end had to be redesigned in order to support the emerging X25 protocol that came from the world of telecommunications. This gave rise to another front-end, the Datanet, running on a Honeywell machine, the Mini-6.

In parallel, we invested this work in the OSI standardisation process. The idea was that Bull[20] should be ahead in the implementation of the OSI architecture and protocols.

Itw: Did you bet on OSI rather than the Internet? How did you go along with the further developments of the Internet?

Michel Élie: Before the mid-1980s the Internet was more or less ignored by computer manufacturers. Honeywell-Bull (HB) played the card of OSI standards and invested in implementing on all product lines the emerging OSI architecture and standards. I was responsible for the HB architecture team in France until 1988. Our policy was to prevent the IBM SNA (Systems Network Architecture) from becoming a de facto standard. And in a sense we succeeded eventually, at the end of the decade. At this time, the US industry department and some big users did promote OSI standards. But the US DoD strongly backed the Internet and the introduction by Tim

Berners-Lee and Robert Cailliau of the World Wide Web strongly weighed in favour of Internet, which finally prevailed.

Itw: What was your involvement with the Internet as a user?

Michel Élie: In 1988 I joined the Research Department of Bull led by Gérard Roucairol, who came from research in mathematics. I was in charge of research exploitation, specifically in the field of networks, between France and the United States (for instance, between Bull and MIT). A few years later, every researcher wanted to be connected to the Internet and exchange freely with other researchers outside the company in order to test their programs or algorithms. This was not part of corporate culture ... and became a hot topic.

In 1997 I retired and took part in working groups about Internet regulation with Isabelle Falque-Pierrotin[21]: self-regulation was then favoured... We were really invested in this issue, and we came up with an Observatory of the Uses of the Internet (OUI) with other people who were interested in the Internet, based on voluntary participation. Soon after came the time of the Internet bubble and most participants ended up with paid work and could not participate any more. Still, we did experiments on Internet use conducted by Master-level students under the super-vision of their professor. The idea was to observe non-commercial uses of the Internet. To this day, we see Internet as a toolbox offering leverage for the development of social uses. This is why we should maintain net neutrality.

Itw: What lessons could be drawn from the ARPANET experience?

Michel Élie: The idea of making profit from the network was completely absent. It was an idyllic world where people just shared, and the NWG was the main apostle of this. For instance, Lawrence Roberts, the project manager, immediately accepted that the specifications would be open. The NWG was strongly opposed to computer manufacturers and their influence on the shape of networks. The UCLA computer centre was running IBM computers and my colleagues were resisting any interference from a computer manufacturer in the ARPANET specifications. The same went later for Cyclades in France: the tight link between the CII and the network researchers was not publicised. Manufacturers were synonymous with captive clients, who had to live in their world. This was an argument in the OSI versus SNA war, and that is why OSI was strongly supported by users.

I had the chance to participate in the beginning of the Internet adventure. We designed a tool, which in a relatively small time produced big changes in our societies and lives. I am proud of it, but sometimes regret our lack of anticipation in regard to threats to private life, security, and the inequities and deviant uses it also generated. Looking back at the extraordinary Internet developments in the last fifty years and my own activities, I can make the following remarks on its evolution.

The first major step was at the end of the 1980s: the World Wide Web allowed any user to browse human knowledge. At the same time, mass-produced personal computers allowed access of end users to network technology and data content. Ethernet was an important driver for workstation dissemination. The deregulation of telecommunications paved the way for innovative entrepreneurs. With the installation of computer-based PABX, the cost of communications dropped.

The second was in the early 1990s: the opening of the Web to commercial uses gave an enormous commercial advantage to those nations and enterprises, which controlled the Internet and its applications, mainly the US. However, the exclusive use of English slowed down and filtered Internet users. The US dominated Internet management. I was in favour of an international regulation of the Internet by the ITU (International Telecommunication Union) or some other specific international organisation. I discussed the issue with an Internet company manager who told me: "the USA gave the Internet to the world, which entitles them to some return." In fact the US government and enterprises did have an extremely high return on investment...

The third was in 2008, the launch of the smartphone, which realised the dream of engineers of the second half of the twentieth century: the merger of telecommunications and information technology and their uses.

This led to a fourth major step with the development of social networks with now well-known pros and cons. Another recent major step is the opening of applications to voice control and the asymptotic increase of connected objects.

Today, users are caught by their own desires and gullibility. They are the captives of big empires, GAFA, which have little concern for their negative impacts on society. They want to forge a society that serves their business interests. There are late reactions from governments and users.

Personally speaking, I invest my time, knowledge and efforts, as a volunteer, in trying to promote the concept of "the commons," the use of free software, cooperative work among non-profit organisations and a more equitable society: goals that were already latent in the mind of the ARPANET project participants.

The ARPANET anniversary should emphasise the non-profit, social and societal sides of network developments and uses. It should be an opportunity to stress that the urgency seems not to be in technology but in re-humanizing the Internet and its uses in order to serve social needs all over the earth: let the Internet be human again!

Itw: Gérard Le Lann, you also took part in the ARPANET, but some years after Michel Élie.

Gérard Le Lann: Indeed, my involvement followed that of Michel Élie. Michel saw the very beginnings of the ARPANET. I became a contributor to the ARPANET project when TCP/IP was being defined, with an interest in the problems of synchronisation and flow control in end-to-end protocols.

Starting in 1972, my work was initially focused on the first protocols designed for the ARPANET (the NCP protocol) and for the Cyclades network. I had joined the Cyclades project to create a team in Rennes (Brittany, France), where I could take advantage of a well-organised computer center. I decided on a specific work program after learning that a Simula-67 compiler was available. What about developing an event-based simulator aimed at revealing the causes of those malfunctions exhibited by the early Cyclades protocols – inspired by NCP to some extent?

That turned out to be a good idea. Simula-67 happened to be the first object-oriented language ever created, and programming in Simula-67 was incredibly pleasant and efficient. Simulations were focused on the transport layer (layer 4), while on the ARPANET side, they were studying the problems on layers 3 and 4. (The layering was not yet very clear.) I chose to consider only the end-to-end connections between computers and not the packet switching nodes (ARPANET IMPs or Cigale nodes).[22] This made it possible to look at end-to-end synchronisation problems without being exposed to artificial limitations proper to a specific network layer.

I then got in touch with the ARPANET teams. When Louis Pouzin hired me, he mentioned his intent to have someone from the Cyclades project immersed in one ARPANET site. This was actually an ideal prospect.

Before joining Cyclades, I had spent three years at CERN,[23] working in an international environment and sharing my office with an English colleague. I wanted to face a stiffer challenge, from scientific and societal standpoints.

So I toured the ARPANET centers in spring 1973. DARPA (Washington), BBN (Cambridge, MA), Stanford University (Palo Alto, CA), and UCLA (Los Angeles, CA) were on my list.

Vint Cerf had just been appointed Professor at the Stanford's Digital Systems Lab. When I met Vint, I knew I had made my choice: top-level scientific discussions and human contact. I had brought along my simulation results. Vint told me they were extremely useful, since NCP was to be replaced by some other protocols (TCP and IP were in the works). So I came to Stanford in June 1973, for a year, to work on synchronisation problems, flow control, error control, and abnormal end-to-end connection failures.

Itw: Vinton Cerf had just been appointed to Stanford. Did he have a team?

Gérard Le Lann: Yes. Shortly after obtaining his PhD at UCLA, Vint started teaching at Stanford and was awarded DARPA funding. He quickly built his team (half a dozen PhD students and one or two engineers in charge of logistics, installation of the IMP, FTP and email software).

Itw: You mention DARPA financing ...

Gérard Le Lann: Yes, the financing was funnelled through DARPA, coming from the Department of Defense. In the late 1960s, encouraged by the work by Leonard Kleinrock (then at MIT) and Rand Corporation, DARPA launched the ARPANET project. Later on, when it became obvious that packet-switching was opening up tremendous opportunities, the National Science Foundation and the computing industry joined forces with DARPA. TCP/IP became a commodity technology in 1983, when DARPA decided to put the technology in the public domain.

Itw: Funding was military, but the project was not classified; moreover, foreign researchers were welcome among the teams ...

Gérard Le Lann: During the ARPANET years, there was also some funding from DARPA awarded to non-US teams, which had connections to the ARPANET, the Norwegians notably. The British and the French had their own national budgets. Bringing in researchers has always been a DARPA and a US policy. To the best of my knowledge, ARPANET's developments were not classified. There might have been some confidentiality clauses or patents related to the work conducted by BBN or a few ARPANET teams.

Itw: When you arrived at Stanford, after working at CERN and in France, did you discover a different working atmosphere?

Gérard Le Lann: Yes. CERN is a highly international organisation. But it is huge, and I was hired to join a team already structured, and wasn't really asked to be innovative. The only creative work I conducted was to rewrite portions of the operating system of the CII 10070 (the French name for the US XDS Sigma 7) in order to make it fit to process real-time tasks having to meet very tight timing constraints. This computer had to keep up with inputs generated by 8 mini-computers located along the particle accelerator, in charge of snapshotting the particle beam. (Thanks to these "photos," physicists could test their conjectures regarding fundamental physics theories.)

The big difference with Stanford was that I could bring something new. The whole of Vint's team was constantly brainstorming, investigating fundamental questions regarding time-varying and error-prone inter-process communication. In fact, without knowing it at that time, we were uncovering that *terra incognita* which went by the name of "distributed computing" years later. To some extent, we were computer scientists learning that our discipline had been so far focused on a special case, centralised systems, and that the time had come for a mental revolution akin to relativistic physics: the hypothesis according to which processes share the same space/time referential should be abandoned. In distributed systems, there is no central locus of control. Some "global state" being necessary for endowing any system with desired properties, specific (distributed) algorithms had to be devised to this end.

Itw: After that, your research became actually oriented towards distributed computing?

Gérard Le Lann: That is right. TCP was being designed, and the famous RFCs addressed fundamental questions. The foundations had been laid. A specific example comes to mind. If I remember well, it is Ray Tomlinson[24] who, with the alternating bit protocol, proposed a primitive version of the sliding window scheme on which I was working (Le Lann & Le Goff, 1978). The hypothesis that there may be only one packet in transit had been abandoned and we had to find a scheme whereby multiple packets in transit on a full-duplex connection could be designated unambiguously in the absence of a "natural" time/frame referential and in the presence of failures (packets had to be repeated, which raised the need to know whether any given packet had previously been received or whether it was a new one).

To put it simply, network protocols in the ARPANET age were posing problems of cardinality 2 (end-to-end), whereas distributed algorithms are needed for solving problems of any cardinality greater than 2.

Itw: How were the work and research themes distributed and organised within the teams?

Gérard Le Lann: As far as I was concerned, besides my work on TCP, I had total freedom. For example, while in Vint's team, I became interested in the work conducted in nearby Xerox PARC, which led to Ethernet. Also, I was reading papers on the ring developed at Irvine University (CA). Both topics had a definite influence on my work related to real-time local area networks. PhD students were offered a choice, among the themes selected by Vint. Presentations were organised on a weekly basis. Everyone picked a theme according to his desire, in connection to open problems or published papers. We were looking for solutions, and there was some kind of scientific competitive spirit in the air, as well as the conviction that we could expose any "crazy" ideas and get immediate feedback. This kind of "thinking" was specific to the birth of Silicon Valley.

Itw: Is this spirit specific to the USA?

Gérard Le Lann: The sharing of speculative inroads is specific to research. In the USA, it was easier than elsewhere to engage massive research efforts that would attract attention, bringing in the best researchers. Awareness of emerging topics was not widespread in France at that time. When I returned to France in 1974, I started teaching a course on computer networks at the University of Rennes. In 1977, one of the professors at that university had still not understood much of it. His vision was that "issues of bits per second, message loss rates, and reliable message deliveries are not related to computing, but to physics." Clearly, there was a huge cultural gap between French and US universities at that time.

Itw: Wasn't it too difficult to return to France?

Gérard Le Lann: I was honest. I had promised Louis Pouzin I would come back to the Cyclades team, even if the temptation was great indeed to stay in the USA. We were offered golden job opportunities in those early days of emerging Silicon Valley.

Itw: How did you promote the work done in the USA?

Gérard Le Lann: I published a journal paper based on my work in France and at Stanford four years after I left Stanford. I was not very interested in publishing on past work, and I was deeply invested in my research on distributed algorithms.

In the USA, I saw and learned how to conduct disruptive research: don't follow the crowd, think by yourself, and when you are confident enough in your findings, take your responsibilities and publish/propagate, even if you break away from dominant or trendy topics.

Itw: Your contribution to the ARPANET was recognised as your name was put on the Stanford "Birth of the Internet" plaque ...

Gérard Le Lann: Yes. Unfortunately I was unable to attend the celebration that took place on this occasion in July 2005.

Itw: Returning to France, did you operate a knowledge transfer?

Gérard Le Lann: Indeed. What had I brought into my nets? Layered architectures, the importance of properly separating physics (transmissions, links, computers) and virtual/logical structures (connections, processes, system models). In 1977, I published a pioneering paper on distributed computing (a distributed algorithm for fault-tolerant mutual exclusion, based on the concept of a virtual ring).[25] I brought back information on how routing would be done in the future Internet. And knowledge relative to what would become an area of very high visibility: local area networks.

Itw: Do you remember other Europeans who worked directly within the ARPANET?

Gérard Le Lann: Europeans who immersed themselves in ARPANET teams? I do not remember, but there were significant contributions by Europeans. The idea of layered protocols was adopted by everyone and led to the OSI project at the International Organization for Standardization, in which the foreign community was mobilised. I had a lot of discussions with Hubert Zimmermann on the layered model,[26] but I quickly gave up because I was more interested in my more theoretical research program. One of the members of Cyclades, Jean Le Bihan, proposed in 1978 that I should join the Sirius project he was conducting on distributed data-bases, which I did, for I could then work on distributed algorithmic issues such as concurrency control and the serializability theory. As far as OSI was concerned, the problem was closed for me. And I have a personal bias: I hate standards committee meetings.[27] I think they take too long to achieve convergence and, very often, good ideas come from the outside. So many would-be standards have been dis-carded only a few years after they became official! John McQuillan said something I liked very much in the 1980s: "Standards are great, there are so many you can choose from"! Standards rest on human-centric agreements, which explains why some standards are flawed, notably those resting on "solutions" that violate impos-sibility results. Current standards for inter-vehicular cooperative schemes based on wireless radio communications aimed at autonomous/automated vehicles are an example – terrestrial and aerial autonomic vehicular networks are my current area of research.

Itw: Do you have any regrets about elements that were not thought of at the time of ARPANET?

Gérard Le Lann: Cyberattacks, privacy threats and illegitimate cyber-espionage were not foreseen at that time. We had the firm conviction that we were developing a tool that would serve humanity, and no one really thought it could be misused. There are no encryption algorithms, no pseudonym schemes in the ARPANET protocols' "DNA." These issues have gained higher visibility since the advent of mobile wireless network-ing. We know that we are vulnerable in cyberspace via our smartphones. Matters are much more worrying with upcoming "connected" automated vehicles. With currently adopted solutions, these vehicles are equivalent to smartphones-on-wheels, making us vulnerable in the physical space: smartphones-on-wheels may kill.

Itw: If we had to conclude on what remains of ARPANET?

Gérard Le Lann: Today, everything runs on TCP/IP, Internet would not have existed without ARPANET (and external contributions, notably from France and the UK), and Internet is not dead, contrary to recurrent dogmatic "predictions"! More than anything else, packet-switching has been THE crucial revolutionary technology, experimented first with ARPANET. Without packet-switching, none of those cyber-services we rely on daily nowadays, none of those technologies that have emerged recently (e.g. IoT) would have come into existence.

Itw: In 2013, at the École Militaire[28] in Paris, after you were awarded the Willis Lamb Prize by the French Academy of Sciences, you gave a lecture with Bob Metcalfe and Vint Cerf and I remember that there were also references made to applications in the energy sector.

Gérard Le Lann: Yes indeed, Bob Metcalfe had outlined the idea of a future Enernet, an open network based on energy packet-switching, where energy packets could be produced, disseminated, traded, and consumed anywhere, anytime. The future will tell whether something close to Enernet can be deployed. We have many challenges to think about. In the list of new ground-breaking technologies, one finds mobile optical communications—passive optics and active optics (visible light commu-nications). They can serve to solve fundamental problems left open with radio technol-ogies. Just one quick example: naming in spontaneous open mobile networks, where no advance knowledge of neighbours, membership, geolocations or velocities, is available. Optical communications also have a decisive advantage over radio communications: they can be privacy-preserving by design. As regards personal data protection, with the GDPR,[29] the Europeans are ahead this time, I believe.

Notes

1. See for example Mckenzie (2011).
2. "Donald W. Davies and Derek L.A. Barber: An Interview Conducted by Janet Abbate", IEEE History Center, 17 March 1996 (https://ethw.org/Oral-History:Donald_Davies_&_Derek_Barber); see also Abbate (1999).
3. This symposium, supported by the "Délégation à l'informatique," the government authority for computer science, was of major importance (Mounier-Kuhn, 2002). AFIRO (Association française de l'informatique et de la recherche opérationnelle) was a scholarly society for computing and operations research. Active in the second half of the 1960s, it merged with several other academic and industry associations, eventually becoming the current "Societé Informatique de France" (SIF – French Computer Science Society).
4. The packets of information do not follow each other in the packet-switching network; rather, datagrams take various routes depending on the availability of switches and lines, and are reassembled at their destination in order to recreate the original message.
5. This phrase is used in Davies and Bressan (2010).
6. The Open Systems Interconnection (OSI) is an open layered network architecture developed and discussed by computer scientists within the International Organization for Standardization (ISO). The OSI was indeed seen as a source of independence for some European players, while IBM was developing EARN (the European Academic and Research Network), which was an equivalent to the American university IBM-supported network Bitnet. A group of experts proposed an ambitious project for an OSI network to the European Commission, supported by COSINE (Cooperation for Open Systems Interconnection Networking in Europe). See Russell (2014), as well as Badouard and Schafer (2014).
7. Short for the French École supérieure d'électricité. This prestigious engineering school is known today as CentraleSupélec.
8. Fearing US leadership in the field of computing, the French President Charles de Gaulle launched the "Plan Calcul" to support the French computer industry and computer science research. This resulted in the creation of the CII (Compagnie Internationale pour l'Informatique) and the creation of a research center, IRIA (which then became INRIA in 1979).
9. Town located in the south-western suburbs of Paris.
10. François-Henri Raymond was a pioneer of the French computer industry and scientific world. He founded the SEA in 1948, which merged with the CAE to form the CII, before becoming the Chair of Programming at the Conservatoire National des Arts et Métiers in 1973.
11. This former NATO camp was put under the CII's authority in 1967 by the French government. It hosted software development as well as commercial and sales services. See http://www.feb-patrimoine.com/projet/usines/louveciennes.htm.
12. *Salon des industries et du commerce de bureau*. SICOB is a French professional trade show for office automation, computing, networks and telecommunications.
13. This text is available thanks to the Wayback Machine at: https://web.archive.org/ web/ 20040304032735/ http://www.mids.org/pay/mn/1003/crocker.html
14. Network Working Group, Steve Crocker, "Documentation Conventions", RFC-3, 4689, April 1969. http://www.hjp.at/doc/rfc/rfc3.txt

15. Under their supervision, Michel Élie completed a Master's thesis entitled "General purpose computer networks" at UCLA in 1970.
16. Internet Assigned Numbers Authority.
17. See Élie (1970).
18. Published as "Le réseau d'ordinateurs de l'Arpa et les réseaux généraux d'ordinateurs", *RIRO*, B-2 1971, p. 19–42. This was the first French-written paper on the ARPANET.
19. Maurice Allègre had been State Delegate for Computing since 1968.
20. Bull was a pioneering French computer manufacturer. Among the many acquisitions and other transformations, it was bought by Honeywell in 1970 and merged with CII in 1975 – but the name "Bull" has remained in use. Michel Élie and Philippe Picard testified about their experience with open systems at Bull (Élie & Picard, 2017).
21. Isabelle Falque-Pierrotin is currently Chair of the CNIL (the French Data Protection Authority) in France. She served as Chair of the interministerial Commission on Internet Affairs in 1996, and was appointed then as an expert adviser for the OECD in 1997. She was general rapporteur for the report by the French State Council on "Internet and Digital Networks" from 1997 to 1998. From 2001 to December 2010, she was Chair of the Advisory Board and General Delegate of the French Internet Rights Forum.
    See: http://ec.europa.eu/justice/article-29/structure/chairman/index_en.htm
22. Cigale is the sub-network of the Cyclades network (Schafer, 2012).
23. CERN is the European Organization for Nuclear Research, established in 1954 and located on the France-Switzerland border.
24. One of the acknowledged inventors of email techniques for distributed networks (see Leiner et al., 1997; Salus, 1995).
25. Le Lann (1977).
26. Hubert Zimmermann, a contributor from the Cyclades team, was strongly involved in the OSI architecture (Schafer, 2012; Russell, 2014).
27. OSI was supported and developed within standard-making organizations and known for methods involving long specification processes. See Russell (2014).
28. The École Militaire is a military college in the centre of Paris, founded in 1750.
29. GDPR (General Data Protection Regulation) was adopted by the European Union in April 2016, and applicable from May 2018.

References

Abbate, J. (1999). *Inventing the Internet*. Cambridge MA: The MIT Press.
Badouard, R., & Schafer, V. (2014). Internet: A political issue for Europe (1970s – 2010s). In J. Bishop (Ed). *Transforming politics and policy in the digital age* (pp. 69–84). Hershey: IGI Global.
Beltran, A., & Griset, P. (2007). *Histoire d'un pionnier de l'informatique. 40 ans de recherches à l'INRIA*. Les Ulis: EDP Sciences.

Davies, H., & Bressan, B. (2010). *A History of international research networking, the people who made it happen*. Weinheim: Wiley-Blackwell.

Élie, M. (1970). Proposal for a Network Interchange language. NWG RFC No 51, 4 May. https://www.rfc-editor.org/rfc/rfc51.pdf

Élie, M. (1972). Décomposition et représentation de la fonction de transport de l'information dans un réseau. ACM/IRIA Workshop « Réseaux D'ordinateurs ».

Élie, M., & Zimmermann, H. (1973). Vers une approche systématique des protocoles sur un réseau d'ordinateurs. Application au réseau Cyclades. AFCET Congress, Rennes, 277 296.

Élie, M., & Picard, P. (2017). Unix et les systèmes ouverts dans Bull, avant l'Internet. *Cahiers d'histoire du Cnam, 7-8*(2), 133–153.

Griset, P. (ed.) (1998). *Informatique, politique industrielle, Europe: entre Plan Calcul et Unidata*. Paris: Institut d'histoire de l'industrie/Éditions Rive Droite.

Le Lann, G. (1977). Distributed systems – Towards a formal approach. In IFIP Congress (pp. 155–160). Toronto: North-Holland pub.

Le Lann, G., & Le Goff, H. (1978). Verification and evaluation of communication protocols. *Computer Networks, 2*(1), 50–69.

Leiner, B. M., Cerf, V. G., Clark, D. D., Kahn, R. E., Kleinrock, L., Lynch, D. C. … Wolff, S. S. (1997). The past and future history of the Internet. *Communications of the ACM, 40*(2), 102–108.

Mailland, J., & Driscoll, K. (2017). *Minitel: Welcome to the internet*. Cambridge, MA: The MIT Press.

Mckenzie, A. (2011). INWG and the conception of the internet: An eyewitness account. *IEEE Annals of the History of Computing, 33*(1), 66–71.

Mounier-Kuhn, P.-E. (2002). Les premiers réseaux informatiques en France. *Entreprises et Histoire, 29*(1), 10–20.

Mounier-Kuhn, P.-E. (1998). *L'informatique en France de la seconde Guerre Mondiale au Plan Calcul. L'émergence d'une science*. Paris: Presses de l'Université Paris-Sorbonne.

Neumann, C., Petitgirard, L., & Paloque-Bergès, C. (2016). Le Cnam. Un lieu d'accueil, de débat et d'institutionnalisation pour les sciences et techniques de l'informatique. *TSI, 35*(4–5), 584–600.

Paloque-Bergès, C., & Petitgirard, L. (2017). La recherche sur les systèmes, des pivots dans l'histoire de l'informatique. *Special Double Issue of Cahiers D'histoire du Cnam*, Vol. *7-8*, 1–2.

Russell, A. (2014). *Open standards and the digital age. History, ideology, and networks*. Cambridge UK: Cambridge University Press.

Russell, A. L., & Schafer, V. (2014). In the shadow of ARPANET and Internet: Louis Pouzin and the Cyclades network in the 1970s. *Technology and Culture, 55*(4), 880–907.

Schafer, V. (2012). *La France en réseaux (années 1960-1980)*. Paris: Nuvis.

Schafer, V., & Thierry, B. (2012). *Le Minitel. L'enfance numérique de la France*. Paris: Nuvis.

Salus, P. H. (1995). *Casting the net: From ARPANET to Internet and Beyond…* Addison-Wesley: Longman Publishing Co., Inc.

Siles, I. (2017). 25 years of the Internet in Central America: An interview with Guy de Téramond. *Internet Histories, 1*(4), 349–358.

Zimmermann, H., & Élie, M. (1974). Transport Protocol. Standard Host-Host Protocol for heterogeneous computer networks, INWG#61.

25 Years of the Internet in Central America: an interview with Guy de Téramond

Ignacio Siles

ABSTRACT

January 2018 marks the 25th anniversary of the first dedicated Internet connection in Central America. Little is known about the conditions that characterised the early development of the Internet in this part of the globe. In this interview, made on 23 June 2017, Guy de Téramond, more commonly known as "The Father of the Internet in Central America", recalls some of the main events that led the connection to BITNET and the Internet in this region. De Téramond talks about the motivations, challenges and satisfactions involved in regional connection projects in countries like Costa Rica, El Salvador, Guatemala, Honduras, Nicaragua and Panama, during the 1990s; the role of the Organization of American States; the foundation of academic networks in Central America; and the privatisation of telecommunications in the region. These discussions are updated by addressing the contemporary state of these academic projects and some of the main challenges faced by countries of the Central American region in the global geopolitics and governance of the Internet.

Introduction

Guy de Téramond is widely known as "The Father of the Internet in Central America". During the past few months, while I have researched the Internet connection process of countries in the region, I have heard engineers describe him also as "The Network Hero", and "The ideologist, philosopher and strategist of the Internet in Central America". As a joke, de Téramond says that it would be more appropriate to refer to him as "The 'Grandfather' of the Internet in the region". The joke hides a very distinctive feature of his character: he likes to highlight the achievements of others rather than his own.

Taken together, these nicknames try to capture his crucial role in the connection of several Central American and Caribbean countries to the Internet during the 1990s (de Téramond, 1994, 2005; Internet History Library, 2015). First, he led the connection of Costa Rica to BITNET (in 1990) and the Internet (in 1993). Then, during the following years, and thanks to a project funded by the Organization of American States (OAS) led by Dr Saúl Hahn,[1] de Téramond travelled with a small group of Costa Rican engineers to set up Internet access points or support local projects in Nicaragua (1994), Panama (1994),

Honduras (1995), Jamaica (1995), Guatemala (1995), El Salvador (1996) and Belize (1997). He also gave technical advice and training in countries like Bahamas and Trinidad and Tobago.

During the 1990 and the 2000 decades, de Téramond was the leader of the regional connection to the Internet (Siles, 2008, 2012). He founded the first academic network based on Internet protocols in the region (CRNet), which first connected Costa Rica to the Internet and then countries like Nicaragua and Panama. Between 2000 and 2002, he was appointed as Minister of Science and Technology in Costa Rica. His work in this Ministry was key to develop a broadband infrastructure in the country, based on the academic model he implemented years before. In addition, he has been honoured with prestigious awards such as the Guggenheim Fellowship (1986), the Fulbright Research Award (1983) and the Leonid Medallion (1997).

De Téramond was born in Biarritz, France, in 1945, son to a French father and a Costa Rican mother. De Téramond has double nationality and has alternated periods of study and residency in both countries. After the end of the Second World War, his family moved to Costa Rica. De Téramond started as an engineering student at Universidad de Costa Rica (UCR). However, he gradually discovered that his greatest interests lay in the field of Physics. When these interests consolidated, he decided to change his major. De Téramond received a scholarship from the French Government, with which he travelled to Grenoble (during a year) and subsequently to Paris. At the Université Paris-Orsay, he earned a PhD degree in Theoretical Physics (1977). Thanks to his work in this field, de Téramond carried out several research internships in the United States and Europe in the late 1970s and 1980s, in places such as Stanford University and Harvard University. It was during this time that he began using academic computing networks such as BITNET and the Internet. When he returned to Costa Rica in the late 1980s, de Téramond started a crusade to connect the country to these networks.

To commemorate the 25th anniversary of the establishment of the first dedicated Internet connection in Central America, in January 1993 at Universidad de Costa Rica, I interviewed Guy de Téramond (aka "don Guy") on 23 June 2017, in the facilities of NIC Costa Rica, the organisation that manages the country's Internet top-level domain (TLD), to discuss some of the key moments that marked this story. The interview was edited for readability.

"Don Guy", what inspired you to connect Costa Rica to the Internet when you came back from the United States in the late 80s? What convinced you to start this process?

I had worked for a while with a group of people who were doing some experiments in Switzerland and we had an interesting cooperation. Part of my job was to continue the collaboration with them from Stanford University. It was then that I said: "This is what will allow me to go back to Costa Rica one day, this kind of instruments!" It was not such a difficult step because the systems that UCR had were IBM 4381s, which had the same operating system (used in BITNET). We essentially needed a link. There were some opposing forces in the country and abroad, big interests, related to telecommunications. As one of my collaborators said: "It is a mined field from A to Z." One realises that this might have not happened.

What motivated you to make it all the way to the end?

I think what was at stake was huge. It was the future. And these were such powerful instruments, and the change they entailed was so great, that any effort was worthwhile. It also helped a lot to have the support of partners. At that time, there were leading figures in the government who expressed their support. One of these days I was thinking: where did we get the determination and the strength? I really do not know… I guess we were obsessed with this project and we just wanted to go ahead no matter what.

It is not always easy to describe what the Internet is, even today. How did you convince those allies back then? How did you persuade these contributors to finance the project, which must have been one of the most significant challenges at the time?

You cannot convince someone if you are not deeply convinced yourself. But if you are a strong believer, you become an evangelist. I think the group that was working on this clearly saw where the development of the technology was going and we did not waste any time in fruitless discussions. Let me tell you an anecdote. We had some meetings at *Consejo Nacional de Rectores* (the institution that manages public higher education in Costa Rica) every week, where we discussed for hours: "What is the path to follow? Is it this technology or that one?" For us, it was clear that it had to be Internet because it was the only protocol that allowed us to connect everything with everything. It was as simple as that. In the second or third meeting, I lost my patience and blurted out: "Look, for some of us it is very clear that this technology is the way to move forward, so I will ask you respectfully to let me go out while you think a little more about this, and if you conclude that this is the way to go, please call me. Otherwise, please do not call me." If you are totally convinced about something it becomes more powerful, and it can inspire others. There was an additional motivation element: scientists in the country needed this instrument.

You brought together those collaborations in a specific project: CRNet (the network that interconnected research and academic institutions in Costa Rica through Internet protocols). Why was this network established and how was this achieved?

Strategic alliances are important. Circumstances play a determining role to succeed. This project could not have happened in another time. That is what happened with the previous efforts that failed to establish the connection. It was the right time because of the circumstances and the fact that we took advantage of the experiences of others in their previous attempts. A series of circumstances worked to our advantage. Naturally, with someone who manages to communicate with others. It was an effort to communicate the potential of this technology to all sectors but, essentially, to researchers who knew they needed more than getting in a line to receive a fax. Here, decisive circumstances intervened: the project would have been impossible had it not been for the availability of PanAmSat Corporation's new satellite. It was a new company that was outside of Intelsat's monopoly. With Intelsat, we wouldn't have gone anywhere…

Why?

Because Intelsat was a government consortium managed by its representatives in each country. Its representatives in each country were the PTTs (postal, telegraph and telephone services). If you tried to communicate with Intelsat, you would have not gone past the secretary who picked up the phone. It was impenetrable. Then, we had the great luck that, at that moment, PanAmSat, a very small company, launched its satellite, the first digital communications satellite in the world. It was a company that wanted to experiment with new things. I met the engineer who oversaw this project and we talked extensively. He even came to Costa Rica when we wanted to extend the project to Latin America. We had plans that never took place. We wanted to use a satellite transponder to cover Latin America entirely. That was discussed at a conference in Rio de Janeiro in 1992. The idea was to rent the transponder at a price that would have allowed us connections of higher capacity. The motto of the company was TTBB: "Truth and technology will prevail over bureaucracy and bullshit." Then came extraordinary circumstances. The state telecommunications institution (in Costa Rica) requested PanAmSat to disconnect us (CRNet). But they did not know that the engineer we knew had become the director of the company. I wrote him a message and he said: "Don't worry. I'll fix it. Who should I write to?" And he stopped the issue right there. Otherwise, they would have damaged us.

Returning to the previous question about CRNet, the Internet project was not only a project of UCR. UCR was naturally the leader but, at that time, National Science Foundation, which managed Internet connections in the world, had established as a requirement that the Internet needed to be a country project. BITNET required little bandwidth, we had a link of 19.2 Kbps, which was minimal. For example, the link that connects my house today is a thousand times greater, but, with only that link of 19.2 Kbps, we connected with the world through email. BITNET was based on storage and forward, that is, it was not interactive. The Internet does require a lot more bandwidth. With the Internet, we increased to 64 Kbps, which seemed like a marvel at the time. Today, that is nothing, obviously, applications consume much more capacity nowadays, because of graphics. Therefore, we needed to share the costs with other institutions. We could not see the Internet as separate from CRNet. It was the same project. We needed to share the costs with other institutions.

After this experience in Costa Rica, you and your team travelled to Central America to help connect countries to the Internet with the support of OAS, specifically Saúl Hahn and his RedHuCyT project. It seems to me that the regional perspective was there since the beginning of the project.

Of course, because that is the nature of the networks.

Please tell us more about this process.

First, a year before (in 1992), we connected the Technological University of Panama to BITNET. The Panama UTPVM1 node used the connection to UCR's node, UCRVM2, through storage and forward, to Florida Atlantic University's node in the United States. We had a lot of empathy with this group in Panama and, when we were asked to help, we immediately supported them. We did not ask them to share costs because that was how BITNET worked: from one node to the next, a computer-to-computer connection, the messages were stored, sent to the next node, and then forwarded to the following nodes. Even if there were too many emails, they were sent based on the available capacity. BITNET technologies were relatively simple and IBM's operating systems were those used at universities at the time.

How did the process of connecting these countries unfold?

Saúl Hahn had an extraordinary role. Dr Hahn is a mathematician with a PhD from New York University. He worked at *Universidad Nacional Autónoma de México*, and then worked for IBM Mexico. We had an excellent working relationship and eventually a great friendship, which continues even today. Saúl worked for the Department of Science and Technology of OAS and, on one occasion, in the early 1990s, we talked in Washington and spent some time thinking what would be a good strategy to propel the Internet in Latin America. Saúl played an extraordinary role in the development of the Internet throughout the continent. His role has not been fully recognised. He has been one of the best collaborators I have ever had. Saúl is a person of great integrity, knowledge, and training. In this meeting we had in Washington in the early 90s, we came to the conclusion that we had to support directly the universities in the region, although there were other options, including NGOs, which certainly had an important role, including in Costa Rica. We thought that those options were not going to have the necessary conditions for scaling up these projects. On the contrary, universities had computer centres, engineers, technicians and students: supporting them thus meant investing in something much more stable, with growth potential, and a significantly higher multiplication factor. Saúl's project focused on supporting universities. Dr Hahn had a budget close to a million dollars for Latin America, which is a lot and is too little. To connect a single country cost $50.000, but it needed to be done from the Dominican Republic to countries in the South (of Latin America). Of course, larger countries, such as Mexico, Argentina and Chile, had less support because they were more organised. But, for the other countries, this meant a fundamental support. For example, in the case of Paraguay, the first satellite antenna ever installed was donated by OAS.

My impression is that there are actors who have not been fully recognized, such as Dr Hahn, partly for political reasons and for being under the umbrella of OAS. But Saúl is a very independent person and played a very important role. In these processes, developing local knowledge is very important, and I believe Saúl's project helped significantly universities to master the technologies. In other countries and regions, such as Africa, the process was different and the European transnationals controlled telecommunications – and still do – because they did not have a professional group with this kind of knowledge. There were also countries in Latin America, such as Chile, Mexico, Argentina and Brazil, which have had an extraordinary role on the Internet. But I am certain that the OAS project did help Latin America to have an important degree of independence in Internet-related aspects.

Once you specified the equipment necessary for each case, OAS sent it to each country and you travelled to establish the connection to the Internet. You stayed for a few days and offered training seminars for local engineers. Tell us about these experiences.

Exactly. UCR was the intermediary between OAS and the other countries. This partly answers your previous question. Part of the motivation was the change and the multiplicative factor entailed by accessing the Internet. We could talk for hours and hours about all the experiences in Central America. Some of them were very difficult.

In what ways?

In Costa Rica, we had to face a (telecommunications) monopoly. However, in Central America, the situation was much more complicated, because there were not only monopolies, but monopolies under military regimes. They saw the Internet connection as a serious intrusion into their affairs. Let me just tell one story about the Internet connection in Honduras. We were always travelling with basic equipment, such as welding equipment. In Honduras, we found a very old and out-dated Siemens equipment. When we got to see it, we asked ourselves: where do we connect it? It was very old; there was no way to technically connect it to the routing device, a V35 interface. We were about to be embarrassed because, the very next day, they had already planned a ceremony to celebrate the connection to the Internet.

How did you resolve it?

We did two things. On the one hand, Roger Brenes, an engineer who was part of the team, spent all night testing a cable, all possible connections, and welding each one of them. The number of possibilities is a factorial number. Roger spent all night trying each possibility. On the other hand, I had a very basic laptop computer, one of the first laptops, and I knew a Swedish engineer by chance. Then, since this was a Swedish equipment, I sent him a message, saying: "Here we are, we have the connector on one side and the equipment on the other. If you could get us a diagram, please send it". That was around 8 pm and, at 4 am, he replied with the diagram. But Roger had already managed to solve it. In this way, we established the connection to the Internet in Honduras, just before the inaugural event. My collaborators were pale for not having slept all night. This illustrates some of the problems we had to face in Central America. Central America had a tumultuous period of conflict and was thus very polarized. We had lots of issues, more political than technical.

How did the uses of the technology evolve during those early years?

At that time, the Internet was essentially a scientific instrument and what changed everything was the Web. At the beginning, using the Internet was more complicated. Thanks to the graphical interface of the Web, the way of accessing the information distributed around the world changed. Information could be accessed immediately just by typing. This completely changed the paradigm. But the basic protocols of communication are the same, TCP/IP, only a graphical interface was added. It was a gradual process. Everyone began to see that this had an unthinkable potential, which gave us much more motivation to propel this technology.

There were privatisation processes taking place in the field of telecommunications when the Internet connection in Central America was first established. How did this shape the development of the Internet in the region? In the case of Costa Rica, for instance, in 2000 you started working at the Ministry of Science and Technology (MICIT), and led a project of broadband connection with the help of an important public institution (Instituto Costarricense de Electricidad, ICE).

Around 2000, we saw that CRNet no longer made sense. Why did we keep it? First, because no one else was carrying out this endeavour (developing the academic Internet). We also wanted to support an institution that contributed greatly to the country's development, rather than looking for limited interests. It was clear that it was not the role of universities to go around with routers and cables all over Central America. This was no longer their role. At the Ministry of Science and Technology, we supported ICE, and it was important to see that an institution like ICE was going to take the project into its hands. We always saw ICE as an institution with some deficiencies, but also with great qualities. It was the institution called to continue this project, especially considering the upcoming opening of the telecommunications market (which occurred between 2007 and 2008).

These processes can have very positive elements if they are handled with balance. The previous privatisation bill (in 2000) lacked this balance, and indeed it amounted to an appropriation of key state assets. On the contrary, it was very important to have a powerful infrastructure in place, with great capacity and low prices, before the opening of the telecoms in 2007. Not everyone agreed with the idea of ICE assuming a leading role in the development of the Internet in the country. When the market finally opened for private participation, some companies in the United States did not offer their services in Costa Rica because the ground was already covered. To open the market is essential and competition is healthy. In this way, in 2007, the country was able to use ICE's broadband IP network (known as the Advanced Internet Network, the joint project between MICIT and ICE) for mobile 3G connections; ICE was thus prepared for competition. By opening the market, the number of broadband and cellular connections multiplied, while keeping a leading role for ICE and a balanced environment for the telecoms.

How has the Internet evolved in the region after these events?

In Costa Rica, the role of academia is still important, but in a different way. In the 1990s, the National Science Academy (*Academia Nacional de Ciencias*) was given the responsibility to handle the top-level domain. It is a transparent place, free of certain interests. The management of the top-level domain is handled by NIC (Network Information Center) Costa Rica, a project of ANC, and this is increasingly a critical issue. First, because the management of these technologies is becoming increasingly more complex. This has allowed us to keep an extraordinary group of talented engineers and to conduct several parallel projects. The National Science Academy has an Executive Director and a board of directors. This board of directors consists of four members of the Academy, among whom I am. The management of the TLD has become very important, especially because of security issues. You must use a secure TLD for many things. The Internet has become largely transactional: there are thousands of transactions in a bank each minute. If there is a problem, it is a catastrophe. A secure TLD, for example, guarantees that, when you access the bank via the Internet, you can establish a session that cannot be intercepted by an agent in the middle. If it is intercepted, you are entering your password into a computer that can be 900 miles away and someone will be watching you.

Recently, we established an Internet Exchange Point (IXP) at NIC Costa Rica. When you switched calls from one operator to another, the traffic used to go outside the country at a large cost and with latency. All the operators in the country can now interconnect at the IXP. This is an interesting issue, because this project had never succeeded in the past; the operators wanted a neutral entity, and that is precisely what ANC and NIC can offer. This project is managed by the operators. What we achieved was to help them reach consensus on several issues, to establish basic rules that all the operators could accept. The costs are shared among all of them with great benefits, since local traffic does not have to go outside the country. It is also important that the country has control over its own communications and that the traffic is not exchanged outside the country. For this project, we have had funding from Internet Society and some other organisations. This has given us optimal equipment to establish high-speed Internet connections. Our IXP is called CRIX, which means Costa Rica Internet Exchange. Large companies that are responsible for a high percentage of Internet traffic in the world, such as Google, Akamai, and now Netflix, are installing their servers at CRIX. What kind of benefits is this going to have? The user gains in low latency and a faster response, but it should also be reflected in the costs.

Something I wanted to say is that, although the country (Costa Rica) has improved a lot, we are not doing very well when it comes to the capacity of the links, according to worldwide rankings. And I think we should send a clear message: in annual reports, we have been falling. This is not what we want after all the effort that was put into this in the past. We need to considerably broaden the capacity of the links. We should multiply cell phone links and fixed connections by a factor of 10. Although enormous efforts have been made so far, this is something that we are not doing very well.

What explains this situation?

I think it has been a matter of self-complacency. There have not been enough challenges. It is important to open up more the spectrum, but you should multiply it by a factor of 10. Operators are installing fibre optic everywhere, which means that the infrastructure is there, but now the costs need to go down. There is no longer an excuse to keep the costs so high. There are projects in other places, for example, in Barcelona, where high-capacity connections are available for 30 euros per month. We must lower the costs. Moreover, there is the digital divide. The purpose is not necessarily to offer free Internet, which is not sustainable. What is important is to have low costs to connect everybody. It is not about giving away connections.

At NIC, we have a project to measure the capacity of Internet connections. The idea is to have equipment distributed throughout the country, especially in primary and secondary schools. With this equipment, we are going to create a database that is going to be public. It is a project that we are doing together with Brazil. It is important to have objective and independent statistics. This project will also allow us to detect network vulnerabilities, which brings us to another great chapter that is the security in the network.

For a region like Central America, the geopolitics of the Internet are an important issue.

Something important was that Costa Rica hosted the 43rd meeting of ICANN (Internet Corporation for Assigned Names and Numbers) in 2012. One thousand seven hundred people from all over the world participated. This meeting was inaugurated by President Laura Chinchilla. The speech she gave was extraordinary, and focused on the Internet. This speech helped a lot to establish the country's position on Internet governance. This was complemented by the creation of the Internet Advisory Council (in Costa Rica) which meets twice a year and where all sectors of the country are represented: judiciary, access providers, civil society, telecommunications companies, the academic and commercial sectors... all areas have their representatives in this Council. Something interesting is that, in this Council, they discussed what the country's position was going to be for the Dubai meeting in 2012.

At this meeting, in Dubai, convened by the International Telecommunications Union (ITU), a new treaty for Internet governance was proposed, which gave governments extensive power for Internet control and censorship. Eighty-nine countries signed the agreement, 55 countries opposed it and some abstained. Some countries that signed this agreement did not know what they were signing. Costa Rica was among the few countries of the region that opposed it, despite the pressures exerted on our representatives. China and Russia were the great proponents, for obvious reasons. The Internet became a geopolitical issue in important ways. We have a serious issue here, because the Internet is a powerful instrument that authoritarian regimes do not like a lot. Our Advisory Council has the mission to preserve freedom on the Internet in a clear way and, in the case of Dubai's conference, it played an important role in advancing a well-informed country position. The original idea of the Internet was that every device in the network could be connected to any other device so that traffic could flow freely. Unfortunately, this is not the case today. There are areas of opacity, where there is simply no connection with the rest of the Internet. We live in a time in which authoritarianism has returned in ways we had not seen in a while. What a challenge!

From that point of view, it is essential that an organization can convene the parties to agree on certain positions about the Internet, which can have important consequences at a global level. Granting the administration of the top-level domain to a scientific academy was a decision made over 25 years ago but it still has serious implications today.

Yes, it would not be the same otherwise. It is also a non-profit operation under the support of the National System of Science and Technology of the country.

If I understand it correctly, you see these recent events and the role of NIC Costa Rica as part of the same story that began in the early 90s, which established the Internet in the country and in Central America.

Yes, that is what I would like to convey...

Note

1. From 1987 to 2006, Dr Saúl Hahn was Chief of the Science and Technology Division at the Organization of American States. Starting in 1991, he led the Hemisphere Wide University Scientific and Technological Network (RedHUCyT), which contributed greatly to the development of the Internet in Latin America. His role in this process is further discussed on pages 5 and 6.

Acknowledgments

I thank Massiel Calderón and Susan Leitón for their assistance conducting and translating this interview.

Disclosure statement

No potential conflict of interest was reported by the author.

References

de Téramond, G. (1994). Interconexión de Costa Rica a las grandes redes de investigación Bitnet e Internet [The interconnection of Costa Rica to the big research networks Bitnet and the Internet]. In *Ideario de la ciencia y la tecnologia: Hacia el nuevo milenio* [Ideal for science and technology: Toward the new millennium] (pp. 61–86). San José: Ministerio de Ciencia y Tecnología.

de Téramond, G. (2005, April 7). *The Advanced Internet Project in Costa Rica. Infrastructure for the new knowledge society: A case study*. Paper presented at the Seminar on Latin American, Caribbean and Asian Strategies for Science, Technology and Competitiveness IDB Meeting, Okinawa, Japan.

Internet History Library. (2015). A history of networking in Costa Rica. Retrieved from http://www.internet-history.info/media-library/mediaitem/2296-a-history-of-networking-in-costa-rica.html

Siles, I. (2008). *Por un sueño en.red.ado. Una historia de Internet en Costa Rica (1990-2005)*. San José: Editorial de la Universidad de Costa Rica.

Siles, I. (2012). Establishing the internet in Costa Rica: Co-optation and the closure of technological controversies. *The Information Society, 28*(1), 13–23.

The real "poor man's Arpanet"? A conversation about Unix networks with Kilnam Chon, godfather of the Asian Internet

Camille Paloque-Bergès

ABSTRACT
Chon is an archetypal figure of Internet pioneer – and more specifically of "Global connector", as he is acknowledged in the Internet Hall of Fame. He is a computer scientist who, thanks to an exemplary international academic trajectory and good socio-professional and political connections, got an early taste of Internet technologies. He played a leading role when South Korea joined the global race in technological innovation, and is generally considered key to the entrance of the Internet on the Asian continent. I wanted to discuss with Chon about the hypothesis that himself and his peers from South Korea and Asia got a kickstart from Unix culture and did initially follow UUCP routes, in close connection with their Internet pioneering.

Introduction

Kilnam Chon is representative of a first-generation of digital networks pioneers who not only made history but actively strived to participate in its writing. I met him when he presented the *Asian Internet histories* collection – which he edited, largely co-wrote and made available as well as updatable online (Chon 2015) – at the "Networking history roundtable", an event that tackled issues of historiography facing the increasing importance of software.[1] Based on oral histories gathered from his numerous contacts during his career, the collection is "a project that involved 100 people, for five years. We interviewed almost everyone in Asia, we missed only the people who passed away. This is a global Internet history. It would not be a book, but a collection of regional histories. People have to work on this".[2]

Chon is an archetypal figure of Internet pioneer – and more specifically of "Global connector", as he is acknowledged in the Internet Hall of Fame.[3] He is a computer scientist who, thanks to an exemplary international academic trajectory and good socio-professional and political connections, got an early taste of Internet technologies. He played a leading role when South Korea "passionately embraced the Internet as an attempt to join the 'advanced world'" (Kang & Marchenko, 2018), and is generally considered key to the entrance of the Internet on the Asian continent. His achieve-ments are multiple, but he made a name by developing in 1982, as a professor at Korea Advanced Institute of Science and Technology (KAIST), the System Development Network (SDN), one of the early "notable" international computerized communication networks (Quarterman & Hoskins, 1986).

His Internet story is global indeed, in that it mimics many of those in countries all over the industrialized world – with variations relative to the Korean context, especially the transformations and heritage of the Park Cheong-hee administration (1962–1979), a military regime that invested profusely in domestic elite scientists and engineers in an effort to accelerate industrial development. Like many of Chon's international homologue peers, the first adventures in computer networking he ini-tiated started with a collaboration between departments of Computer Science and schools of technology and engineering: in this case the Seoul National university, KAIST (Korea Advanced Institute of Science and Technology) and KIET (Korea Institute of Electronics Technology)[4]. It then continued with a cooperation with the American National Science Foundation International Connection Program, with Chon "pursuing aggressively connectivity" to CSNET connectivity (Malamud, 1993, p. 406), the TCP-IP-based international Computer Science network using the Internet, followed by the creation of KREONet (Korea Research Environment Open Network) which was based on the same networking model. This led to obtaining the first country code official top-level domain, .kr, in 1986 (Chon et al., 2007; Lee, 2016). He is also representative of a generation of committed computer scientists building the first bricks of interna-tional Internet governance, by initiating and co-organizing the PCCS (Pacific Computer Communications Symposium), a precocious Internet global conference held in Seoul in 1985, or the Academia Network Committee in 1988[5]. In the same vein, crucial were his involvement in PACCOM (Pacific Communications Networking Project) in 1989; or other regional initiatives such as the JWCC (Joint Workshop on Computer Communications), at first between Japan and South Korea, which evolved into the ICOIN (International Conference on Information Networks). Finally, in this period he was also very active in the CCITT standards organizations, and at the heart of the Open system interconnection debate (the ISO-based standard supported by the International Telecommunication Union) and discussions about national standards (Malamud, 1993, pp. 376–377). Eventually, the early 1990s saw the transfer of these technological and political efforts to a telecom company: SDN (now connecting 15 universities through South Korea) and its South-East Asian extensions called HANANet, which became in 1992 a commercial Internet service, JORNET, within Korea Telecom (KT).

But this global history is also archetypal in that it is twofold. The story unraveled in the following interview could also be titled: "How South Korea (like many) did not connect to the Arpanet". Indeed, it was not until 1986-1988, when formal agreements were made between the NSF and non-US computer scientists, local universities and governments – often through a CSNet collaboration and IP domain national names selective distribution, that official international Internet connections became opera-tional. With the exception of UK and Sweden, both of which were early involved in the Arpanet project, non-US countries were not until then invited to the TCP-IP net-work, even when the Arpanet became the Internet in 1983.[6] Meanwhile, facing the relative closure of the Arpanet/Internet world, for reasons having to do as much with US foreign policy than with a sociology of science and technology (King et al., 1997), computer scientists, engineers and amateurs fostered alternative solutions. Among them, and one of the relative most popular in the 1980s and early 1990s in the academia world, was the international distributed UUCP network based on machines running on the Unix system, itself a largely adopted operating system on multi-user minicomputers in universities and industries. Indeed, behind the trophy of a first-time Internet in Asia hide the achievements of the Unix community. Usenet, the computerized social application running on top of it from 1979 (and opened to international users in 1981), was nicknamed the "poor-man's Arpanet" (Hauben & Hauben, 1998, p. 7). Self-labeled the "commonfolk of the computer science community" (*ibid.*) – a hyperbolic expression that translates a friendly competition about digital resources and infrastructures between several worlds of experimental computer networking at the time, this community not only played a very active role in paving the way for the Internet, but also opened and managed its own networks (UUCPNet and Usenet). These were symbiotically linked with the experience of "being on the Internet" in the dozen following years (*ibid.*; Hauben, 2007; Hauben et al., 2007; Kelty, 2008; Schafer et al., 2015; Paloque-Bergès, 2017). In order to see behind the "Internet hall of fame" scene, I wanted to discuss with Chon about the idea that, most probably, himself and his peers from South Korea and Asia did initially follow the same UUCP routes in close connection with their Internet pioneering.

Thus, SDN's Internet pioneer connections were actually a local area network running on TCP-IP for most of the 1980s. If the South Korean network "had international links initially" (Chon et al., 2007), it was not based on the famous Internet protocol suite: "SDN was connected to the mcvax in the Netherlands in August 1983 by using UUCP (Unix-to-Unix-Copy), and in October of the same year, it was connected to the hplabs in the United States. Since UUCP was a protocol that was already installed in UNIX computers, there was the advantage of not having to install additional protocols, and thus SDN Connectivity could be expanded not only to overseas computers but also to domestic computer nodes with relative ease" (*ibid.*).[7] Exotic names such as "mcvax" and "hplabs" are crucial to understanding the initial international mapping of the Internet, or rather, the map that would welcome the Internet TCP-IP nodes and links later on. They are the names of major hubs in the distributed network of Unix machines: at the National Center for Mathematics and Computer Science (CWI) in Amsterdam and at the research labs of Hewlett-Packard in New Jersey, USA – two great crossroads, also called "backbones", supporting the distribution of UUCP data in Europe and the United states. In Asia, the first and main backbone was for a while "sorak", Kilnam Chon's own machine at KAIST (Chon, 1985).

The *Asia Internet histories* collection does reference Unix networks, especially in the first volume set in the 1980s, when they were very active. They appear within European pioneers' testimonies featured in Chapters 3, 6 and 7; also, in Asian pathfinders' testimonies in a surprisingly geographical diverse fashion: Japan, India, China, Australia, Hong Kong, Kazakhstan, Thailand, and Indonesia.[8] The role they played is also underlined in the organization of the Pacific Computer Communications Symposium (chapter 5), and shows in the bibliography and sources of the collection. Of particular interest for our interview is the deployment of AsiaNet, a project submitted by Chon to his peers during the NUS/UNESCO Workshop of 1984 (vol. 1, chapter 4). It was launched the same year, extending Usenet to the Asian continent, with 5 initial participating countries in addition to South Korea: Australia, Indonesia, Japan, Hong Kong, and Singapore, every one of which redistributing data locally or regionally (Chon et al., 2007; Lee, 2016). UUCP-based AsiaNet was building the routemap for the future operational use of TCP-IP when leased lines were finally opened later on, following the PACCOM Project (Chon et al., 2007; Lee, 2016). Korean's reputation of being precociously familiar with issues of digital citizenship may find some of its roots within early experiences of Usenet as a breeding ground for "netizens" – "citizens of the net", in the words of the Haubens (who are the most vocal heralders and chroniclers of the then-popular social network): "The netizens of South Korea [...] deserve particular mention. They are helping to shape the democratic practices that extend what is understood as democracy and citizenship" (Hauben et al., 2007, p. 14; see also in the same volume Chon et al., 2007). Of course, this is to be read in the light of the following years after the military regime ended in 1970, that kickstarted the fast technological development of the country–which the Haubens, in their efforts to promote Usenet as a democratic tool, do not mention.

When South Korea has been remarked for its notable accelerated advances in digital technology and culture (Yoon, 2018; Kang 2017), in the economy of social media and digital platforms (Jin, 2017), this early AsiaNet experience also might have helped the South Korea become familiar with usage-related aspects–for instance related to the governance of user communities and social issues like "net abuse" and "game addiction" (Chon et al., 2013; Lee, 2016). But this interpretation should be put into perspective with the larger "discursive construction of digital Korea" (Kang, 2009): the promotion and redefinition of the country as an IT superpower through technology-driven nationalism, striving for innovation in a globalized world. Indeed, Chon's testimony comes across as a "standard history" (Yang, 2017), with a celebrationist tone which itself is part of this construction. The following interview reveals Kilnam Chon as an agent and force of the "Internet power" strategy put forward by the South Korean government, as a "subject *in* history" seeing himself as an "subject *of* history", according to Yang's fitting words (*ibid.*). However, I might add that this standard history is false-bottomed: behind the promotion of a pioneering technology expertise, another story is told, this time a little off the side. For instance, reasons for choosing in the search of domestic and independent computer technologies (especially the national South Korean PC) are found in the tight budget of academia – in South Korea like elsewhere, where Unix's very moderate cost, almost free, was a great incentive for its adoption. Thus, matters of geopolitical and global market strategies are left to "an expertise of the poor", so to say, where necessity is, again, mother of invention.[9] Similarly, in the networking worlds, Unix promoters and adopters work as outriders who are literal pathfinders, opening with reduced means the digital routes mapping the future success of the Internet. In this, no governmental strategies or formal policy decision, but choices influenced by a global community, meshed with a local context of striving developments and international, often informal, contacts, discussions and negotiations.

Interview

Thank you for agreeing to this interview, Kilnam Chon.[10] *As we discussed before, you are of the Unix generation, and this is key to your actual first steps in connecting South Korea internationally. My general intention is to enquire about Unix culture globally and locally (from technical culture to social networking and politics) and its role in the spreading of early digital networks. About you especially, an inaugural inductee acknowledged in the Internet Hall of Fame as a "Global Connector", I am wondering if and how your experience with Unix was relevant to your contribution to helping to network a big part of Asia and to your participation in internet histories in general. So, I suggest we start by talking about how you got into networking in the first place and how you discovered Unix. Was it as a young computer science researcher?*

Yes, the question of how interworking came from within Unix is a relevant area, I have to think about it. (*Thinks about it for a while*). Ok.

Let's go back to the 1960s. I finished my bachelor degree in Japan and then I went to the US, at UCLA, in 1966. Actually, I was born in Japan, even if my parents were Korean. This choice of UCLA had an impact as two years later, in 1968, it was there that the Arpanet project started. Of course, I didn't know UCLA was going to start this project. After my master degree there, and before the Arpanet started, I worked in a company involved in networking. In the USA, there were so many projects in that area, by major companies: IBM, DEC, and Aerospace companies. And the size of these projects was much bigger. Arpanet was not a big project, but it was funded by the US Government.

My PHD in UCLA was finished in 1974, not in the field of networking but of operation of research which has to do with applied math in probability or stochastic processes.[11] After that, somehow, I ended up working at Jet Propulsion Laboratory (JPL/ NASA), in the area of networking. JPL was in charge of sending a spacecraft in the outer space for the US, to go Mars, Jupiter, or Saturn. We had to communicate. Sending commands, for instance: why don't you go right or left, why don't you take a picture, why don't you take a sample of soil, analyze it and communicate the result back to us... Giving orders to the spacecraft machine was actually networking, because you had to send out all those commands to search for things like water and oxygen. This was a work of very long-distance communications. So, I worked at the mission center, giving orders, getting results, and figuring out how to do all these networking operations.

Then I went to South Korea, in 1979. Having been born in Japan and having studied there and in the US, South Korea in a sense was a new country to me. I became in charge of the National Computer Development Project for Industry. Indeed, South Korea had decided to get into the Information and Communication technology industry, especially in the domains of semi-conductors, computers, and telephone switching systems. I was first put in charge of the computer developments, more precisely to develop various computer systems including personal computers and mini-computers. After a lot of study, we chose open systems, including the Unix operating systems, and publicly available processors such as ones from Intel and Motorola, because we may not have been able to compete globally with proprietary hardware and software.

In terms of software, the question was: are we going to develop our own operating system or to use something else? We chose publicly available operating systems such as Unix and CP/M because we thought we couldn't compete with proprietary operating systems globally. It was a policy decision. At that time, there were several operating systems for personal computers. But for open multi-user operating systems, there was only Unix, and its source code was available.[12]

About the hardware, again we had a choice to make. Most did develop their own processors, but I suggested that we again use a commercial micro-processor, like Intel and Motorola, rather than develop our own proprietary processor.

At the hardware level, what kind of Unix-compatible machines did you use? Because at that time Unix could only be installed on a couple machines, like DEC's PDPs and VAXes.[13] Did you import any of these machines for tests and was it difficult? In France, for instance, importing those machines would face legal constraints.

Technically, you could port Unix to any processor. For a VAX and PDP 11/70, you would get Unix from AT&T. Anything else would require software development, but it was not that difficult if you had good engineering. The purpose was to develop our own computer, we had to port Unix on our own machine. At first, for development machines, we had to have VAXes or PDPs, which were working Unix machines, indeed; but then you could work on your own computer. Thus, we decided that Unix would become some kind of national porting system.

We could have faced the same issues that were raised in France. The French government wanted the French to buy BULL computers,[14] and not American computers (*laughs*). But we couldn't have the same approach, so I said no. Many of those European countries, like France or Germany, cared about their domestic market. Not us. But we had to export, whatever computer we made. We had to start our initial market, so we started the government computerization project that today you would call "e-government". For this, we used Unix and we were probably the first in the world to use Unix for that purpose. Korea was not technically advanced, so we asked some experts in the US and elsewhere; they all said no, don't use Unix! (*Laughs.*) But we went ahead and used it anyway. Either you made it your own and tried to make it commercially competitive, otherwise you joined a group to make it easier to do so. And South Korea was not advanced technically enough to support a domestic operating system. But we had to compete on the market, even if it was highly unlikely that we could compete internationally. Who was going to buy a Korean-based OS or a China-based OS in the international markets of the 1980s? Eventually we did a combination of open software and international competitiveness.

What about scientific arguments? The French I interviewed said that an open OS like Unix was easier to experiment and do research on systems, that it facilitated it.[15] Did you have the same experience? Were you already a PHD instructor, a research director, and for what kind of topics? Were you already involved with the Internet?

One topic was computer development, which I just talked about. When I came back to South Korea in 1979, I first worked in the research institute called Korea Institute of Electronics Technology (KIET), similar to INRIA in France, where I stayed for two years and a half to work on the national computer development project. I also started a small project on computer networking from 1980 on. After two and half years at KIET, I decided to move to a university, Korea Advanced Institute of

Science and Technology (KAIST), as a professor. At KAIST, I focused on the Internet and other networking activities. Most of my students worked in the area of networking. KAIST was a place similar to the MIT in the USA, with a focus on research, whether theoretical or practical networking (I chose to do both). I was also in charge of the Internet developments in South Korea. The Internet itself was under development, so it was a research and development project. When the students came to my lab for a master degree they would do mostly development; but for PHDs, it was on networking research and requiring publications.

As previously, when I made the choice of Unix for the industry, I had to choose, or at least propose what I would do in the area of networking. At that time, computer networking was in a serious research phase. Then I recalled that there were already many protocols and I decided we should not develop our own protocol, but choose TCP-IP in addition to OSI (Open System Interconnection) for the networking of the R&D field. That choice was made because we knew many universities would collaborate, like UC Berkeley or MIT. It would be so much easier to work with them, since they were all using the same protocol.

Also, you had connections because you worked there before, so you had a social network.

That's right. They were my alumni at UCLA (*laughs*). And also, there were international standards being developed, especially in Europe – Frenchmen Louis Pouzin and Hubert Zimmerman were working on some of them.[16] OSI was another set of network protocols, and some of them were hybrid, because international open networks were still under development; but they were not "real" networks. The real networks we could use were TCP-IP.

Let's go back to the Unix protocol if we may. The UUCP protocol was already part of the Unix system in the end of the 1970s.[17] Did you use it from the start?

You had to be careful. We already had a Unix system, then UUCP was developed within the Bell Labs for internal use. Then they sort of decided to distribute it through Unix. They didn't really say it was the main network for Unix: that wasn't their intention. UUCP wasn't a core Unix system functionality, it was an add-on. They put a lot of adds-on and many of them were subtle developments too, like Yacc.[18] About 70% or more of the system was composed of adds-on; core Unix was about 20%. We installed these adds-on for simple reasons. If you wanted TCP-IP, you needed a quarter million-dollar computer. Many universities were poor. But you could use UUCP on even the cheapest of computers, as long as it supported Unix. A machine with TCP-IP was very expensive, so within South Korea only about 3 to 5 sites could have TCP-IP and the rest of them were running on UUCP. TCP-IP as a Unix add-on would come later. Before that, you needed an IMP (Interface Message Processor), and the only way to have one was from Arpanet, from BBN (Bolt, Baranek & Newman) more specifically.[19] But BBN never shipped to the overseas, except for one in the United Kingdom, UCL London, that was part of their project, and another one in Norway, a research team that was also part of the Arpanet. Others, like Teus Hagen's team in Europe couldn't get an IMP.[20] The US government stood for this situation, not because of any industrial secret, but because they weren't confident enough to give any good support to overseas sites. The situation changed afterwards once commercial routers, such as from CISCO and Proteon, became available in the mid-1980s, and many organizations started using TCP/IP.

There was big support from the Unix community: if you had a technical question, you could go to them. Did you use the fellowship of Unix as a support system? Before Usenet, which was largely created for such a use at its beginnings, how did you communicate with the community: through conferences, emails…?

It's a big friendly community. The best technical peers are all here, at least in the Unix engineering area – but not in the domain of personal computers for instance. If you had any problem, the community could be asked, and answers would actually come. When the Seoul National University team tried to install TCP-IP on a PDP 11/45, nobody in the world had ever installed Unix on this, and they found out how to by the Unix community.

After I went back to South Korea in 1979, we really started computer networking research and development in 1980. Then in October 1982, we had a meeting in Boston at the USENIX Conference and we agreed to do international UUCP networking. On the American side, there was the "seismo" connection with Rick Adams, and Dave Spiller. In Europe there was Teus Hagen who would connect with "mcvax".[21] I was the only one from Asia, although not a representative. Most of them were Americans, some Canadians, and a few from Europe.

Did you, as in the US and Europe, need a "traditional" telecom network to run UUCP? How was it in Korea 1982? Was it official to plug into? Did you have problems with these telecom networks, especially modems – as in France or in the Netherlands, where they had to import modems somewhat illegally?

Yes, we had a national telecom monopoly like most. But I had an advantage: our project was part of a governmentally funded project; thus I could do many things I wanted to do. We were doing research, not performing services which would have raised more constraints. They just let me do what I wanted, because of my scientific credit. Also, I was helping the government: if they had a technical question they would come to me, so I was needed. To import modems, I would just have to say: "Research! We are testing American modems!" (*Laughs.*) Even in Japan they couldn't do that. Ours is a sort of a special case.

At the Boston USENIX Conference, which was in October 1982, we agreed to make the UUCP international network happen, and they asked if I would support Usenet too – because UUCP was merely email at that time. I didn't know what it was so they invited me to a UNICOM conference in January 1983, in San Diego. I met all these Usenet developers, we talked and I received my tape,[22] then I gave it to Australia, Indonesia and Japan among other countries, in order to create AsiaNet. I used extensively email, that's the only choice when you collaborate with Americans; Usenet was helpful to me to get information, but above all for a couple of technical newsgroups.

Do you think your fellow Korean peers used this mode of communication differently than their American counterparts? Was AsiaNet any different, culturally speaking? Did you participate in Usenet culture more generally (jokes, flames, …)?

Oh, the humor side belonged to my students; it's a question of generation as most of them were in their twenties, so they could talk with each other. I was more in my late thirties, a senior! (*Laughs.*) The seniors would use Usenet for technical discussion and information. But overall, it wasn't really different. At that time there were a lot of messages. Even if you wanted to receive and send news from Usenet, you needed a fortune because the international telephone call costs were prohibitive. And you ended up spending 10 or 20% of your own salary. We could not afford it: it would add up to a quarter million dollar per year. In Europe it was the same. So, we made an agreement with "seismo" (Rick Adams): he sent a tape including the news, weekly, by postal mail. This way, you only spent 10 or 20 000 dollars. We could send news via the network, but not receive them because of the cost. Most news came from the USA; so as long as you didn't receive many news, the budget costs were doable. Korea was a poor country: we received like 5 newsgroups; Japan was much richer, so they got about 20 newsgroups.

In these first years, there was actually very little online activities. Most of the content seemed to have been received, read composed "offline" after or before being sent out.

Yes, from online connections we got emails, and a few newsgroups only. I received content from Rick Adams, then I sent out copies of his tape through to Indonesia, Hong Kong, and in this general direction, because I felt kind of sorry to ask Rick to send it to 10 countries in Asia. Eventually, Japan and Australia received a tape directly from Rick. We stopped receiving these tapes when we got leased lines, at the end of the 1980s. One guy in Tokyo had to receive it online, because he needed imme- diate replies – and tapes 10 to 20 days via postal mail. Eventually Tokyo University asked "How is this so much?? Do you call the USA that often?" (*Laughs.*) We were asked to stop using it so much.

This money issue is very interesting, because early network histories have underlined the importance of academia-supported networking experiments as publicly funded, admit- tedly niche, experimental, confidential and complicated, but without consideration for who is actually paying and how. How did you fund all this, however constrained your budget was? Was it a research budget?

No, we may have gotten no problem getting permission, but we got no money. I had to pay for all Korean-related topics from my research project accounts: the bill came to me. So, I had to have other professional projects to fund it. Our country was still a developing country! We were just slightly better off than many countries in Africa and Asia. After the experimental phase, we had to do two things: technical development and usage development. We had to ask users to use networking more, because they had to get used to it. What kind of users? Whoever made sense: some from the computer science field, some from the activists' world. We had to build up traffic. We had to use the computer network or it would have died. If you have many stakeholders, it's better. If you only have computer scientists, it won't work. You need telecom people, company people, activists… It's very different then in Europe where it is mostly settled in academia.

Eventually, it got so big that after 4 or 5 years, we had to charge. But charging didn't really help. It was a nightmare. My administrator was complaining: "How can we pay this bill, what will happen this month?" (*Laughs.*) At the same time our stu- dents were downloading a lot of software… One of them downloaded Smalltalk,[23] it cost us 7000 dollars! (*Laughs.*) These were fun times.

You mentioned activists. I talked with early Internet activists in Japan, who told me there were other communication networks they used, like Nifty and other PC networks; same in France with the Minitel or elsewhere with Bulletin Board systems (BBS) and other telematic experiments.[24] *Were there equivalents in Korea and how much interaction happened between the UUCP/Usenet world and these community networks? Was there a difference between PC people and Unix people?*

PC networks, like BBS, were almost exclusively domestic. But 50% of UUCP traffic in Asia was going international. Usenet newsfeeds became international by default, and PC networks had no money to connect to the overseas. So, I told the activists "If you want to connect internationally, we can give you an account: use ours". They could use any machines they had, even PCs, because we gave them technical support. If there was anything possible, we could do it, "Asian style" I guess. Europeans tend to segment people, some kind of segregation. Not in Asia.

Epilogue

I would have liked to hear more about the interactions between powerful people like Kilnam Chon and the activists, amateurs and other "everyday people" uses of these young digital networks, but sadly there was no more time – and my interlocutor seemed a little bit reluctant to go there. I will redirect the reader to the in-depth analysis of South Korean user culture by Jo (2017), for a comprehensive look into small-scale and everyday experiments with tinkering and plugging into digital networks through dial up telecom technologies.

If Unix users are still representative of a homogeneous demographics and sociology of digital early-conceivers and adopters (male, educated, with a good grasp of international and industrial stakes in science and technology), at their own scale they do insert some diversion in the coherent narratives of the all-winning Internet story. Their achievements are interesting not so much because they are the forgotten "first", but because they had to deal with relatively simple means in a context of growingly complex technologies. Their work highlight correlations like the power of social connections meshed into lower levels of technological achievements (material and money concerns below the official programs and funding), the strained relationships between people who work for, within, but also against and at the margins of institutions...[25] South Korea as a developing country in the early 1980s, in the midst of a transition in the modes of production that is both is crisis and in reconfiguration (Yang, 2017), is of particular interest in that fashion.

Notes

1. SIGCIS symposium "Command Lines: Software, power and performance", 2017, Computer History Museum, Silicon Valley USA [http://meetings.sigcis.org/uploads/6/3/6/8/6368912/command_lines_program.pdf]. The roundtable was organized and directed by Marc Weber who I wish to thank warmly here for making this encounter possible.
2. Quoted from Chon's presentation at the SIGCIS roundtable.
3. Kilnam Chon is one of the three Asians in this first wave of inductees, along with Japanese Toru Takahashi and Singaporean Tan Tin Wee [https://www.internethalloffame.org/search/node/kilnam%20chon].
4. Presently ETRI, Electronics and Telecommunications Research Institute.

5. Kilnam Chon et al. (2007): "As the use of the Internet expanded to domestic and then to the international networks, there was a need to establish a mechanism to systematically and efficiently manage Korea's domestic Internet use. Thus the ANC (Academic Network Committee) was formed in 1988 as the association that would perform this function. The ANC was composed of the ANC Steering Committee, consisting of representatives of ANC and other necessary committee members, and its technical subcommittee, the SG-INET, consisting of members involved in the everyday operations of networks. The ANC assumed the role of representing the Korean Internet society, and was involved in managing the use and assignment of domestic domain names and IP addresses as well as connections with overseas networks, and represented Korea in international network associations. The ANC changed its name to KNC (Korea Network Committee) in 1994 and then to NNC (Number and Name Committee) in 1998, and continued to operate as a civil organization establishing and recommending domestic Internet policies" (p. 27).

6. Cf. the special issue about Arpanet of *Internet Histories*, 3/1, 2019 [https://www.tandfonline.com/doi/abs/10.1080/24701475.2018.1560921].

7. From 1983, SDN was connected to various sites in Asia in addition to North America (hplabs and seismo in USA, CDNET in Canada), and Europe (mcvax in the Netherlands).

8. The Asian pioneers interviewed in the collection are, in order of appearance in the first volume: Hu Daoyuan, Abhaya Induruwa, Daeyoung Kim, and Shigeki Got.

9. An analysis about the success of "Korean Inc." – the South Korean semiconductor industry – highlights, with a study about innovation governance, the "*complex* and *unorthodox* interactions between state actions and market dynamics" in order to question the "concept of the national system of innovation" that fed the official history of computer technologies in South Korea (Kim, 1998).

10. NB on editorial choices: the interview transcript was edited for proper written English and readability. An audio recording is available for check.

11. A similar trajectory, from operation of research (« *recherche opérationnelle* ») to networking (« *réseaux* ») was observed in a study of a Unix users research team pioneering computer data networks in France in the same period. The results of this study were partially published in English in Paloque-Bergès (2017); but for more details about the prosopography of these players, see the French publication: Paloque-Bergès and Petitgirard (2017), a double volume in which the latter tackles the history of Unix (with articles in both English and French).

12. For more on the sharing of Unix code, paving the way for free software and open-source culture, see Kelty (2008).

13. They were the "workhorses machines of early Unix culture", according to Open source guru Eric S. Raymond (2001, p. 9). See also Paloque-Bergès (2017), *op. cit.*

14. The BULL company was the computer constructor champion in the midst of the French government's planning for the computer industry in the 1960s ("Plan calcul"). See Mounier-Kuhn (2014).

15. See Note 10.

16. For more on Louis Pouzin, see Russell and Schafer (2014); and Valérie Schafer's important work on the issue in the lineage of her PHD thesis, published in many articles in French and English.

17. UUCP (Unix-to-Unix Copy Protocol) was written by Mike Lesk in 1976 at AT&T's Bell labs – where Unix was originally developed, and propagated with the release of the popular 7th version of Unix in 1979. It allowed data transfers, such as mail, newsgroups and BBS groups. See Kelty (2008).

18. Yacc was written by Stephen C. Johnson, also at Bell labs; it was a popular compiler program for Unix, released in the 3rd version in 1975.

19. For more on IMPs (Interface Message Processor) and BBN (Bolt Baranek & Newman), crucial elements in the Arpanet project, see the seminal Abbate (2000); on IMPs more

specifically, a recent article by McKelvey and Driscoll (2019) sheds a new light on their socio-technical interaction with the telecom, when the standard Internet history usually refers to IMPs as its own project rooted in computer science experiments separate from existing telecom infrastructures.

20. See Paloque-Bergès (2017).
21. *Ibid.* Early UUCP networks' nodes were identified after the Unix machines nicknamed by their administrators.
22. Before and in the early times of data networks, magnetic tapes were often used to store software (and data) and were distributed hand to hand through specialists' conferences.
23. Smalltalk was a programming language developed in the 1970s for educational purposes, opening to modern developments in computing.
24. See for instance Mailland and Driscoll (2017), and Driscoll (2016).
25. In my article "How EUNET hacked European digital networks and disappears", currently under review, I analyze the ambivalences of Unix networks and players in the management of academic resources, technologies and knowledge, in the midst of the European Community becoming the European Union (1980s) and pushing for the digitalization of its knowledge infrastructures.

Disclosure statement

No potential conflict of interest was reported by the authors.

Funding

This work was supported by Computer History Museum.

References

Abbate, J. (2000). *Inventing the Internet*. MIT press.
Chon, K. (1985, October). National and Regional Computer Networks for Academic and Research Committee in the Pacific Region. In *Pacific Computer Communications' 85, Proceedings of a Symposium*.
Chon, K. (2015). *An Asia Internet History Second Decade (1991–2000)*. Seoul National University Press.
Chon, K., Park, H. J., Hur, J. H., & Kang, K. (2013). A history of computer networking and the internet in Korea [History of communications]. *IEEE Communications Magazine, 51*(2), 10–15.
Chon, K., Park, H., Kang, K., & Lee, Y. (2007). A brief history of the Internet in Korea. *The Amateur Computerist, 15*(2), 26.
Driscoll, K. (2016). Social media's dial-up roots. *IEEE Spectrum, 53*(11), 54–60. https://doi.org/10.1109/MSPEC.2016.7607028
Hauben, R. (2007). International and Scientific Origins of the Internet and the Emergence of the Netizens. *The Amateur Computerist, 15*(2), 4–18.
Hauben, R., Hauben, J., Zorn, W., Chon, K., & Ekeland, A. (2007). The origin and early development of the Internet and of the netizen: Their impact on science and society. In W. Shrum, K. Benson, W. Bijker, & K. Brunnstein (Eds.), *Past, present and future of research in the information society* (pp. 47–62). Springer.
Hauben, M., & Hauben, R. (1998). The evolution of UseNet: A poor man's Arpanet. *First Monday, 3*(7). https://doi.org/10.5210/fm.v3i7.605

Jin, D. Y. (2017). Rise of platform imperialism in the Networked Korean Society: A critical analysis of the corporate sphere. *Asiascape: Digital Asia*, *4*(3), 209–232. https://doi.org/10.1163/22142312-12340078

Jo, D. (2017). H-Mail and Early configuration of online user culture in Korea. In G. Goggin & M. McLelland (Eds.), *Routledge companion to global internet histories* (p. 197). Routledge.

Kang, I. (2017). Technology, culture, and meanings: how the discourses of progress and modernity have shaped South Korea's Internet diffusion. *Media, Culture & Society*, *39*(5), 727–739.

Kang, I., & Marchenko, A. N. (2018). *The Internet is plural: The sociopolitical shaping of the Russian and Korean 'Internets* [Paper presentation]. International Conference on Internet Science, Springer.

Kelty, C. M. (2008). *Two bits: The cultural significance of free software*. Duke University Press.

Kim, S. R. (1998). The Korean system of innovation and the semiconductor industry: A governance perspective1. *Industrial and Corporate Change*, *7*(2), 275–309. https://doi.org/10.1093/icc/7.2.275

King, J. L., Grinter, R. E., & Pickering, J. M. (1997). The rise and fall of Netville: The saga of a cyberspace construction boomtown in the great divide. *Electronic Markets*, *7*(1), 21–24. https://doi.org/10.1080/10196789700000008

Lee, K. S. (2016). On the historiography of the Korean Internet: issues raised by the historical dialectic of structure and agency. *The Information Society*, *32*(3), 217–222. https://doi.org/10.1080/01972243.2016.1153011

Mailland, J., & Driscoll, K. (2017). *Minitel: Welcome to the Internet*. MIT Press.

Malamud, C. (1993). *Exploring the Internet. A technical travelogue*. Prentice-Hall.

McKelvey, F., & Driscoll, K. (2019). ARPANET and its boundary devices: modems, IMPs, and the inter-structuralism of infrastructures. *Internet Histories*, *3*(1), 31–50. https://doi.org/10.1080/24701475.2018.1548138

Mounier-Kuhn, P.-E. (2014). From general electric to bull: A case of managerial knowledge transfer (1956–1970). *Entreprises et Histoire*, *75*(2), 42–56. https://doi.org/10.3917/eh.075.0042

Paloque-Bergès, C. (2017). Mapping a French Internet experience: A decade of Unix Networks Cooperation (1983–1993). In G. Goggin & M. McLelland (Eds.), *Routledge companion to global Internet histories* (pp. 153–170). Routledge.

Paloque-Bergès, C., & Petitgirard, L. (2017). La recherche sur les systèmes: des pivots dans l'histoire de l'informatique. *Special Double Issue of Cahiers D'histoire du Cnam*, *7–8*(1–2).

Quarterman, J. S., & Hoskins, J. C. (1986). Notable Computer networks. *Communications of the ACM*, *29*(10), 932–971. nohttps://doi.org/10.1145/6617.6618

Raymond, E. S. (2001). *The Cathedral & the Bazaar: Musings on Linux and open source by an accidental revolutionary*. O'Reilly Media Inc.

Russell, A. L., & Schafer, V. (2014). In the shadow of ARPANET and Internet: Louis Pouzin and the Cyclades Network in the 1970s. *Technology and Culture*, *55*(4), 880–907. https://doi.org/10.1353/tech.2014.0096

Schafer, V., Paloque-Bergès, C., & Georges, F. (2015). La culture Internet au risque du Web. *CIRCAV*, (24), 15–30.

Yang, S. (2017). Networking South Korea: Internet, nation, and new subjects. *Media, Culture & Society*, *39*(5), 740–749. https://doi.org/10.1177/0163443717709443

Yoon, K. (2018). Digital media and culture in Korea. In Dal Yong JIN and Nojin Kwak. Lexington Books (Eds.), *Communication, digital media, and popular culture in Korea: Contemporary research and future prospects* (pp. 283–300).

"The internet and the European market" from a multidisciplinary perspective: a "round-doc" discussion

Valérie Schafer, Andreas Fickers, David Howarth, Francesca Musiani, Julia Pohle and Dwayne Winseck

ABSTRACT

David Howarth, Francesca Musiani, Julia Pohle and Dwayne Winseck were invited to discuss the main topic of this special issue, "The internet and the EU market." This conversation at the crossroads of several research areas (communication studies, sociology, science and technology studies and political science) brought together leading experts who shared their experience, research and expertise on the internet, European integration, governance issues, etc. They referred to several topics that are addressed in the papers in this issue, such as the taxation of digital services, net neutrality and the openness of networks, as they discussed questions related to the realities and limits of the notion of "Digital Europe", changing discourses on the EU's digital economy, the concept of European governance and the turning points and key events in the relationship between the internet and the EU market since the 1990s.

Valérie Schafer and Andreas Fickers: It is not always easy to address questions in the field of internet studies from a Europe-wide perspective. What do you see as being the reasons for this, what issues does it raise, and what methodological and scientific challenges need to be overcome?

David Howarth: First, "internet studies" is a problematic term. There are so many potential disciplinary and sub-disciplinary perspectives on the internet – history, sociology, political science, economics, law, etc. In my own field (political science), I know of research institutes focused specifically on the internet and even on specific dimensions of the internet (e.g. social media) (as at the University of Oxford). Therefore, I find the term unhelpful. It reminds me of "European studies" or "area studies" more generally. In my own research area, "EU studies" exists and there are associations/conferences dedicated to the study of the EU from a number of disciplinary perspectives, but political science dominates these multi-disciplinary associations (EUSA in the US and UACES in the UK/EU), for better or worse. Each discipline has its own methodological and scientific (epistemological) challenges. Therefore, I have trouble identifying challenges that are specific to studying the internet per se, rather than challenges regarding specific disciplinary perspectives on studying the internet.

Dwayne Winseck: For a very long time the internet has been cast and studied as primarily an American invention. This is probably due to the reality that the US did play the leading role in its development and the outsized influence of US scholars on special topic domains. That said, even early researchers/internet historians like Janet Abbate noted that the development of the internet was not just an American or linear affair but that it also involved competing conceptions of what computer networking would/could be, and also that British, French and Swiss interests, from engineers and technical experts to telcos, computer hardware and software firms and governments, were also involved. Recent scholarship on "the French internet" (Driscoll & Mailland), "the Russian internet" (Peters), "the Chinese internet" (too many to list), "the Chilean internet" (Golumbia), "the Canadian internet" (Daniels), etc. have begun to rectify this and give us a more international/global view of the internet and its development. The distinction between the generic internet vs the desktop vs mobile internet as well the platformisation of the internet is also adding to the tendency to realise that there is more than one internet, and that these internets have and are taking shape outside the US, with wildly divergent development trajectories. Discussions of "the federated internet" (Noam) lend themselves to a similar view, and that view is now being girded by the much more aggressive approach the EU is taking to internet regulation: the GDPR,[1] numerous government-inspired "codes of conduct" governing internet content regulation, the RTBF,[2] revisions to the e-Commerce Directive revamping copyright, and the EU's unique and enduring stance on net neutrality (along with Canada, India and others) also lend support to the idea that there are new ways to think about the internet beyond US-centric views. These emergent realities will take some time to take deeper root and dislodge a kind of American hegemony over "internet studies".

Francesca Musiani: I believe this also has to do with the problematic status of the entity "Europe" as a political entity in addition to an economic one. Some avenues for dialogue on internet policy/governance issues exist at the European level (e.g. EuroDIG[3]) and, of course, some important directives or reforms of existing European law on the internet have entered into force in recent years (the primary example being the General Data Protection Regulation); however, Europe keeps on having a complicated time between the enduring influence of the United States as internet governance's dominant political-economic entity, the pursuit of often heterogeneous goals at the national level by Member States, and the centralising pushes of some previously more open countries such as Russia and of long-term voluntarily insulated ones such as China.

Julia Pohle: The internet is a global network of networks, which affects all parts of the world; however, much like globalisation, the digital transformation does not have the same effect in each country and for each society or community. This is particularly true at the global level, where digital connectedness has led to new modes of inclusion and exclusion. But also, within the European Union, the digital transformation takes different forms in its highly developed Member States. Specific uses, developments and policies are strongly influenced by traditions, norms, values and institutions, which vary from country to country. For the field of internet regulation – my field of research – these variations have resulted in different policy struggles, actor constellations and discourses and, ultimately, in highly diverse regulatory frameworks across Europe. In order to carry out cross-country comparative research and adopt a Europe-wide perspective on internet policy, we need to take the different influencing factors and their effects into account.

Is the notion of "Digital Europe" an expectation, a discourse, a fantasy or a reality?

Dwayne Winseck: It is probably all four. Policy frameworks are usually aspirational and visionary as well as being technical and administrative. To my mind, the Digital Europe framework has done a number of important things. It has expanded the idea of synchronising the relationship between the EU as a political and cultural project on the one side and audiovisual media services on the other to communications services, both in terms of infrastructures, markets and what people do with the broadband internet and mobile wireless services at their disposal. EU-wide roaming, for example, and rights portability are excellent additions to what it means to be an EU citizen and nicely go beyond mere trade regimes to set out a fairly expansive set of public interests that citizens and consumers can expect from regional integration projects. In my opinion, this would bode well for the political and cultural legitimacy of the EU against charges of its technocratic elitism. Of critical importance to academics and participants in both markets and policy processes, it seems to me that the Digital Europe framework has propelled vast improvements in the coverage and availability of data on a wide range of measures with respect to mobile wireless and broadband (wireline) coverage, adoption, speeds, prices, market structure, etc. These have been more frequently published as well. They are also much easier to access, download and use then they have been in the past and relative to most of what takes place in the US and Canada. There's also a stronger integration across both data from the communications and audiovisual media fields *and* the research studies, reports and other publications associated with them. In other words, there is a quality and coherence to data and policy documents that surpasses past standards by a long shot. Lastly, I wonder if something in the Digital Europe framework, and all of the things just mentioned, haven't girded policy-makers' spines so that they can take more aggressive stances with respect to, for example, market concentration, the role of digital platforms with respect to AVMS services, privacy and data protection, EU-wide mobile roaming and policy-making in general. In this sense, might it have helped propel the "return of the state" – at both the EU level and amongst its Member States?

Would you agree with Dwayne that the notion of "Digital Europe" is all four: an expectation, a discourse, a fantasy and a reality?

Francesca Musiani: Yes, some of all this, I believe. It is an expectation inasmuch as the notion of a "European digital sovereignty" – often cited but rarely achieved – is seen as a crucial goal to pursue if an alternative to the United-States-based internet giants is to be found. There have been cycles of European-funded research projects that pursued this objective, especially when it came to search engines (Quaero, Theseus,[4] etc.). It is a (performative) discourse, as this notion of European specificity and the possibility of Europe being a sovereign entity comes back regularly in the speeches and declarations of different Member States, and as such, it is the "motivational" backbone for a number of cooperation and coordination initiatives between them.

Julia Pohle: I agree that the notion of "Digital Europe" is most of the above – and even more: it is a term used by the European digital technology industry and the European Commission to frame their vision of a European digital industry built on policies and regulations that prioritise the interests of European citizens, countries and companies. It is first and foremost, therefore, an economy-centred strategy and discourse aimed at strengthening Europe's economic leadership in the digital era and creating a digital industry based on European norms and values. While such a position is still far from being the reality (and as such remains a fantasy), current usage of the term also brings the broader idea of the "digital" within the confines of the much narrower concept of a "digital economy". It thus supports the assumption that the digital transformation is primarily an economic transformation rather than a socio-technical process of change that reaches far beyond the economic sphere.

David Howarth: This is a "slippery" term, the contours of which are far from clear. However, as an academic who is principally interested in European Union economic governance, I see the concept as – above all – an invented term to sum up a number of macro- and micro-economic policy goals, which are more or less clearly defined. Thus, "Digital Europe" is a form of discourse and an expectation. See the Digital Europe Programme.[5]

There is a specific EU policy goal agreed by the Council of Ministers/Commission which involves funding for projects that can be categorised (more or less precisely) into one or more broad goals: "The programme will boost investments in supercomputing, artificial intelligence, cybersecurity, advanced digital skills, and ensuring a wide use of digital technologies across the economy and society. Its goal is to improve Europe's competitiveness in the global digital economy and increase its technological autonomy." Needless to write, these policy goals – like ALL EU policy goals – beg a lot of questions. The 1992 project of the Single European Act was to complete the Single Market by 1992. Since then we have had a series of EU efforts to "complete" or, more modestly, "advance" the "Single Market". Of course, the term "single" is a misnomer because we are far from a "single" market in a huge range of areas. In 2010, an Israeli colleague and I guest-edited a special edition of the high-ranking *Journal of European Public Policy* on the "never-ending completion of the European single market".

Since the Bangemann report in the mid-1990s, the internet has been full of promise for the EU. Has the discourse remained resolutely optimistic, or on the contrary has it now become more realistic and pragmatic?

David Howarth: I have not followed the development of EU (notably Commission) official discourse on the internet. However, I have followed EU (notably Commission) official discourse on the Single Market. This remains consistently optimistic but also consistently vague. At the same time, the EU insists on pragmatism but the manner in which pragmatism should delimit optimistic goals is always frustratingly vague. There are constant shifts – on the issues/policy areas emphasised – but there are also com-mon/consistent themes. The Lisbon process, for example (both its first and second revised iterations), promised to transform Europe into the most "advanced knowledge-based economy" in the world. The central role of ICT (thus the internet) in this process is obvious but always elusively defined. A potentially useful study would be to look at all the specifically internet-related projects funded in full or in part by the EU and to look at the outcomes of these projects in terms of the stated goals of "Digital Europe". Has that ever been undertaken? A kind of academic "audit" of internet-related funded projects would help both academics and policy-makers understand the relationship with real-world developments and goals and allow a more targeted cri-tique of both the goals and the manner in which they have de facto been interpreted to date.

Julia Pohle: At the time of the Bangemann report, citizens, governments, the private sector and the European institutions were united by their belief in the very optimistic and techno-deterministic discourse about an "information society" that would bring economic prosperity and social well-being to Europe through technological progress. Today, we need to distinguish between various more nuanced discourses, which are promoted by different actors. The European Commission and many governments still primarily emphasise the benefits of the digital transformation for the European econ-omy and its consumers. Yet they have become more pragmatic with the realisation that simply promoting technological progress and market liberalisation will not lead us into this bright future; instead we need effective policies and a strong regulatory framework in order to both protect and promote the European market. But other actors within governments and many citizens across Europe are increasingly con-cerned about the risks that a globalised digital economy holds for fundamental rights and for the self-determination of European countries, companies and citizens. This gives them a somewhat pessimistic view that fails to recognise the advantages of digital technology.

Dwayne Winseck: Based on the discussion above, I think that the discussion has become much more realistic and pragmatic. Policy-makers seem to be recognising reality and acting accordingly rather than turning a blind eye or wishing things like market dominance – whether in terms of mobile markets, search, shopping or operat-ing systems – away. Of course, there are always new imaginaries of what might be that are excessively optimistic and even fantastic. Today those are being occupied by the likes of, for example, 5 G, IoT,[6] big data, AI and ML,[7] etc. However, even here, the discourse and actions being taken seem better grounded, although a healthy degree of scepticism is needed on this point.

Can we talk about the concept of "European governance"?

Dwayne Winseck: Absolutely, and for better or worse. I've already mentioned several things above: a reasonably robust net neutrality framework (albeit with too many loopholes and blind spots), the GDPR, the four mobile wireless carrier policy, broad-band extension programmes and funding, RTBF, updates and planned overhauls of the e-Commerce Directive and numerous "codes of conduct" are all evidence of this. Many of these initiatives, in my view, are desirable, but I worry a great deal about the vast increase in the use of "codes of conduct" that lack a firm basis in the rule of law, that delegate too much power to private actors that already have too much power, and that generally jostle very uneasily with the ECHR[8] Article 10, UDHR[9] Article 19, etc. It is also the case that some European actors have far too much clout in EU policy-making, which I would say is exemplified by ETNO[10] in telecoms and internet infrastructure policy and regulation, and by media, publishing and cultural industry groups when it comes to audiovisual media, copyright and other such policies.

David Howarth: My answer is also yes. There is a huge body of literature on this that also reflects an even larger body of literature on the concept of "governance" in political science. Different political scientists define "governance"/the contours of governance differently. Different political scientists also define the relationship between "government" and "governance" differently. In the European context, the concept of "governance" also has a "multi-level" nature, which can make its effective analysis/ understanding even more challenging.

Francesca Musiani: While I am a little bit unsure of whether we can talk about European governance, I am quite sure we can safely talk about the notion of European digital sovereignty, which I mentioned above, as a goal towards which the EU regularly tends. I believe there is now a consensus in Europe that if the economic and political dominance of the US and China – the first established, the second emerging – is to be countered satisfactorily, European states cannot fight the battle on their own. The GDPR has perhaps been Europe's strongest action so far in grounding the control of data flows "on rules rather than force alone",[11] and the prime example of a project of European digital sovereignty that has turned into an actual governance action.

What do you see as being the main turning points/key events in the relationship between the internet and the EU market since the 1990s?

David Howarth: This definitely goes beyond my knowledge. However, I would point to the Lisbon Process I and II (as I note above). Both Lisbon I and II placed digital services (the internet) at the forefront of EU internal market policy concerns. Lisbon I might then be described as a turning point by placing the internet at the heart of market developments. I would also point to EU (meaning Commission and collective Member State) efforts to reach agreements on the taxation of digital services. The precise "turning point" here is more difficult to determine but it might be the October 2017 European Council that first placed squarely on the agenda the need for an "effective and fair taxation system for the digital era" – but this followed on from the Digital Summit of September 2017. To date, there has been a failure to reach an agreement in the Council on a "digital services tax", but the issue is clearly on the agenda. Other possible "turning points" are more difficult to define. Some might relate to major EU funding decisions but the relative importance of these decisions can only be determined in the future (i.e. when we can assess their impact). EU competition policy decisions have also had a significant impact upon the internet in Europe (Microsoft and web browsers, etc.). I write as a political economist. I fully recognise that there are a number of other major EU agreements regarding the internet that must also be considered to be major turning points in other areas of concern. The General Data Protection Regulation of 2016 is of great significance (notably re human rights). However, the turning point linked to data protection and the internet came earlier (probably in November 2014) when the Commission released guidelines on the "right to be forgotten". Even before this move, Google had eliminated hundreds of thousands of websites. Thus, the precise turning point is difficult to define but the issue is of immense importance.

Dwayne Winseck: I would point out the steady move to a stronger regulatory framework for net neutrality, beginning around 2006 and culminating in the 2016 Net Neutrality Framework/Guidelines – the 2000 to 2015 or so period in which strong intermediary liability protection rules limited the scope of copyright claimants' demands and ability to use ISPs and other intermediaries in the processes of identifying, blocking access to and taking down allegedly infringing content. The steadily increasing delegation of more and more obligations on ISPs and other intermediaries with respect to copyright since around 2011 has, as many critics feared, opened the floodgates for enrolling far more actors in such processes across a much wider purview. The updates to the AVMS Directive[12] in 2010 and 2016, I believe, also seemed to be well placed and reserved in their scope, i.e. they refused to sweep everything into their remit and left much scope for countries to chart their own relatively autonomous course. I thought that this was a thoughtful way of approaching audiovisual media policy "in the internet age" which stood as a smart touchstone for other countries like my own, Canada, where efforts to update AVMS policy have been much more ham-fisted and constrained to the visions and interests of industry insiders.

Julia Pohle: It is difficult to identify specific turning points, since shifts in discourses and perceptions do not occur all of a sudden but happen over time. As well as the burst of the dot-com bubble in 2000, which certainly dampened the initial enthusiasm for the digital economy, a number of other episodes have led to a more reflective and nuanced vision of a digital economy. Interestingly, several of them are related to citizens standing up for their rights in a digitally connected world, e.g. the huge protests against the Anti-Counterfeiting Trade Agreement (ACTA) in 2012 and its subsequent rejection by the European Parliament. Another such episode was initiated by Edward Snowden's disclosure of mass surveillance practices by US intelligence agencies and their European partners. The massive outcry that followed the Snowden revelations did not actually lead to more effective protections against these surveillance practices for European consumers – and it caused both the French and German governments and the European Commission to publicly call for "digital sovereignty" and to adopt economic policies and strategies that in many ways appear almost protectionist.

Debates and controversies regarding EU market integration in the area of the internet and EU-wide regulatory issues and challenges regarding the internet and the web are numerous. Is the EU market a microcosm of the tensions that the internet and its stakeholders have to face at the global level?

David Howarth: Yes! On taxation, data protection and competition policy issues (among many others). Through its policy and rule-making in intergovernmental fora (the Council) and at a supranational level, the EU can lead the way on international efforts in these areas. More generally, the role of the digital economy and the internet specifically in the context of Europe's relative economic decline (notably in relation to Asia) is an issue of considerable preoccupation, at least in the EU!

Dwayne Winseck: Yes, it is, but it is also playing a lead role in showing what a more active role for the state in relation to the internet might look like within the context of market economies and liberal democracy. Its approach to all of the issues already mentioned – market concentration/dominance, privacy and data protection, copyright, AI/ML policy,[13] a broader conception of consumer and citizen rights (rights portability, regional roaming), etc. – all mark out a fairly capacious view of internet policy and regulation. The lesson it offers portends a kind of EU internet that is steeped neither in Californian ideology nor in Chinese or Russian authoritarianism, to paraphrase Macron at IGF[14] in 2018.

Francesca Musiani: The EU market is certainly an opportunity for the researcher to observe how debates unfold around critical issues of internet governance such as net neutrality, the protection of personal data and the preservation of "communication rights" and "internet rights" such as access and diversity. It is a microcosm of how these tensions take shape at the global level as, within Europe, Member States are often not in agreement about a common position that should be upheld "in the name of Europe", or about the instruments that should enforce governance on a particular issue. A clear example is net neutrality: while there is a common EU framework for it in the form of a set of directives that entered into force in the early 2000s, some Member States have passed stronger national laws or are in the process of doing so, with former Commissioner Neelie Kroes famously declaring that an "uncoordinated, country-by-country basis [would] slow down the creation of a Digital Single Market".

Julia Pohle: As I said earlier, normative frameworks and societal contexts vary significantly across the EU Member States. Policy-making in Europe also involves a larger number of stakeholder groups with differing and often competing interests. Accordingly, EU policy-making on the digital economy certainly reflects many of the tensions that actors also face at the global level, whether in international organisations such as WIPO[15] and the ITU, in global multi-stakeholder processes, e.g. within ICANN, or during trade negotiations, e.g. within the WTO. However, in contrast to global controversies, interactions and debates at the EU level are confined by the norms and values on which the European Union is built. While actors at the global level might have to renegotiate the specific meaning of even the most fundamental principles, such as freedom of expression or privacy, the "space of possibilities" in the European field is much more clearly defined. Of course, this does not mean that there are fewer tensions in European policy debates, but the gaps between contrasting positions might be easier to bridge.

Looking more closely at the topic of this journal issue, "The internet and the EU market", what do you see as being promising avenues for future research, and what are the main scientific issues that need to be addressed?

Dwayne Winseck: A key area of research on the internet and the EU market will need to flesh out the issues above and dig deeper into the histories, development and uses of prototype computer networks and the early internet in the EU. The role of the various EU Member States and the key players in setting the terms of debates over the main issues outlined above will also be important, with particular attention needing to be paid to the tensions between internet policy and industrial policy, to the excessive influence of some business constituencies over other interests, including in business and public interest advocacy groups, to how the technocratic tendency of EU policy-making discourages wider participation in internet policy and, thereby, undercuts its own legitimacy, to how regulatory capture works in the EU context, etc.

Julia Pohle: A tendency that we can observe in recent years in Europe and other parts of the world is a growing nationalisation of internet policy. Moving away from the belief that the internet as a global network needs global policies, norms and agreements, countries are increasingly trying to regulate the digital transformation – including the digital economy – at the national or regional level. But what does it mean for the development of the global internet if its regulatory framework becomes increasingly fragmented? What new power constellations can we observe when value-based policy issues, such as data protection, intermediary liability and freedom of expression, are part of bilateral and plurilateral negotiations between individual governments and stipulated in instruments such as trade agreements? How can democratic countries join forces against a US-dominated platform capitalism if they are primarily occupied with the protection of their national digital economy? In my view, these and similar questions are the most pressing issues that researchers interested in the political dimension of the internet need to address in the years to come.

David Howarth: The taxation of digital services is one of the major political economy issues of our time and touches upon a range of other topics of controversy – tax avoidance, growing inequalities, and more vaguely "globalisation", to name a few. Few political scientists/political economists work on tax policies at the EU – there are only a handful of book-length studies and the best known are now dated. Many are focused on the topic of so-called "harmful tax competition" or on VAT issues. There is also (more descriptive) work by legal scholars. I would love to work on this topic. Why is agreement on EU legislation in this area so elusive? What are the different preferences of the different EU Member States? But … alas … I only have so many hours in the day.

Francesca Musiani: Europe first has the opportunity to shape, or to further develop (along the lines of what the CAPS programme has done), a research programme that advances the state of knowledge on the sharing economy, peer-to-peer production and decentralised architectures. If researchers can be mobilised in political arenas to account for the opportunities and challenges of distributed networks, the objective should also be to produce prototypes, which take into account the social and organisational dimensions in addition to the technical dimension. Europe should also be able to consider and encourage – and good research can help in this regard – the development of companies that offer "truly" alternative systems. Faced with the dominance of centralised clouds, whose server farms are very often hosted on US territory, it would be desirable that the "technological independence" of Europe, envisaged as an integral part of its digital *habeas corpus*, includes P2P and decentralised solutions, rather than considering as an alternative the promotion … of the centralised European cloud, something that is most often put forward.

Notes

1. General Data Protection Regulation.
2. The right to be forgotten.

3. See https://www.eurodig.org. The European Dialogue on Internet Governance (EuroDIG) is an open multi-stakeholder platform created in 2008 by several organisations, government representatives and experts. It aims to foster dialogue and collaboration with the internet community on public policy for the internet.
4. See https://atelier.bnpparibas/en/prospective/article/age-european-search-engines-quaero-theseus-pharos
5. European Commission website: https://ec.europa.eu/digital-single-market/en/news/digital-europe-programme-proposed-eu92-billion-funding-2021-2027 "As part of the next long-term EU budget – the Multiannual Financial Framework – the Commission has proposed the Digital Europe programme, the EU's programme focused on building the strategic digital capacities of the EU and on facilitating the wide deployment of digital technologies, to be used by Europe's citizens and businesses. With a planned overall budget of €9.2 billion, it will shape and support the digital transformation of Europe's society and economy."
6. Internet of Things.
7. Machine Learning.
8. European Convention on Human Rights.
9. Universal Declaration of Human Rights.
10. European Telecommunications Network Operators' Association (https://etno.eu).
11. See https://www.ecfr.eu/article/commentary_reality_bytes_europes_bid_for_digital_sovereignty
12. Audiovisual Media Services Directive.
13. On artificial intelligence and machine learning.
14. Internet Governance Forum.
15. World Intellectual Property Organization.

Disclosure statement

No potential conflict of interest was reported by the author(s).

Viviane Reding on her action in the field of the information society and media (2004–2010) Interview by Elena Danescu

Elena Danescu (iD)

ABSTRACT

The following pages are taken from a long interview (more than eight hours of footage in total) that Viviane Reding granted us in 2015 in connection with the "Pierre Werner and Europe" research project. Drawing on more than 40 years' experience in politics, Viviane Reding spoke about her career, the role of Luxembourg and Luxembourgers in the European integration process, and various key events in which she played a part. In these extracts, she discusses her role as a member of the first and second Barroso Commissions (2004-2009 and 2010-2014) and her efforts to help build an information and knowledge society in Europe, one that serves citizens and protects their rights and fundamental freedoms. Her achievements in this respect include capping mobile phone roaming charges (they were subsequently abolished in 2017), advocating for the introduction of a single emergency number (112) in all EU countries, launching the Europeana digital library, and spearheading a programme to use technological innovation for climate and energy solutions. She also describes the process of developing a Digital Agenda for Europe to improve the continent's digital competitiveness compared with the United States, China and Japan – a complex and challenging task given the context of globalisation and the divergent interests of the various stakeholders (research, industry, consumers, etc.). Finally, she mentions the reform of personal data protection that she initiated (leading to the GDPR, adopted in April 2016).

"If we think small, we stay small"

Viviane Reding, *Interview*, 3rd session, Luxembourg, 4 December 2015

In the early 1950s, the historiography of European integration adopted the phrase "fathers of Europe" – most probably by analogy with the Founding Fathers of the United States, who signed the Declaration of Independence in 1776 (Bossuat, 2001). But what role have women played in the European project? In the decades from the

1950s to the 1970s, leadership in Europe was predominantly male, since women were involved only rarely in politics in the six Member States. Even if we can identify some women who contributed to the beginnings of the European project alongside the founders, they did not play a decisive role. The journalist, feminist and Europeanist Louise Weiss (1893-1983) was a leading light in her era, but she was not involved politically in the European integration process.

The situation changed at the dawn of the 1980s, when women began to take on leadership roles in European politics. In 1979, French politician Simone Veil (1927-2017) was elected as President of the first European Parliament formed following direct universal suffrage – many of whose members were also women. That same year, Margaret Thatcher (1925-2013) became Prime Minister of the United Kingdom and played a prominent part in European integration. After Thatcher, Angela Merkel, Chancellor of the Federal Republic of Germany since 2005, is only the second woman with sufficient executive power to have a decisive influence in the process of building a united Europe. In 1989, the Parliamentary Assembly of the Council of Europe appointed the French politician Catherine Lalumière as the organisation's first female Secretary General. The European Commission, which had long remained a "men's only club", opened up to women, with France's Christiane Scrivener becoming Commissioner for Taxation and Greece's Vasso Papandreou Commissioner for Social Affairs in 1989.[1] From 1993 to 1995, only one of the 17 European Commissioners was female; this progressed to 5 out of a total of 20 Commissioners from 1995 to 2004, and 10 out of 28 in the 2014 Juncker Commission. The election of Germany's Ursula von der Leyen as the first female President of the European Commission in July 2019 clearly marks a paradigm shift.

In the line of women who have helped build Europe, Luxembourg's Viviane Reding (born on 27 April 1951 in Esch-sur-Alzette) is a key figure. After her studies, including a PhD in Human Science at Paris Sorbonne University, she worked as a journalist at the *Luxemburger Wort* for more than 20 years and chaired the Luxembourg Union of Journalists. She joined the Christian Social People's Party (CSV) and was elected to the Luxembourg Chamber of Deputies (1979-1989 and since 2018), where she particularly focused on social affairs and international relations, before becoming a Member of the European Parliament for three terms (1981-1999 and 2014-2018) and turning her attention to social affairs, employment and the working environment, as well as civil liberties. In 1999, she became a Member of the European Commission, where she also served three terms. In the Prodi Commission (1999-2004), as Commissioner for Education, Culture, Youth, Media and Sport, she opened up the Erasmus programme to the rest of the world, launched the eLearning programme as a key part of the *eEurope* initiative (highlighting the educational potential of the internet), initiated the reform of the "Television Without Frontiers" Directive (which in 2007 became the Audiovisual Media Services Directive) and introduced a system for funding independent audiovisual production, which not only boosted the European film industry but also promoted European creativity, culture and values throughout the world. In the first Barroso Commission (2004-2009), she was given a pioneering portfolio – Information Society and Media – which encompassed telecommunications, innovation, technological research and the digital economy. Her major achievements – which had a direct impact on the daily lives of hundreds of millions of Europeans – include capping mobile phone roaming charges (they were subsequently abolished in 2017), advocating for the introduction of a single emergency number (112) in all EU countries, launching the Europeana digital library, and spearheading a programme to use technological innovation for climate and energy solutions. In the second Barroso Commission (2010-2014) she became the First Vice-President of the European Commission, responsible for Justice, Fundamental Rights and Citizenship. She introduced a "Europe of Justice", based on a package of 50 new laws, and took a stand – threatening sanctions – against Member States that tried to hinder the free movement of citizens (especially France, the United Kingdom and the Netherlands) and against the dismantling of independent judicial systems (in Hungary and Romania). She is committed to promoting the role of women on the boards of directors of listed companies, and she initiated the reform of personal data protection, considered as a fundamental right (the resulting GDPR was adopted in April 2016).

The following pages are taken from a long interview (more than eight hours of footage in total) that Viviane Reding granted us in 2015 in connection with the "Pierre Werner and Europe" research project. Drawing on more than 40 years' experience in politics, Viviane Reding spoke about her career, the role of Luxembourg and Luxembourgers in the European integration process, various historical events in which she played a part, and especially her pioneering, decisive action in building an information and knowledge society in Europe.

I would like to thank Viviane Reding for her willingness to read through the interview from today's perspective and update it as necessary. I am also grateful to Sarah Cooper for contributing her linguistic expertise to this paper.

Elena Danescu

Elena Danescu: Your first term ended in 2004, but you were reappointed in the new Commission headed by José Manuel Barroso, which took office on 22 November 2004. In this new Commission, you were responsible for the information society and media. Could you tell us about how this new Commission was formed and the fact that you were reappointed in virtually the same areas of responsibility as before?

Viviane Reding: No, the areas were completely different. The information society is all about the Internet, communication, cable, telephony, broadband, frequencies and such like. It also covers technological research, which accounts for one-third of European research expenses. So I entered an extremely technical and industrial field with a great deal of economic power – it had nothing to do with culture. I did hold on to areas such as television and cinema, and I tried to incorporate those into the digitisation of Europe. Concerning the task I was entrusted with, I had to learn a great deal, because I didn't know much about the infrastructure aspects – which are vital if the content is to reach people –, about communication technology and research into all the new areas of state-of-the-art technology. To develop new technological fields, the Commission created technological research platforms. The technology we see in cars today was developed on those platforms – the eCall initiative, new materials, new communication technology systems, nanotechnology, etc. I organised all of those areas on the basis of technological research platforms, my aim being to encourage high-tech industry, small start-ups and university researchers to work together. The technological platforms were a huge success and truly advanced technology in all the areas we know today.

ED

What did you find most difficult at the start of this term, in which you had so much to do and to discover?

VR

In a very short time, I had to learn about many new fields, such as the telecoms market, technology, frequencies, cable, new communication methods and satellites. All of that was new to me. Fortunately, I had developed effective learning methods throughout my life. I also adopted this learning approach when preparing for my hearing, when I was asked complicated questions on technology. Subsequently these areas became a passion of mine.

ED

You worked with President Barroso. How would you describe his personality and working methods in comparison with the previous President, Romano Prodi?
   […]

VR

He gave commissioners a great deal of freedom in their respective areas, but he also made the Commission work as a real college. By that I mean that decisions on all political subjects were taken by all the commissioners together. President Barroso made use of his presidential prerogatives in areas such as foreign affairs and for major international issues. But he granted a lot of freedom in the areas covered directly by the commissioners. If a commissioner took risks and he felt that those risks were worthwhile, he backed the commissioner. For example, when I decided to reduce roaming fees, going against the entire industry and most of the ministers, President Barroso supported me. He gave very strong support to his commissioners when he thought that their initiative was worthwhile.

ED

You mentioned roaming fees. Thanks to you, 500 million Europeans now benefit from these reduced fees. They also have you to thank for the common emergency number, 112. You masterminded these proposals. How did you come up with these ideas and turn them into reality?

VR

I always thought of the single market when developing my approach. We Europeans have an enormous asset in the form of a market of 500 million potential consumers. And we need this asset if we want to invest in the development of our economy and have the jobs and employment that go with it. Taking advantage of this single market and breaking down the barriers that still exist within it have always been on my agenda. Concerning telephony, we quite simply needed to create an open telephony and internet market. So I carried out a major reform, opening the telecoms market to competition. I wanted to give a chance to small companies so that they could also enter the market. I was convinced that competition generates new ideas, technological progress, better offers for citizens and price cuts. And for me, as a Luxembourger, roaming charges were a complete non-sense. When you live in a small country surrounded by other countries, you need to take advantage of your freedom of movement. But each time you cross a border (which doesn't actually exist anymore), you come across a telephony border linked to high costs. It makes absolutely no sense. So I had analyses carried out to establish whether there were any objective reasons why roaming was so expensive. All the evidence showed that there weren't. It was simply a question of higher net earnings for the major operators, whereas their costs were extremely low. I said, "That won't do. We have to cut these punitive fees," and so I started the process of cutting the fees, step by step.

It was David against Goliath. The telecom ministers were against me, and so were the finance ministers and, of course, all the major telecom operators. Most of the commissioners were not happy either. The political battles were never-ending. The European Parliament, however, was on my side. It understood the need to open up the market and enable the free movement of communication in the interest of consumers. The media were also on my side, because journalists were furious about the fees they had to pay when reporting from abroad. So I drew strength from Parliament and the media to win this fierce battle.

ED

What are your thoughts on the claims that the first Barroso Commission, and in fact the second Barroso Commission, were ultra-liberal, as often asserted by the press, whereas the … ?

VR

That's just nonsense. The Commission at that time comprised a large number of Christian Democrats, a large number of Socialists and a few Liberals. And no decision is taken by a single commissioner; the College always decides collectively. Since the majority of members of this Commission were Socialists and Christian Democrats, the decisions were rounded off, so to speak, to be more balanced. The Barroso Commission was certainly not ultra-liberal.

ED

I would like to ask you a question about your achievements as Media Commissioner. You have repeatedly stated that we need information, not propaganda. How does the diversity of the media and of information channels help to provide citizens with reliable information?

VR

That's the big question, isn't it? Because most media, those which are read or watched by the biggest audiences (television and the Internet), are short-message media. On top of that, most media in Europe, except public TV and radio, are privately owned. And journalists are certainly not eager to publish "propaganda"! But there are problems. Because media inform the public too rarely about the decision-making process in Council and in Parliament (the two co-legislators for all EU legislation). There is a lot of talk about the noise of politics, but very little about why and how political action is carried out. The European Parliament is a joint decision-maker on all laws adopted at European level, which are then implemented in the Member States. Parliament therefore carries out an enormous amount of legislative work and wields an enormous amount of power. And yet the media hardly mention this. But if someone shouts or makes a dramatic gesture in the plenary session at the European Parliament, this ends up in the news. As a result, people think that the European Parliament is there for shouting, for making dramatic gestures and impressive outbursts. They don't realise that Parliament spends the vast majority of its time working, making laws, influencing political leaders and shaping the Europe of the future. Unfortunately, this gets overlooked because only a minority of citizens read serious newspapers, which sometimes report on the work being carried out by Parliament. The situation is getting worse and worse, because on technological platforms the news isn't even squeezed into a few sentences any more, it's squeezed into a few words. This naturally distorts the information delivered to citizens. People are ill-informed and therefore ready to believe the simplistic anti-European propaganda of populists.

ED

What image do the media convey of Europe's institutions and citizens? Do you think that the immediacy of the media and the faster pace of people's lives call for more education and explanations on this matter?

VR

Yes, but how can we do that? As a former journalist, interested in political communication, I have been analysing the major channels of information provided to European citizens for decades. In general, the media pounce on the latest news. These subjects have a life cycle of a few days. Then the media move on to something else. But it sometimes takes years for a decision to be taken, to be applied, for a law to come into effect and reach citizens. And yet citizens rarely have the opportunity to follow this process. There's also a whole host of private lobbying bodies that spout a load of rubbish and invest a great deal of money to ensure that their message is widely disseminated. People are puzzled, they are starting to believe anything and get worked up by lobbying propaganda based on commercial or ideological interests. If you add to this the fact that most information has a "local" character, you understand why it is so difficult to get a meaningful European message across.

[…]

ED

Would you agree that this media profusion, together with the technical nature of EU jargon, is making European citizens apathetic about getting involved?

VR

When we explain procedures and political developments to citizens, they are really interested and say, "Why didn't anyone tell us that before?" We can explain complicated things using simple language. As great philosophers said from the outset, centuries ago, "Whatever is well conceived can be clearly said." So we don't need to hide behind acronyms and technocratic language, we can easily explain what is at stake. Each time I explained the reasons for and the progress of an issue, people were interested and happy that someone was taking them seriously. The problem is that when we explain the problems to each citizen on an individual basis, we only reach a minority of citizens.

[…]

ED

In the context of globalisation and the digital economy, the Internet economy, which you supported, is undeniably dominated by the interests of the United States. Google, Facebook, Twitter and YouTube are just some examples. How does this situation affect European policy in this field as well as the sovereignty of the Member States?

VR

For the time being, we seem to have lost part of our digital sovereignty, and I'm choosing my words very carefully. We haven't managed to consolidate enough strong proponents of digital technology in Europe. Why is this so? Because our market is divided. I meet talented young entrepreneurs who, instead of battling with 28 different regulations to gain access to the 500-million-strong European market, go to the US, where they have unimpeded access to a market of 300 million people. The second problem is that we haven't managed to develop enough risk capital in Europe to invest in these new businesses. The third problem is that we can't accept that an entrepreneur who went bankrupt could do better second time around. Anyone who doesn't succeed at the first attempt here in Europe is considered a failure. That's foolish; we need to encourage creativity, entrepreneurship and risk-taking. We need to help young people develop their own business. The EU Commission has finally come up with the idea of turning Europe into a digital market. "Hallelujah!", I say. It would have been better to do this 10 years ago, when I already wanted to move in this direction. But it's better late than not at all. We have to make the most of our excellent research capabilities and give talent a real chance if we want to boost capacity-building. A strong capital market is also essential.

ED

This digital field is also a challenge in terms of regulation, particularly in the Transatlantic Trade and Investment Partnership – TTIP – between the EU and the US that you mentioned earlier. Do you think that Europe still has a chance with the United States?

VR

Yes, of course! We have the world's biggest organised economy. We have the world's biggest securities market. Europe makes the most external and internal investments worldwide. We will have full capacity if we can just manage to break down the artificial barriers that still prevent us from taking advantage of our single market. That is why I put forward a reform of the legislation on the protection of personal data. Today we have 28 different systems that contradict each other and prevent our industries from using the market as one. The General Data Protection Regulation, or GDPR, is built on the principle of one market and one law for everyone, including US companies who want to set up on our territory. I put this proposal forward in January 2012. It has been adopted and is now starting to be applied. These uniform rules for the entire territory will be the basis for a true digital single market.

At the time, I also put forward a reform of contract law. In e-commerce, we see that people buy within their own countries but not in others, because they fear that contract law is different in other countries and they are not sure which would be the competent court in the event of a problem. I suggested reforming our contract law so that people and companies can make purchases throughout Europe under a single contract with the same cross-border consumer protection regulations. This still hasn't been accepted by the governments. You see, the governments are often a real obstacle to creating a true single market. Opening up the markets and granting access to start-ups and SMEs will help them grow into big businesses. I hope that the Juncker Plan, in collaboration with the European Investment Bank, will turn Europe into a unique area for digital development. We will only be able to regain our digital independence if this project succeeds.

   […]

ED

In this globalised landscape, what did you perceive to be the strengths of this digital economy in Europe, and what were the potential pitfalls for Europe?

VR

It was very clear for me. The pitfalls were that we wouldn't embrace the digital economy fast enough and that we would end up lagging behind. This would be a lost opportunity, because we have excellent engineers, excellent researchers and excellent companies. But if they don't manage to jump onto the digital bandwagon they will not survive. I was already thinking of our strong automotive industry and the need for electric cars. I realised that if we didn't manage to integrate digital technology into our automotive sector, our global flagship industry would fall behind.

We had seen this happen to our mobile phone industry. Europe had invented mobiles and was the world leader at the time, but as mobile technology developed further into high-tech instruments, US iPhones took the lead. As for the Internet, were we going to retain our leading position, or weren't we? I wanted us to move fast so that Europe wouldn't end up lagging behind the US today and Asian countries in future.

ED

The private sector undeniably plays a pioneering role in the digital domain, and your initiatives were immediately followed by consumers but less so by the Member States, which failed to offer top-quality public services that kept pace with the digital age. What were the main problems that you encountered in this regard vis-à-vis the public authorities, and how did you overcome them?

VR

It was in the public authorities' interests to take action in three areas. The first was e-government: digitising public administration in order to have archives, to speed up response times for citizens and to do away with red tape. Paper files were obsolete; it was time to create electronic files. But of course the opposition came from the administrations themselves. They simply didn't have officials who were trained in new technologies. The administrative bodies themselves slowed things down. The second area was e-learning – learning beyond physical books by using e-books, by training trainers and teachers electronically and enabling them to give their pupils and students information via effective online channels. Educators could pack a huge amount of knowledge into their classes, but they needed to know where to find it and how to pass it on, and they knew little about that. At the time I set up information networks for teachers which they could use for support, where they could download lessons, but the use made of these tools was minimal. The third area that I saw as an element of the future was e-health, quite simply because hospitals need to be connected. Instead of doing a blood test or an X-ray five or six times, the tests need to be networked, also between physicians and hospitals. Doctors need to be able to look at the results on a screen rather than on paper and compare them easily with other tests to avoid mistakes and reach a diagnosis more quickly. Hospitals need to be interconnected not just internally but also with other hospitals in the same town or region. But there are still huge obstacles to accomplishing this feat today, at a time when the population is ageing and we need efficiency more than ever. Without efficient digitisation, our expenses are at risk of going through the roof.

That's also why I've always insisted that we should roll out broadband not only in town and city centres, but also beyond. If we want to keep people in their villages, especially disabled or elderly people, if we want to maintain village life, there needs to be this link between villages and towns: educational links, health links, transport links. When I look at the figures, I am saddened to see the huge delay in providing broadband coverage without "white spots", mostly in rural areas. With 5G implemented and 6G in the research stages, our 4G coverage is still deficient, not to mention our high-speed Internet ...

ED

What progress has been made with regard to the European Commission initiatives that you instigated in favour of pan-European public services such as e-identity and e-signatures?

VR

It's quite technical. The e-signature worked. What didn't work so fast was e-government in national and regional administrations. We should have carried out large-scale professional training, lifelong learning, but then who would have done it? Because we were also lacking the teachers ... Only large companies had the capacity to move forward. Only researchers had the capacity to move forward. But in terms of our capacity as a society – local administrations, government administrations, hospitals, schools – we were still in the pre-Internet age.

ED

You stressed the importance of public-private partnerships to drive these matters forward. In which areas do these partnerships play the most prominent role and what are the areas of divergence between the public and private sectors?

VR

The public sector always tries to maintain a certain amount of control. But when the public sector works with the private sector – and the private sector tends to be more oriented towards technologies – it feels as though it is losing its power, so it has a tendency to resist innovation in general. Public-private partnerships worked well, however, in the field of technological research. In order to move forward in research – and we are excellent in this field – we had to boost cooperation and partnerships. But universities weren't used to working with companies. That is why I created technology platforms, which enabled universities, large companies, small companies and start-ups to work together in a given area (for instance nanotechnologies). This enabled the best minds to join forces until their joint efforts reached market stage. I created a dozen technology platforms between 2004 and 2006, bringing together intelligence and resources … I allocated solid resources to these platforms. The result was extraordinary. The project took off very quickly indeed. Engineers and researchers, whether from universities or companies, quickly understood the value of working together.

The collaborative approach was a driving force: the researchers progressed much more quickly than if they hadn't worked together. And today we are seeing results in the automotive industry, in new materials incorporated into our aeroplanes and helicopters, to name but a few. It's a real success story!

ED

You also accompanied this process with a major information campaign whereby society and consumers were constantly kept abreast of all these developments and therefore subscribed to these innovative initiatives. But we also mentioned the public authorities earlier. In the context of the digital environment, the Member States are not all equal, and competitiveness gaps widen further when the pace is faster than in the normal economy. What did you do to reduce the digital divide between the Member States?

VR

I mentioned this digital divide earlier when talking about broadband, because rural areas often had no Internet connection or a slow connection which made it impossible to use the Internet in an efficient way. I also saw that there were huge differences between the Member States. For example, Italy, Greece, Hungary, even France at the time, were incredibly far behind. France decided to move forward, propelled by its companies. So it made a giant leap forward. Others continued to lag behind; even Germany had many "white spots" with no coverage.

Benelux in general was very good indeed, as were the Scandinavian countries and the UK. So I had my champions and my stragglers. And some stragglers failed to understand that the only way to develop their economy was to invest in high-speed networks. That is why I travelled around Europe with my maps featuring "white zones" that showed the regions lagging behind. The dawdlers didn't really appreciate the fact that I was travelling around with these maps. Few of them wanted to move forward, fewer still wanted cross-border investments to be made. I always said, "To have high-speed broadband we mustn't stop at borders, we have to cross borders." But we were faced with the problem of frequency auctions, since the frequencies belonged to the governments, which thought more about how much they could raise at auction than about technological development. Within governments, the responsibility for frequencies was often in the hands not of telecommunications ministers but of finance ministers. And finance ministers were primarily interested in selling these frequencies in order to fill the state coffers. They weren't interested in whether the sale was effective in creating the networks we needed. This problem still persists today. The reforms put forward by the Commission to date have not succeeded in creating a pan-European approach to ensure full coverage of the European market and enable the most efficient technology to be used (whether telecoms, cable or satellites), according to density (towns/cities or rural areas) and geography (flat or mountainous regions). On islands or mountains, working via satellites could be an alternative. Unfortunately, this overview of how to develop very high-speed broadband has still not sunk in among governments, which often think on a small national scale rather than striving to develop the European area together.

ED

This is also a matter of digital sovereignty, a concept that you have worked on a great deal recently. Isn't there a contradiction between Europe's digital sovereignty compared to the rest of the world and the digital sovereignty of each Member State, which thinks – as you say – on a "national" scale?

VR

If we only think on a "national" scale, we lose sovereignty, we give ground to the digital giants, which unfortunately are not European. We are now starting to build strong European digital companies. They are finding it difficult to achieve a global dimension from the outset, because they are hampered by contradictory laws on European territory. We need uniform pan-European legislation. We have the world's biggest organised economy, but we can only be competitive if we stop this Balkanisation and create a single law for the entire continent. How many times have I seen this scenario repeat itself in Europe? We help young entrepreneurs with brilliant ideas to create their own start-ups. We support them with seed money, but when they want to get their "baby" off the ground, they don't have the geographical scale needed. So they head to the US where they have immediate access to the entire US market and the risk capital that goes with it. Europe is reluctant to take risks. But fortune favours the bold. And if we don't move beyond our small national sovereignties, they will be defeated by their own making, so it's a lose-lose situation. We are unfortunately lagging behind because of this small-minded conservatism and this ethos of "I will create my little territory and build a big wall around it". We need to think on a larger, pan-European scale and try to actually remove barriers. We are also too slow in creating appropriate legal instruments under the "one continent, one rule" principle. Take for example our data protection legislation, which forms the basis of our digital market. It has taken four years to be approved and will take three more years to be implemented. I put this proposal forward in January 2012, and yet it won't be implemented until 2018. We lose time, although it makes good sense to have one rule for all companies throughout the continent. But, my goodness, it's hard to get this message across! We always tend to think small, but we can't grow if we carry on thinking small.
   […]

ED

In July 2009, you launched the Digital Agenda for Europe, together with a series of legislative measures. Could you elaborate further on the content of this strategy and its contribution to digital competitiveness, and give us an assessment of its implementation?

VR

The Digital Agenda was a nudge in the right direction to help governments realise that they were lagging behind. It was made up of several levels, the aim being to encourage investment in high-speed networks. It took the year 2015 and Juncker's initiatives, in collaboration with the European Investment Bank, to put this item strongly on the agenda and generate investment. I am sure a future Commission will invest even more funds to encourage the growth of the "digital market". Fortunately, as regards the technology platforms that I mentioned earlier, we were able to set them up because they operated under a public-private partnership. Concerning investment in risk capital, I tried to encourage the involvement of business angels (individuals who invest in risk capital). But Europe was difficult, because "risk" capital does not have a good reputation. I tried to overcome the hurdles.

Mentalities are only starting to change now because everybody realises that the major players are no longer European. The fact that these major players are also attacking our automotive industry gave Germany a wake-up call. Driverless cars, autonomous cars, electric cars, etc. have been developed in Silicon Valley. That gave us food for thought: we realised that if we don't make rapid progress now, we will not manage to catch up. And in the long term, this will mean that our flagship industry, the automotive industry, will suffer. Fortunately, we are still at the cutting edge of progress when it comes to research and innovation.

ED

When it comes to globalisation and the digital economy, the Internet economy is clearly dominated by US economic interests, as you pointed out earlier. What impact does this situation have on Europe's policy in this field and on rules under international agreements, particularly TTIP?

VR

Before negotiations began on TTIP, we had had bilateral negotiations with the US for many years to ensure that the US and its companies would apply European law when they were in Europe. What a horrendous thing to say! We were negotiating so that the Americans would apply European rules in Europe. Can you imagine what would happen if we, Europeans, didn't apply American rules in the US? It would be unthinkable!

In Europe, personal data is protected by law, and this legislation is developed on the basis of the European Treaties. The Charter of Fundamental Rights also protects these rights. US companies were acting as though there were no rules in Europe. That's why the European Court condemned several US companies for failing to comply with European law. This prompted me to review the European data protection regulations and come up with one law for the whole continent, which applies to all companies operating in the EU, whether they are European, Chinese or American. That's one thing. The second point is linked to security: whenever there is a danger to society, the police forces and secret services should naturally be able to have the information they need. In Europe, there are laws governing access to this information. But the US administration forces US companies based on European territory to give out all the personal data that they have collected, without judicial decision. We have been negotiating for years to resolve this issue. You may have heard of "Safe Harbour", an agreement put on the table by the Commission so that US companies could send personal data between the US and Europe and vice versa, so that trading could work between a parent company and a subsidiary. The handling of this matter was also called into question by the Court of Justice, which said, "In practice, the Americans are not sticking to the law." The agreement was eliminated.

We had to renegotiate an agreement between the US and Europe on how to treat personal data and how companies operating in Europe should comply with European rules. The same applies to TTIP. It's not a new negotiation; it's a situation we've been dealing with for a very long time. Of course, we will have to reinforce European standards in TTIP. We have major disagreements with the US on many issues. All these problems have to be regulated in the TTIP agreement, and it should all be dealt with in such a way that it does not contradict our fundamental rights.

Note

1. See Denéchère, 2007 (especially the accounts by Simone Veil, Yvette Roudy and Marie-Claude Vayssade).

Disclosure statement

No potential conflict of interest was reported by the author(s).

ORCID

Elena Danescu http://orcid.org/0000-0003-3915-7200

References

Bossuat, G. (2001). *Les fondateurs de l'Europe unie*. Belin. doi:10.1086/ahr/87.3.790
Denéchère, Y. (2007). *Ces Françaises qui ont fait l'Europe*. Audibert.

Section III

The web and digital cultures

Behind the scenes: an interview with Pierre Beyssac

Camille Paloque-Bergés, Victoria Peuvrelle and Valérie Schafer

ABSTRACT
Pierre Beyssac, who launched EU.org around 1995 and was the co-founder of Gandi, a French company which profoundly disrupted that country's growing market of domain names, reflects on his path from the 1980s to the beginning of the 2000s. He was one of these discreet but central players of the French Web scene of the 1990s and 2000s, who experienced these tremendous times as a user, then as a "pro-am" and finally as a web professional.

Pierre Beyssac, who launched EU.org around 1995 and was the co-founder of Gandi, a French company which profoundly disrupted that country's growing market of domain names, reflects on his path from the 1980s to the beginning of the 2000s. He was one of these discreet but central players of the French Web scene of the 1990s and 2000s, who experienced these tremendous times as a user, then as a "pro-am"[1] and finally as a web professional.

As a player and witness, he testifies to various aspects of the history of the Internet and of the Web: those of the DNS system and naming, but also of the issues of openness and freedom of information that were raised in the digital field, of the evolving governance and regulation of the Internet, and of the adoption of the Web by the general public at the end of the 1990s. He also enlightens continuities that overpass protocols and networks, from the Minitel to Usenet and then the Web.

His taste and passion for microcomputing, the role of users' and amateurs' associations, the DIY and tinkering of the 1990s, are evident, as much as the promises of the Net economy, the turn to the commercial web, the politicisation of the debates dedicated to the Internet and the confrontation between traditional players and newcomers in the digital field.[2]

Interviewer[3]: Thank you for joining us today. Let's start with a quite simple question: how did you discover programming, networks, Internet and the Web?

Pierre Beyssac: I discovered computing pretty early on. Without going into too many details, my father, who was not a computer scientist but was interested in computers, would take me to the National Library to punch holes in punch cards. I must have been between 6 and 8 years old. He would sit me down in front of the big keypunch machine and tell me "go ahead". We would type in some words, it was like a typewriter you know, but with capitals only. Once I spent a day writing "My name is Pierre Beyssac", because there was an area where a space was missing... So, I rewrote it 80 times, which of course did not change anything [laughs]! My father would also take me to the ENSMP[4] in Fontainebleau. All this was between 1972 and 1975.

But I really started giving programming a go when microcomputing appeared. I was in middle school by then, in Clermont-Ferrand.[5] Magazines like Jeux et Stratégie [Games and Strategies] discussed microcomputing, others like Sciences and Vie [Sciences and Life] also touched on the subject of electronics. The FNAC store[6] had only just arrived in Clermont-Ferrand and I first saw microcomputers there. We thought they were typewriters since we had never seen them. I remember there was an Apple II, a Commodore PET 2001, a clone of TRS80 and so on... All the big names of the time were there! We would try to find a spot on the machines, and there was a super cool salesman that would let us use the machine for hours. We would hack software too... That is when I thought: "I like this." Then there were the first Microtel Clubs. They had the first Goupils, managed by France Télécom, but we were rather free to do whatever we wanted. The computers were not as powerful as the Apple II was but we had a modem, a device that I had never used before. Then the Minitel[7] arrived, in 1984 I think. Just having a free access to a phonebook online was incredible. I would hook up the Minitel to my computer and scan the pages. That way I could find the cheaper communications.

You connected your Minitel to your computer?

Yes, and we eventually bought one computer, an Apple II. When we arrived in Paris in July 1981 my dad saw that I would spend my days at the Microtel computer club of Issy-les-Moulineaux.[8] Every Saturday I would take the earliest train there to be sure to get the machine I wanted. The aim was mostly to test new games. After a couple of months of back and forth my dad started thinking that it would be a good idea to buy one. At the time an Apple II cost 13,900 French francs – pretty much a month's salary – so between my savings, those of my brothers, and my dad, we were finally able to afford one at Christmas 1981.

In 1984 I was fiddling with electronics to connect my Minitel to the Apple II. You had to actually write the code and ask the machine to manage a serial port, because the Apple II did not have one... But it was not too complicated. When the two machines were connected the Apple II could send commands to the Minitel and start automated queries on it. We even hacked into a completely unprotected Unix machine once. Thankfully I stopped hacking in that way before I did anything too bad...

Then, after my baccalauréat, I went at the IUT (University Institute of Technology) from 1984 to 1986 at Orsay. It was half management information and half whatever else.

Was Orsay an important centre at the time for computing as it is then?

Yes, but we saw it from afar. IUTs did not have much money, we had few computers and used old terminals. We used the notable PL1 language, which we would run on the computing centre of the Orsay University (the CIRCE[9]). We would have a punch card to indicate that we had prepared the evening's practical exercises, it was then sent to the CIRCE from the IUT to run during the night. We had to be really careful because one misplaced character meant a lost day of work. That was my first contact with the computing centre.

Did you learn about networks?

Yes of course, we learned the basics of the X25 protocol, the role of wires on serial ports. At the time there were very few IBMs but we had some, we did accounting, Cobol, PL1, no C but a PL1 derivative called "PL16" which ran on Solar 16 (a small French mainframe, the IUT had one), and a little teleprocessing but it was more theoretical. The studies were at the border between accounting and networks.

At the time, was there a professional environment linked to networks? Were people speaking about those yet?

Not really, not at the time. It was not a hot topic. The Minitel itself had not even really come out. The situation was still blurry. Networks appeared later, when I was at the SupElec engineering school.[10] We then started having access to BITnet, a weird thing based on virtual punch cards that would enable data transfers and emails. This was originally an IBM protocol. SupElec was very DEC oriented, DEC with VMS and with Ultrix.[11] We were connected to the European Academic Research Network, which was interconnected with the addresses of ARPANET. Not that it was already Internet at the time – that was between 1987 and 1991, as I only really started having access to it in 1989. I had an Amiga computer, which was the closest thing to a professional computer because it allowed to program in C and you could use UUCP[12] and loads of fun stuff like that. There was even a UNIX version but no one could afford it. I could see the newsgroups on this computer, so when I arrived on BITnet I subscribed to all the corresponding groups. I actually overloaded the university's server and got reprimanded for it; coming back from the Easter Holidays one day I got asked into the systems administrator's office because he had had to cut-off my email due to the amount of traffic. I had subscribed to Amiga distribution lists.

To what extent was this use of networks popular in your school?

It was not generalised, but we were definitely a few. Information did not really migrate much, it was not as simple to pass information along as it is now, it was really word of mouth.

How long did your studies last? What happened next?

Mine lasted for four years. First of all, in the middle of my studies I started contacting an association called FNET[13] because I realised that I would not have an email address anymore once I was going to finish my studies, and that bugged me. I wanted to find an email provider for a decent price, so I called FNET. A very nice person on the phone told me that it was not too expensive; only 2200 francs (app. 350 euros) per annum, plus a per volume tariff… Simultaneously there was UUNET,[14] which gave an unlimited access for 432$ per annum, but you had to pay the phone bill for the USA too. In the end, I did not choose either of these because I could not afford it, so I used the school's amenities until I left it, and then I ended up in one of Thales' subsidiaries, now thalesIS. They worked on European projects, and I got a professional classic address, which allowed me to wait. When I would tell my IT coworkers I wanted a personal address they did not understand what I would do with a personal email address. And that is when I fell upon what was not yet called the AFAU (Association Française des Amateurs de Usenet – French Association of the Usenet Amateurs), of which I am now the president. The idea was to get an email, Usenet and news access for a decent price. It was kind of a smaller equivalent to the ISP FDN

(French Data Network). At the time it was difficult to get access to Usenet news in France, because you may access them but you were not supposed to disseminate them. Many underground channels existed to disseminate the news whilst dissimulating their origin. We had a friend that worked in one of these informatics companies working in pair with research, who would put the magnetic strips on his personal computer every night and make the news available for the price of a local communication in metropolitan France, plus a small subscription fee. All of this happened around November 1993, when I started having a personal address and access to news and Usenet. I had a small modem from February 1993 (bootlegged from a trip to Canada) but did not have much use for it until I managed to get email thanks to the AFAU.

Could you tell us more about this AFAU association?

In the beginning it was informal, and a little later we created a formal association under the 1901 law, to have a little bit of means through membership contributions. At that time the AFAU was based at Vincent Archer's home, but it then migrated over to Laurent Chemla's company called Brainstrom. Then Laurent got a 64 kbit/second connection for professionals, so little by little we got more and more means to have better connectivity and pay less.

When did the Web arrive in your life?

[...] When I get my first Unix, I would get one floppy disk a day. At the time all of this was sufficient, we did not need more. There were protocols like Gopher, but they were very confidential and did not provide much information. I heard about Mosaic for the first time in 1993, when a colleague came back from a trip to the States and told me he had seen this new thing, which gives access to graphics. Otherwise I do not think I have ever directly seen Mosaic, because I did not have an IP access at the time. The first navigator I saw was Netscape; it was sent from a friend from Angers[15] via the phone. It took about 45 minutes for the image to load, but I witnessed the first Netscape. That happened around 1995.

In 1993 people did not think much about the Web. In 1994 people thought of making their first servers but were not sure of what to do with them. The Web really started around 1994–1995 with Yahoo! In June 1994, the first IP connections for the general public arrived in France – until then the most advanced you could get was RENATER.[16] FNET also existed but the debit was much smaller and it was expensive. Companies went through FNET, but mostly for email.

In June 1994, Francenet, Worldnet and CalvaCom[17] probably made a deal with Oléane[18] because all three opened only days apart. All three companies went through Oléane and a transfix link, which was very expensive at the time. Transfix was the commercial name of France Télécom leased digital lines. It allowed you to send data between two points. France Télécom did not care or have to know whether it was IP or anything else, they just handled bits. So, Oléane used it to deliver IP connectivity to their professional customers. Before, no one had personal access, as the Web was used for professional uses. FDN started in 1991 and contacted FNET like everyone else. FNET provided a full package: the DNS, the .fr, the distribution of IP addresses, then the services: email, Usenet, and for the richer, the IP access. FDN also wanted a .fr and asked FNET, but FNET declined, arguing that FDN was not based in France since they were not using FNET and were with a US provider. When RENATER and, a bit later, Oléane started, there was more and more pressure to dissociate .fr and FNET, and little by little what became the Afnic[19] was created. Monetisation occurred in 1995 or 1996. There were a whole bunch of people who needed domain names and it was not necessarily legitimate for them to obtain them for free, NIC-France[20] thus started asking for payment, and at the time you paid once upon registration only. I do not know when that changed. So FDN got a .org, and their .fr when NIC-France opened to other providers.

I started giving a go at FDN in 1994: It happened through Usenet, when I got in touch with Christian Paulus, the president of FDN at the time. FDN had benefited from a 64 kb/second RENATER access that arrived at Christian Paulus' place (near place Gambetta, in Paris). He had started creating PPP access for FDN with a software for NEXT, because FDN at the time was based on NEXT machines, similarly to Oléane actually, but it was not working. So I found myself debugging it, and little by little, within a week or two we improved the thing. Once it was reliable in mid-July 1994 FDN started proposing associative IP accesses, and that became my first IP access! I became a member of FDN. It already had their server, FDN.fr. Libération[21] was using their service, and Valentin Lacambre, Jean-Claude Michot (co-founder of France-Teaser[22]) and others were amongst their members. You thus had some players acting as a bridge between the Minitel and the Internet. It became especially relevant since downloading existed on the Minitel at the time; you would connect the Minitel to the computer, connect to the 3615 and request for a software to be downloaded. It marked a change from the old floppy disks.

FDN had assemblies maybe once a year and though I cannot remember much of what we talked about, there were discussions on how to deal with volunteers running a non-profit association which was providing a service for companies that were making money. It could be problematic and thus raised philosophical questions. But the problem went away by itself when companies started buying themselves professional access with the decrease of prices around 1996. At the same time France Telecom was preparing their loss of monopoly, so prices for local communications were rising, by increments.

At the time, you were still working in a company...

Yes, I stayed there until 1996, then left to join Hervé Schauer, who was one of the first to be a consultant in the Internet field, specialised in Unix, networks and security consultancy. Antivirus consultancy already existed at the time but was not deemed very serious. His firm provided professional security, and it came before all the other less acute consultancy firms. At the time Windows NT appeared, but Unix was seen as one of the big professional systems that were going to keep the market and Linux did not really exist yet (it was not much on the radar of commercial users/corporations, who still used classical Unix systems). There were tensions on who would win the market. I started working for Hervé, because I actually knew him through mutual friends and through Usenet. It was a small crowd. That is actually how he recruited many people, through these networks.

What was your role?

I was a consultant. I would go to clients and install the Internet and firewalls. It was interesting. I did not do much training because I was installing equipment for people who already knew about it all, and knew what they wanted but simply needed a bit of help in installing or updating their system.

Were your different activities linked or would you keep clear barriers between them?

The borders were definitely fluid. I would answer personal emails at work, and professional emails at home in the evening. It was always kind of the same crowd though, and because I decided to make my job out of my passion, I was never able to keep clear barriers.

You linked your passion to your profession, but did you encounter any opposition?

Well, it was difficult at the time because Internet was clearly coming from research and came through concentric circles: first you had the IT research sector, then research more generally, then the companies working with the researchers, then the IT companies in general, and we could see it all grow and knew it was going to reach the general public, but we did not know to which extent. We could definitely see an exponential evolution though. Commercial services were being created, in which we sometimes participated. But there was a fear at the time that this would change the nature of the initial network, which was based in universities and was highly collaborative. It was not easy to navigate through all that without, well, losing your soul [laughs].

When did Gandi come into play?

Well before Gandi there was EU.org that provided the contacts that eventually led to Gandi.

EU.org dates back to the time when it was really difficult to have a .fr address. Somewhere during the first half of the 1990s Christophe Wolfhugel reserved fr.net, which gave me my first address email: fasterix.frmug.fr.net (it later became .org). I chose fasterix because I originally wanted Asterix, but thought the rights holders would pester me and I added an –f to avoid any problems. Fr.net was reserved by Christophe Wolfhugel to counter the limits of the .fr. He would redistribute it freely to those who wanted it.

EU.org's goal was also to provide domains without being a university, etc. I launched it around 1995 when I found NSI (Network Solutions, Inc., later bought by Versign), the contractor handling the InterNIC, the US organ in charge of distributing IP addresses and domain names with the suffix .com, .org, .edu, .net, .mil, .gov (now operated by Verisign). In the case of .mil and .gov you had to be transparent and show clean hands, with .edu you had to demonstrate that you were an educational organisation, but .com, .org and .net were completely open and anyone could request them. At the time you had to fill in a small text form and send it via email, and then you would wait. It was free.

So what was the problem with .fr?

In order to obtain a .fr, one either had to be an FNET client at a time (initially, circa 1993), or to demonstrate that one had a residence in France. A company could provide a Kbis (company registration certificate). But a private person could not register a .fr. If you were an association I do not even know what you had to do and for universities you had to be affiliated to the ministry of education I guess. There were many rules like that for the .fr.

How did you do it with EU.org?

I found the DNS servers, which was not very simple at the time. The first was at FDN. I also had a friend that hosted the first machine for EU.org's server. That was really a "muddling through" strategy.

I had to wait three months for the answer from Internic: because it was free, there was a growing demand, and it was probably done by hand. I must have asked for my domain in the Spring of 1995, and got an answer in August 1995.

Why EU.org? Did you have a European vision?

Yes, but it was symbolic. Well, originally I had asked .eu, it was free but did not work out. What was funny was that anyone could write to Jon Postel and receive an answer from him.[23] Jon Postel very nicely told me that I could not have .eu because the possible domains were those within the ISO 3166 list – the official international list for country names – and since .eu was not there… apologies, but no. He told me eu.int was available and that I could ask for that. It was managed by Paul Mockapetris, so I went ahead and asked him for eu.int. He told me eu.int is reserved for organs created by international treaties, like NATO, and then asked if I had an international treaty. I answered "oh, no sorry" [laughs]. A few months later he got an official request from the European Union and very nicely asked me if I still wanted eu.int, because the European Union was asking for it. I replied a slightly embarrassed "no I'm good, go ahead, sorry" [laughs].

At the time that I had scanned the ISO 3166 list, I had seen .fx, which meant unassigned mainland France, so I had written again to Jon Postel to ask for .fx. He answered that .fr already existed, and that two first level domain names for a country was not very logical and a bit absurd, so I did not get .fx. I discovered at the time that NIC-France had also configured .fx on its servers, so I was not the first to ask for it. I think an initiative was starting simultaneously in the standardisation bodies to remove .fx from the ISO list.

I finally reserved eu.org and obtained it. At the time I did not know much about the web and worked on the project in my free time. During Spring of 1996 I had something that was rather ready. I had tried to make sure that eu.org worked as well with emails as with the Web, because there were discussions going on at the time concerning the Web. I was inspired by Internic's system, in which you would send an email with standard information such as the demander's name, the name servers, the names requested and automated answering emails. It allowed people who only had an email access to have their own domain name, knowing that they had to possess DNS servers though.

The idea for EU.org was to give anyone who asked a free domain name, but bearing in mind that they still needed a DNS server.

I started a beta in May 1996. The window to open the service was Spring of 1996 though, because obtaining an .fr became a paying service at that time, a few months before .com, .org and .net. I finished and announced it on Usenet in June 1996. A few people registered but the demand was not high due to the technical obstacle of having to possess a DNS server.

Three or four friends were helping with the validation part, because we did not want a completely automated system and wanted to check the names one by one. This was actually not the best of ideas because it was a lot of work…

Were you alone in trying to keep domain names free?

Meryem Marzouki said my initiative was political. Though I did not exactly understand what she meant, it was true in a certain way. I rather saw it as a way to rock the boat, and to help people acquire something that was difficult to obtain, but I did not see it in a grander political sense.

During the Grande Grève [the great general strike] in 1995, we were a few with Laurent [Chemla] to have installed UUCP accesses for Sud Poste.[24] As they were on strike, they had lost their communication means apart from the phone, which rather restricted them, that is why we had installed electronic communications for them.

You mention Laurent Chemla, who will become your associate with Gandi: how did you meet him?

In these groups of Geeks. More specifically in 1993, with the whole gang that had email addresses.

And through the "Estelle Halliday case",[25] Laurent Chemla and Valentin Lacambre met each other. Laurent was very much aware of all these issues concerning free speech. He was also aware of the fact that the legislation was not evolving in the right direction, and therefore of the need to lobby politics in order to avoid a regression in terms of freedom of speech. He had therefore gone and helped defend Valentin in the "Estelle Halliday" case.

Later, Valentin was made aware of the liberalisation of domain names at ICANN, which actually was not that known at the time. Laurent then told him that he knew a person called Pierre Beyssac who already has a bit of experience in that field. And they knew the fourth associate David Nahmias, who was not technical at all but did accounting and was a serial-entrepreneur.

Laurent asked me if I was interested in filing an application to obtain a license and I said yes. David was the one to make us move forward because all of us were engrossed in our own activities. David was the one in charge of all the administrative work. Before Gandi he did a lot of things, he made and sold aluminium ashtrays, sold ice cream and bookcases... or was it bookshops [laughs]?

David pushed us to do all the paperwork so that the project could take shape. We started writing the corporate purpose of the company as "attribution et gestion des noms de domaines internet" [attribution and management of internet domain names], and Laurent noticed that if you switched the first two words you created the word "gandi." We all thought "Bingo", and created the name from that acronym.

The idea was to break the domain name prices and to popularise them in a way that would prevent us from losing our shirts in the affair. We wanted to create an association but it was not possible in the contracts with ICANN; you had to have a company. So, we created a SARL[26], and we looked into how we could manage it like an association, meaning on a voluntary basis. We concluded that the company needed 5000 euros a month, after margins, to run, to cover costs and possibly a person in charge of the secretariat. That number meant selling about 1000 domain names a month.

Were others trying to do the same as you?

Yes there were some. Worldnet had tried to launch attractive prices but they never did much marketing for it... Perhaps because we started before them and they let go of the idea...

At the time .com, .org and .net cost 45$ a year I think and we were positioned at 12€ (excluding taxes) so we strongly broke down prices. May 1996 was when the company was supposed to be created. We filed the application for ICANN, knowing that neither of us knew how to do word processing, so Valentin had printed the forms in A4 and we filled them out by hand. I do not remember if we sent them directly or if we scanned them before, because some parcels were lost and we had to resend the papers twice. Otherwise we were ready; we had developed the software.

We were really complementary: Valentin had the means to host due to Altern, Laurent knew the Web, HTML and SQL (the language used for databases). The latter was the type of language we did not really work on as students because it was management programming. We thought "I will never have to do SQL in my life anyway, it is not worth it"... But later we did in fact need it. So, Laurent knew SQL. Finally, David did all the accounting, and incidentally also prevented the company from going bankrupt by checking the expenses. I was doing the DNS, management of the email, http connection and the connection with the registry Verisign. Our skills were pretty complementary.

I also put up the first methods of payment, which was a whole... Well... Banks you know. A few months after we started, the regional director of the bank told us he wanted to set up a meeting with us. We thought that maybe he wanted to congratulate us for being such good clients because we already had a big volume by then. In fact, he thought we were too good and reprimanded us for making too many transactions at his bank. He was therefore taking enormous risks by accepting to be the credit card gateway and thought of a scenario in which all transactions were refused, which was possible but would have meant all payments were fraudulent. He was afraid, so he asked us to place money in his bank to reassure him. He looked down on us. Valentin had sat down on the ground because he thought it would destabilise the banker [laughs], and actually it was true, it worked pretty well!

I would always have to take a day off when we had meetings like these. We also had other problems with the banks because we had created the company with our own funds and had no investors. We did not put down the minimum required, which was 1€, we put down 7500€ (50,000 F. at the time). However, you needed a bank guarantee of 100,000$ for the Americans. We ended up having to take up personal loans for consumption, like buying a car, because no bank would agree to lend to a company that was starting from nothing. At the time the BPI did not exist yet, it was the BDPME [development bank for SMEs], and the bankers did not want to file up an account because according to them "internet is interesting" but it gave them extra work, so we had to figure it out on our own.

You were really motivated. Did you also think it could potentially work out, and that you would become profitable?

Well, at least personally I thought we could hardly lose money on that one. We were not taking huge risks. We thought it would work out reasonably, but we did not anticipate for it to work that well. That shocked us.

In December of 1999 we were ready. You had to pass a technical validation test with the Americans, which I had done on a Friday evening towards midnight. They asked me "what time is it in Paris?" to which I answered "Well, half past midnight, why?", so even they kind of thought we were crazy [laughs]. The guys from NSI told me to start the validation procedure, but at that point we had not yet given the bank guarantee in order to have the actual access to the production system, neither did we have our system of bank payments. David looked around for business insurances, but they did not understand a thing about what we were doing. Towards mid-February of 2000 we had all the papers sorted. Coincidently at the time building a start-up was not the best idea because a lot of money was evaporating very quickly; that is when the so-called "dotcom crash" started. The bank payments were thus missing and we opened on the sly in 2000, before having finalised them. The very first clients paid by check, given in hand or sent via mail.

How did you spread the word?

We had a mailing list actually, because Valentin must have written about it on the Altern list. We told people to sign up to our mailing list, as we were receiving many queries regarding when we would open, for which we could not give an answer, we therefore told them we would notify them when it was ready. We had between 100 to 500 people waiting for our email. I am not even sure we announced it on Usenet because we did not want to do marketing or spam. We never advertised for it.

Was it possible to buy a .fr then?

No, it was still under the same constraints as before. Individuals could not reserve it, though I believe you could create something with firstname.last.name.fr.

And .com?

Of course. Gandi opened on .com, .org, .net – the domains at ICANN – and later there were no restrictions; individuals could buy them.

.com was the most popular straight away. We had checked the market for domain names at the time in .com, .org, .net and there were around 20–30 million. We did not think any new domain names would be created, knowing there was already a steep growth at the time. But there were about 100 registrars opening at the same time and we were not any worse than the others, so we believed we could equally get 1% of the market. We then calculated how many domains and how much revenue to cover costs that added up to. In these cases we were not creating names but transferring them to Gandi, but that was more difficult to put in place and we were not ready for it when we opened. I set it up during the Easter holidays in 2000 and it opened in May–June of that year. Name creations exploded during that time.

Who were the competitors in France at the time?

There were not many. We were sellers of domain names as such, as we did not want to be dependent on a host, or step on Altern's foot of course. We did not want to be pestered by hosts' problems concerning data volumes, rights and such. We therefore positioned ourselves as sellers of domain names and were alone on that. Otherwise there were plenty of big hosts at the time that were linking domain names to whole hosting packages, but then the domain name itself would be drowned. Otherwise Oléane and France Telecom were selling domains for their pro accounts, but these would pay around 1000–2000 euros a month for a liaison, meaning around 400 a year for the domain names. Prices were very high.

What type of clients were you attracting in the beginning? Individuals? Companies?

Clients were mostly geeks, enlightened amateurs buying up for their friends and family, and a few players that were acquiring names for others and dealing with their paperwork. One person for example was reserving names for administrations that were not capable of paying by check; he would deal with the whole administrative aspect with the client and would buy the domain name from us. It was great for us because we could deal with checks but wanted the least amount of administrative work as possible.

And the company grew rapidly.

Yes, I remember on the opening day of bank payments we were selling 100 domain names a day, meaning we were already earning above what we needed to be viable, as we needed 5000 euros a month, and we had a margin of 6 euros per domain name.

At the time, the distribution was based on a first come-first serve basis, right?

Yes, and there were many abusive reservations, of singers' names for instance. Since it was our policy we would give it to them, and I do not believe we had a choice in our contract with ICANN anyway. What we were not allowed to do was speculate; the registrar was not allowed to reserve names of trademarks and then resell them for an inflated price.

Someone reserved johnnyhalliday.com without any issue once. However, there were cases that needed the involvement of lawyers, because some geniuses were reserving domains of singers' names with .com for 12 euros and would then try to sell it back to them for 1000 euros.

So there were some issues ...

Yes of course, as with any registrars. One time a big group from the CAC40 was in a social conflict with its workers and the opposing party had set up a website with the company's name in the domain name. The CEO was very unhappy and called us. I believe he got Valentin on the phone – I never witnessed it directly, I only know it through Valentin. The CEO had said something in the realm of "Listen, I am in the CAC40, I can put you on your knees with lawyers, so let go of the domain name." Valentin had answered by thanking him, but explaining that we were autonomous, that nothing could be done to us and that we would defend our clients' rights. I am not sure if it went up to the courts or not... It may have actually, and we won. We also wanted to set out a jurisprudence on the fact that the registrar was a technical intermediary, so litigations should be dealt with between the person in possession of the name and the person who believes they are aggrieved.

Once Gandi was created, it grew very rapidly and was a success, right?

Yes, it started growing very rapidly during February 2000. Then Laurent's article "Je suis un voleur" [I'm a thief] appeared in the newspaper Le Monde on 29 April 2000, and preceded the book. He was arguing that he was not doing much; all he did was put a name in a database and sell it for a lot of money though the amount of work put in was minimal.

But was that not downgrading what you were doing?

Yes and no, I am not sure of what to say. It is true that from the point of view of a geek these were simple things – it was also the idea of EU.org. With a PC in the middle of nowhere you could deliver domain names. At the time some were claiming that domain names were a big investment and that you therefore needed a heavy infrastructure, but that was completely false. We wanted people to know that someone was looking after the whole thing.

Le Monde contacted you first?

Well, Laurent had more or less direct contacts with Le Monde through friends that we notably met through the AUI.[27] It was published on the first page of Le Monde, and he explained that he almost felt bad to be so successful though we were not doing anything extraordinary.

It must have indirectly made Gandi even more famous.

Yes, the sales went up to around 500 names a day and were essentially new names, not transfers as we had anticipated. It got to a point when during the summer of 2000 we had to get offices. Up until then the head office was at Valentin's house. Once we ended up with this office, we hired someone to do the paperwork and the accounting, and someone to do the everyday technical maintenance, as well as helping out with customer service, given the sheer volume. In September 2000 I think we had sold 100,000 domains, and it continued to grow after. There was a difficult time in 2002–2003; given the unanticipated success we were not on the same page regarding the vision for the company's future. The situation pacified itself after, because we hired a new director that created a consensus between us all and gave the company a more classical structure.

In parallel, were you still working somewhere else?

Yes, I was in charge of network systems at Telecom Paris-Tech. In 2009 I left for new adventures, I founded Eriomem [an anagram for memory in French], which does cloud storage.

What were your memories from that time? Was it exciting, or did things just happen?

Oh it was rather exciting! There was a visibility that we had not anticipated and an unforeseen impact. We were happy of the success of course, and it was overall positive, notwithstanding the few grey hair it gave us.

And EU.org still exists?

Yes it does. I am figuring out how to distribute the source code so that it becomes open source. Some Austrians are interested in it. I am continuing the agitation.

A new political act?
Yes, exactly [laughs].

Notes

1. Pro-am is a contraction of professional–amateur.
2. This interview is an edited transcription of an interview that was conducted on 20 July 2017, within the FrenchWeb90 project, which was supported by the French National Research Agency. http://web90.hypotheses.org/3840
3. Interviewers are Camille Paloque-Berges, Valérie Schafer and Victoria Peuvrelle.
4. École Nationale Supérieure des Mines de Paris, now known as Mines ParisTech.
5. Clermont-Ferrand is a French city in the Auvergne-Rhône-Alpes region.
6. FNAC is a French retail chain, which is selling cultural and electronic products. In the 1990s it was known for letting users read or test some of its products on the spot.
7. A French Videotex online service launched at the beginning of the 1980s.
8. In the suburb of Paris.
9. CIRCE (Centre Inter-Régional de Calcul Électronique) used to serve as a computing center for many research labs and education structures all over France.

10. The "École Supérieure d'Electricité" is one of France's prestigious Grandes Écoles dedicated to electric energy and information sciences.
11. VMS (Virtual Memory System) is the native operating system of VAX, a DEC machine. Ultrix is DEC's version of UNIX.
12. UNIX-to-UNIX Control Protocol.
13. FNET is the first French provider for UUCP and then Internet (TCP-IP) networks – operating since 1983 by academia-based volunteers in relation with the European organization EUnet. After 1992 it was formalized as a for-profit association. It was then incorporated and bought by a telecom company, Qwest.
14. UUNET is the first international commercial provider for UUCP networks.
15. A city in western France.
16. RENATER (Réseau National deTélécommunications pour la Technologie, l'Enseignement et la Recherche) is both a public interest group and a network born in 1993 for providing networks to the French Research and Education milieu.
17. These three ISPs started their activity quite early in France.
18. A pioneering French ISP funded by Jean-Michel Planche that provided access to private companies.
19. The French Network Information Centre.
20. The ancestor of Afnic.
21. A famous daily newspaper.
22. France-Teaser created the first Minitel servers that allowed connections with Internet.
23. Jon Postel, early contributor of the Internet's RFC standardization documents and TCP-IP protocol, co-founder of the Internet society and administrator of IANA, was a prominent figure, if not a "star" of the Internet pioneer sphere.
24. A famous French trade union, leaning on the far left.
25. On this affair, see the paper by F. Tréguer and P. Petin in this issue. The top model Estelle Halliday filed a complaint against AlternB, the hosting company held by Valentin Lacambre, after a Web user had put naked pictures of her online (these pictures had already been published in a printed magazine and they were then reused by an other people magazine). See http://altern.org/alternb/defense/faq.html
26. Société à responsabilité limitée. This means a "company with limited liability."
27. Association des utilisateurs d'Internet [Association of Internet users].

Acknowledgment

We would like to warmly thank Pierre Beyssac for his testimony.

Disclosure statement

No potential conflict of interest was reported by the authors.

Funding

Agence Nationale de la Recherche [grant number ANR-14-CE29-0012-01].

Interfacing counterculture and digital cultures: an interview with Geert Lovink

Valérie Schafer

ABSTRACT
The famous Dutch media theorist and net activist Geert Lovink stood at the crossroads of several players and stages of cyberculture in the 90s, trying to assemble a disparate crowd of media activists and media artists, programmers, designers, cultural producers and researchers. In this interview he looks back at his involvement in *Mediamatic* magazine from 1989 till 1994, the co-creation of the community access network De Digitale Stad Amsterdam,which started in 1994 as a freenet initiative in Amsterdam and the nettime email list in 1995. He also discusses the spirit of the 90s decade and the role of counter-cultural movements in the genesis and development of digital cultures.

During his entire life Dutch media theorist and net activist, Geert Lovink has been thinking about, and struggling with, the issue of institutionalisation of social movements and independent media. He would probably dislike the fact that he is now described as an "established figure" of media theory and net criticism ... or maybe not, as he made this decision by himself, to act as a bridge between European theories – especially German theory – and others. And he has certainly achieved this.

Geert Lovink stands at the crossroads of several players and stages of 1990s cyberculture, trying to assemble a disparate crowd of media activists and media artists, programmers, designers, cultural producers, and researchers. He is what we might term a "cultural smuggler" or "cultural mediator", who played, and continues to play, an important role in the development of digital culture.

At the time of this interview (13 April 2018),[1] the founding director of the Institute of Network Cultures and the author of numerous books such as *Dark Fiber: Tracking Critical Internet Culture* (2002), *Uncanny Networks* (2002), *My First Recession* (2003), *Zero Comments: Blogging and Critical Internet Culture* (2007), *Networks Without a Cause: A Critique of Social Media* (2012) and *Social Media Abyss, Critical Internet Cultures and the Force of Negation* (2016)[2] was leading a new initiative with the #deletefacebook movement,[3] but he still found time to share his past experiences with counter-cultural movements and digital cultures, looking back at his childhood, the events of 1968 – whose 50th anniversary we are marking this year – his involvement in *Mediamatic* magazine from 1989 till 1994, the co-creation of the community access network De Digitale Stad Amsterdam (DDS), which started in 1994 as a freenet initiative in Amsterdam[4] and the nettime email list in 1995.[5]

Valérie Schafer: First of all, could you tell me when you discovered computers and computer-mediated communications?

Geert Lovink: My first encounter with the world of computers was at the end of my primary school, in the late 1960s. This was a rather intense time for the Magic Centre of Amsterdam and the hippie movement, a rather turbulent time. I got influenced by the promises of computers from the hippie perspective, how people can communicate, influenced by the psychedelic movement, which of course one can read back in Fred Turner's book.[6] This context is closely tied to the questions of how software should look like and how the user should be positioned in there. This topic is something I was really intimately familiar with when I grew up.

VS: Did your parents work in this field?

GL: No, I grew up near the Vondelpark in Amsterdam, behind the Concertgebouw. Almost next door to my primary school was the Hilton hotel where John Lennon and Yoko Ono stayed when the hippies took over the park where I played, in 1969. Of course, I'm not from the '68 generation, I'm younger, from the punk generation, I entered the scene in 1977. But as a child I was very influenced by the counterculture that happened in front of where I grew up. My first direct encounter with computers was somewhat odd. I was 12, 13 years old. With a friend of mine I decided to become a member of a rowing club in Amsterdam. We started rowing on the river Amstel and while we were doing these explorations from the water we came across a strange metal junk yard where the first generation of mainframe computers were dumped and recycled. We could access the yard via the water. We often went there to have a look at these machines. At that time, my friend and I were interested in DIY electronics, in particular transistors. We then traded the large circuit boards we took from there with our friends.

A couple of years later, when I studied political science in Amsterdam at the university, of course I encountered these mainframes again. That was in 1978–1979. We had to learn SPSS and data processing. This was done in the tradition of the Baschwitz institute, which studied public opinion. Kurt Baschwitz is one of the founders of mass communication and he was introducing computers in social sciences. We had to do questionnaires and then process the results using these mainframes.

Around 1983–1984, the personal computer became affordable and available, with the introduction of the IBM PC combined with MS-DOS, the Microsoft operating system. We started to use it. We were running a weekly magazine for the squatter's movement in Amsterdam and very early on we used the computer to do text processing. Friends of mine also started to use the computer to build databases in the early 1980s, to trace neo-Fascist groups and map housing speculators. These were early database and mapping exercises. The use of computers and databases in social movements goes back a really long time. Activists gathered names, dates and observations. There are archives that try to conserve the autonomous social movement heritage and I'm also playing a role in this preservation effort at the International Institute of Social History (IISG),[7] which is in Amsterdam. IISG has extended its archives, which focused on Marx, Bakunin, early trade unions and the Spanish civil war to contemporary movements such as feminism and ecology.

When the squatter's episode of my generation came to a close, in 1987, with the help of my father, I purchased my first personal computer.

VS: Did you feel early on that there was a need to archive this history?

GL: My studies started with a visit to the Institute of Social History. The first paper I wrote, I was 19 years old, was on the history of the provo movement[8] which I had witnessed as a child. Back then I was too young and I couldn't really understand much of it. I went back to the archives, to study that movement 10 or so years later – a movement that had had a big impact on Amsterdam and was foundational to the squatter's movement. Archival work has always been an important task for social movements to pass on collective experiences, images, concepts and debates.

VS: Would you say that your investment in digital cultures and social movements is a continuity of this starting period?

GL: For sure. We're aware of similar struggles before WWII. But we also knew, in particular in the city of Amsterdam that was so severely hit by the Holocaust, that the rupture of WWII and the following decades of conservative reconstruction created a gap in the collective memory. We met few people in our field, only one or two, that were able to bring the memory of the pre-war back. It was a bit more common with the 1960s movement. Memory and its transition from one generation to the next, a strong theme in the work of Bernard Stiegler that I admire, were at the forefront when I grew up.

VS: You bought your own computer in 1987.

GL: It was a big investment: a PC, a huge and heavy monitor and a matrix printer. Before that, there were some collective machines in activist work spaces that we shared, but usually people didn't have a personal computer. We had electronic IBM typewriters. And even some of those machines had small chips and electronic memory: you could formulate a sentence and then print it out. They had very simple text editing capacities. But it was very obvious around that time that the arrival of the computer on our personal desks was going to be a big thing, and it was! We immediately understood that these machines would do nothing if not connected. From the very beginning, already in 1987, it was clear that the computer was not a stand-alone device. This was this big difference between the computer and the typewriter. The computer was from the very beginning conceived as a part of a wider information ecology. But it took a little bit of time.

During this period, it was about connection to Bulletin Boards. My first encounter with Internet itself was during an event in which I got involved as a free radio maker, the famous Galactic Hacker Party in Paradiso in August 1989,[9] just before the fall of the Berlin Wall. There I saw a variety of computer networks such as CompuServe, BBS and the possibilities that the different architectures offered. And Internet at that time was just one of the four or five possible models.

Soon after the same scene around Caroline Nevejan organized the Seropositive Ball,[10] which was a continuation of the Galactic Hacker Party that focused on the gay community which was facing the massive HIV-AIDS crisis at the time. The cultural event was a way to assist the gay movement in establishing global real-time computer networks. Direct relations were important, a network in which one-on-one, but also trans-continental one-to-many and many-to-many communications were made possible.

VS: From your point of view, were networked computers a tool to organize in order to give a voice to their users?

GL: Our theory collective ADILKNO[11] has written a book about this precise question during the period, because this was the main question we struggled with in 1989. The book is entitled *Squatting beyond the media.*[12] It was first published in Dutch and then translated into German and English. *Bewegingsleer* directly addressed the question of how the social movements related to media questions. Is it nearly mediation? Is it only communication? What's the relation between the Event and its image? Are media becoming an intimate part of the way social movements organize themselves? Already at that time we knew that media were becoming a vast separate realm that was taking over every aspect of our daily life, including the political and social struggles.

VS: Did your interest on media theory and net theory start with these movements?

GL: Like many of my generation I started publishing in the student magazine of the high school I attended. The first magazine I founded was the neighborhood bi-weekly of the squatters that lived in the historical canal area (we lived in a baroque house from 1730), called *De Grachtenkrant.* Soon after I was part of a large group that founded *bluf!,* the squatters weekly. During my political sciences study we published several books, two of them on the strategy of the Dutch anti-nuclear movement. Later on, in 1987, we started our own publishing house, related to the movement, called Ravijn. I would still classify my activities along these lines: the self-organization of social movements through (new) media.

Squatting beyond the media was the first book I co-wrote on a computer. In 1987 was an important moment of transition for me personally. Before, I was more an activist. I was in my late twenties, unemployed, I had no idea how I was going to make a living. In that year, I decided to become a media theorist, but I had no idea what this implied. I had definitively burnt all bridges with the university. There was no way I was going back. Hitchhiking between Amsterdam and West-Berlin at the time, I strongly felt I had to make a decision about my life. I could have decided to become a journalist or a cultural producer, but I decided to become a media theorist, in the German tradition.

VS: What did that mean? It wasn't turned to new media.

GL: I was influenced by Klaus Theweleit and Friedrich Kittler, two theorists whose ideas and straight-forward personal writing style really spoke to me. At that time, their topic and angle had a lot to do with processing the Fascist past, the traumatic past of Europe in the period of Fascism and WWII. I was also influenced by Jean Baudrillard, Paul Virilio and Elias Canetti. I was raised at the university as a mass psychologist, this was the period before there was "mass communication". There were a lot of elements that led me into this direction, but what does it mean to be a media theorist … I was completely baffled by this question myself: what are you going to do? You wake up and nobody is going to tell you what to do during the day …

Another encounter with new media happened through video art. There were a lot of initiatives in Amsterdam such as Montevideo and Time-based Arts, it was an open-minded artistic community. Mix this with my squatting background and the junk aesthetics of industrial music that surrounded me, and there you go … In early 1989, I became a member of the editorial board of *Mediamatic* magazine.[13] This was completely new to me as I had a background of political science, maybe philosophy and social movements. The encounter with contemporary art and video art opened up a whole new area for me. It was something that defined all the work I did during the 90 s. That encounter between politics and aesthetics is something I have been doing since then.

VS: The *Mediamatic* magazine was based in …

GL: In Amsterdam. Its design looked very cool. Next to me is the 'Zero One' edition. The topic was hearing and radio. In 1987, when I encountered my existential crisis, I also made the decision that I was going to do radio, which I did from 1987 to 2000. Every week I produced my own theory radio show and next to it developed my own radio theory. Here is the famous *Mediamatic* edition about Otaku. A special feature was that it was bilingual. For the first time my writings were becoming available in English. I developed a bit more of a sensitivity for the English language. Before that, I was totally focused on German which still is my theory and thinking language. Needless to say, that English opened up another field of communication and possibilities for me.

VS: I would like to link this last point with a previous one, as you mentioned BBSs. Were they international or more local BBSs?

GL: You started with local and then you started to connect with others and switched to English. We had close contact with the Chaos computer club in Germany too. In 1990, I had my first modem and started to actively get involved in them. And when I went to Japan in 1990, I also got my first laptop. This first Toshiba laptop was recently exhibited in Leipzig, and I wrote a short piece about it.[14]

VS: Are you interested in media archaeology?

GL: For sure, I always had an interest in it. It's my starting point. The first thing I did in *Mediamatic* was to introduce German media theory of the Kittler circle for an Anglo-Saxon audience. And I'm still doing this today. Maybe this is a Dutch thing? I see building this interface between the specific world of German thinking and the world outside as one of my tasks. Recently I have made the decision that once a year I will write one substantial piece about history. I recently wrote about the exchange in 1984–1985 between the Amsterdam and the Berlin squatter movements in terms of ontology of social movements. One fundamental question raised by Baudrillard was about appearance but also disappearance, and the possibility people have to stage, to perform their own disappearance. Not only to stage their appearance but their disappearance too. Can we leave the stage together or is fragmentation and despair our destiny? To collectively decide it, in the Japanese suicide way, to collectively decide not only your beginning but your end, which is a powerful act. Otherwise other people are doing it for you or you disintegrate and you go through a very painful process. The whole idea of enacting a collective disappearance was a very important element in the first development of social movements.

VS: Did you achieve this collective disappearance in movements like Nettime?

GL: In some cases, the answer is yes, in others, no. If you manage to take control, you can do things like that. But certain structures are very interesting from an institutional perspective. Nettime this was really the case. It was totally non-institutional, but it became an institution of sorts. In a few years into it, we faced a crisis of institutionalization. Today, we also face a crisis of institutionalization for counter-cultural movements because events happen so fast that it is difficult for social and artistic movements, and even for tech movements to establish themselves. Today the issue is no longer about appropriation, the main issue today is that the movement has gone before people realize that they were in fact in a movement. The question of appearance and disappearance is back on the agenda but in a different manner. People are not able to continue the social dynamic because things change too fast. In terms of organization, this is a serious problem because you have to start every time all over again.

VS: You were also involved in the Eastern European events. In 1993, you were one of the co-founders of the Press Now support campaign for independent media in South-East Europe during the war in former Yugoslavia.

GL: This was probably the most politically important event that happened in Europe after the fall of the Berlin Wall. I was 30 years old at the time it happened and was actually in Berlin when the wall fell. I had already an interest in Eastern Europe before that. I knew people. We were in contact with young opposition movements in Hungary, but also in Czechoslovakia, and in East Berlin. For instance, I married a lesbian poet from the scene in 1985 to get her out of the country. This was a big hack, also for myself. It took a year to get her out. Of course, for us, it was really difficult to accept that after the fall of the Iron Curtain, which we had supported, in late 1991, nationalist tensions and civil wars started to emerge. In particular, the disintegration of Yugoslavia, which still is the biggest war of your lifetime and my lifetime in Europe. When this tragedy started, we immediately contacted artists and media activists there that were supporting the antiwar efforts. I was in particular part of the antiwar movement in Zagreb (ARKZIN[15]) and the radio station B92 in Belgrade. We put pressure on the Ministry of Foreign Affairs in The Hague to protect journalists and support independent media. We were acting as a political lobby, like an NGO campaign, out of De Balie.

In 1992, I also decided I could not continue to be unemployed and I quit this minimum existence of living to become a freelancer. I started to teach a little bit, primarily in Eastern Europe. My first teaching in media art and theory was in Bucharest, in Romania, at the art academy. I started to become a little more known, mainly through my writings in English in *Mediamatic* magazine, and most of all in the German-speaking countries, where I published three books, so I was able to get more money, writing pieces, giving lectures.

VS: This activism was through press, radio, new media?

GL: We tried to connect media activists and media artists. I was still a member of *Mediamatic* Magazine. I quit in 1994 after we had a disagreement over the commercial direction of the magazine. At that time, the economic situation started to change when the whole Internet thing was taking off. I had my first modem in 1991 and was part of the *Hack-Tic* scene. I was with Patrice [Riemens] and Caroline [Nevejan] and other main organizers of the hacker party. Early 1993 I had my first Internet account through Hacktic, which was later renamed into XS4ALL.[16] We had Internet access earlier here and there but it was difficult as it was under the monopoly of academic networks that had to be hacked. XS4ALL was rapidly spreading. It all started with the first Next 5 Minutes convention in Paradiso. We brought together the so-called tactical television people who were producing video art and documentaries, and combined that with computer networks and radio, to discuss the media activist strategies. It was all broadcasted live on the Amsterdam cable network. The term tactical media came later.

VS: And the World Wide Web? The Mosaic browser appeared in 1993.

GL: I remember the first time I saw it clearly, it was in the *Mediamatic* office. There, in spring 1994, I saw the first Web page. We used Internet but we didn't have a graphic user interface, we didn't have color monitors at home in the first place. It took a while. Before the WWW we used Telnet to do email, Gopher and IRC. The Internet had already a lot of functionalities but remained green on black, text only.

VS: This field was moving fast. Were there people with technical skills?

GL: Yes, that helped everybody else. I had followed the computer scene since 1983–1984. So, we knew all the players. The problem of access was the most urgent one for a long time. That was our main domain: access for all, we want bandwidth.

VS: It was not just about price but how to get access?

GL: Yes. In 1994, we put everything in place in terms of new institutional initiatives. It started late 1993, when we were preparing the De Digitale Stad, which launched in January 1994. It was text only. There was no World Wide Web version yet, this came in mid-1994. That's what we call the second generation of DDS. It was also the time the ISPs were growing rapidly. DDS moved in the same building as Mediamatic and XS4ALL. By the mid-90s this building consisted of three main players. The computers were there, the band too.

In spring 1994, I also started an Internet art space together with a big group of artists. It was called desk.nl. We rented permanent Internet access together, an ISDN line. In this way we could be online all the time, without dialing in through the phone from our home, sitting there, isolated. In this way we could be online 24/7, think of it as the precursor of the today's co-working spaces. I started desk.nl with the main organizer Walter van der Cruijsen. He found a big room above the experimental jazz club Bimhuis on the Oude Schans. Downstairs there were concerts. In the back room was the editing room of the famous documentary film-maker Johan van der Keuken. The place was low-key but a productive environment packed with interesting characters, it's not really well-known today, but it played an important facilitating role in establishing the Amsterdam tactical media/net art scene. In November 1993, Marleen Stikker (De Balie) and Caroline Nevejan (Paradiso) came together to create a new institution for digital culture, De Waag: Centre for Old and New Media. I was working together with both of them at that time (and still are, in a way). Waag linked two cultures Amsterdam is known for: the centre for debates on culture and politics De Balie and the music temple Paradiso. They were next to each other and they started to collaborate, first through the Galactic Hacker Party, the Seropositive Ball, Next 5 Minutes,[17] and then the next step was to create this new centre, De Waag Society. They found the oldest building in town on the Nieuwmarkt square, from which the Jewish museum had just moved out. It was empty and somehow the city agreed that Waag Society, as it called now, could move in.

VS: Could you tell me a bit more about DDS? It was a big community network, open to the general public?

GL: Yes, and this was a big discussion we had in the past. There were two directions in Internet activism: the "access for us" faction around APC and the universities and us, who demanded "access for all". The Association for Progressive Communication for instance was always for the "access for us". They wanted to give access to NGOs, not especially to the general public. We said: OK, but what about the artists? We refused to make that distinction, that distinction between important political activists and all the others. We didn't want access for some, but access for all. We thought from the beginning in a multidisciplinary way. We thought that the movement could only grow and exist if it had a diversity of skills, agendas and backgrounds.

VS: DDS probably became very popular and less manageable?

GL: Yes, by the end of the 1990s, in the violence of the dotcom mania, it was totally overrun by contradictory expectations and business plans. The late 1990s in Amsterdam was a mad house. There was so much money, so many people were coming to Amsterdam, setting up companies (similar to 2017/2018). Should DDS start to work with venture capital? What was the role of community in all this? Against the commercial violence, the DDS as a 'commons' infrastructure had no chance. As always, our local public access network became way too early.

VS: Did politicians get involved in DDS?

GL: The city funded the experiment at first. Local politicians were not so much present on the Internet but on the local cable channels. Don't forget that the Netherlands in the late 1990s were overrun by neo-liberal privatization. The idea that the city council should do something with Internet access remained an alien idea. The symbol for this absent policy became the sellout of the public access cable network to the American cable company UPC. In the late 90s, we felt that we had lost a valuable public infrastructure that was held by the city of Amsterdam. This privatization was probably more significant than DDS having a future, yes or no.

VS: Related to this changing context, let's talk about the Tulipomania Dotcom conference you organized in 2000.

GL: It was an event happening in Amsterdam (De Balie) and in Frankfurt (Kunstverein), which is one of the main financial centres in Europe. The beginning of the Dotcom Tulipomania conference goes back to the crucial turning point in 1997 when we started to understand the political economy of the Internet. In the early-mid 1990s we had no idea about the coming economic players and their agendas. It was probably after the IPO of Netscape that we started to realize that the game had changed. This was the first Internet company that went in the American stock exchange and it completely surprised us. We were still coming from the idea of public access building out the Internet as a public infrastructure, in line with the university tradition of the Internet as a neutral facility for staff and students. The fact that we were living in a neo-liberal age where everything was going to be privatized, this was really something … maybe we were not surprised, but certainly we were not prepared for the violence, the magnitude of that change in the telecom market. After 1997, the nettime scene looked back at our naive days, the utopian days of the first Internet years, when we discussed so passionately about concepts and possibilities. Already in 1997 we were acutely aware of this loss of innocence.

VS: The year before, John P. Barlow had announced the "Declaration of Independence of Cyberspace".

GL: Barlow came to the second Next 5 Minutes, in January 1996 to discuss this with us. We had set up Nettime in 1995 to facilitate these debates between West and East Europe and the United States. Around that time Pit Schultz and I were building the network and the expertise of the artistic computer network that built on the earlier art network, coordinated out of New York called thing.net. Nettime would not have existed without thing.net. Born in German-speaking countries thing.net was a network of BBS nodes that ran more or less parallel to the Internet. At some point, it got an email gateway. It had no Web interface and ran on separate BBS software. Nettime was a similar discussion forum, especially in the beginning, related to thing.net. Late 1995 we started to interface with a lot of cultural organizations and events that happened. Nettime organized its own meetings and public debated and until 2000 we were part of the European festival circuit. We grew further during our 3-month presence from June to September 1997 at Documenta X in Kassel under Catherine David's supervision, who invited us to do the Hybrid Workspace project in the Orangerie. Just before that we organized the only nettime gathering in Ljubljana, Slovenia. There was so much to discuss, to plan and coordinate. Hybrid Workspace was a network of networks, where cyberfeminists had their own week to come together, the Syndicate networks from Eastern Europe had their time slot, and so on. No One is Illegal was founded there as well. It went on for 3 months. After this turbulent period, we documented all this in the Readme book, edited by nettime and published by Autonomedia in New York.

VS: Who was the nettime audience?

GL: Nettime still exists. It's a classic tactical media mix: artists, activists, programmers, designers, cultural producers and researchers.

VS: How many people participated?

GL: In the first 4 years, nettime had grown. We knew there was going to be a change in the dynamics of the community when you go over 500 members. New people start to show up and the informality slowly disappears. We reached that moment in 1998. It led to a big crisis of governance. There were trolls, there were people we didn't know, people who used it as a stage for their artistic interventions, for their academic work, etc. We struggled with that. Groups started their own lists and debates. And then the Kosovo war happened. I quit soon after. Late 1999 I moved to Australia.

VS: Why did you leave nettime?

GL: We could not find an agreement about the essence of the network. Pit and I had always emphasized the importance of meetings, gatherings, coalitions, notably with the festivals that would debates. But when nettime started growing and became more and more international, this mode of operating became no longer possible. Of course, we encouraged growth, we had the Dutch Nettime, the French Nettime, a Latin-American Nettime, Nettime in Chinese. It was the time of a rapid expansion of the Net itself. We quit, but the community continued. Nettime is now 23 three years old and still going strong with 7000 or more members.

VS: We arrived in late 1990s. You moved to Australia. We won't enter the next decade. Let's close this interview and discuss the spirit of the 1990s decade.

GL: What's so special about this episode was the way in which the utopian, psychedelic elements of cyberculture were combined with a fresh continental post-Cold War European culture of negativity and relativism. We saw it was a turbulent time of change in which French theory played an important role, there were a lot of ideas, about alternative 'interface cultures', people were looking for their own values and things to achieve. This combination defines our 'techno' 90 s. There is certainly a psychedelic element in it. Techno parties, raves, ecstasy … these were important elements in the story. After all, nettime was born in former East-Berlin, in the heart of the techno club scene … This is where we come from. It is important to understand that we aimed for a one-off mix of utopia and the critique, which, of course, is diametrically opposed to the American imagination of happiness, PR and marketing. Even today you can't be utopian and critical at the same time. Either you're a loser, an outsider and a critic, or you sign up for the party and become a YouTube influencer, marketeer or app developer. You can't be both … but that's what we did!

Notes

1. I would like to sincerely thank Gerben Zaagsma and Sarah Cooper (University of Luxembourg) for their help during this transcription and of course Geert Lovink for this generous interview.
2. For a more complete biography: http://networkcultures.org/geert/biography/.
3. Facebook Liberation Army Link List (12 April 2018). Compiled and edited by Geert Lovink & Patricia de Vries (Institute of Network Cultures), *Wired*. https://www.wired.com/beyond-the-beyond/2018/04/facebook-liberation-army-link-list-april-12-2018/
4. See https://waag.org/en/project/digital-city-dds
5. See http://www.nettime.org
6. Turner F. (2006), *From Counterculture to Cyberculture. Stewart Brand, the whole earth network, and the rise of digital utopianism*, Chicago, The University of Chicago Press.
7. https://socialhistory.org
8. A Dutch countercultural movement founded in May 1965 and followed by the hippie movement.
9. https://hart.amsterdam/nl/page/33469/1989-the-galactic-hacker-party. The Galactic Hacker Party was the first public international hacker convention in Europe.
10. To learn more about these events and the history of DDS see Nevejan, C. and Badenoch, A. (2014), How Amsterdam invented the internet: European networks of significance, 1980–1999. In Alberts, G. & Oldenziel, R. (Eds.), *Hacking Europe: From Computer Cultures to Demoscenes*. London: Springer, pp. 179–205.
11. The Foundation for the Advancement of Illegal Knowledge was established in Amsterdam in 1983. See http://thing.desk.nl/bilwet/adilkno/TheMediaArchive/.
12. Adilkno (1994), *Cracking the Movement: Squatting beyond the media*, Automedia. http://thing.desk.nl/bilwet/Cracking/contents.html.
13. This paper magazine, which discussed media, art and television, was published from 1985 to 1999. All issues are available at https://www.mediamatic.net/en/page/10342/mediamatic-magazine.
14. Lovink, G. (2018), "The Story of my First Laptop: the Toshiba DynaBook", blog by Geert Lovink, http://networkcultures.org/geert/2018/01/15/the-story-of-my-first-laptop-the-toshiba-dynabook/.
15. ARKZIN was a periodical published in Zagreb from 1991 to 1998.

16. One of the first ISPs in the Netherlands. Founded in 1993 as an offshoot of the hackers club *Hack-Tic*, it first offered dial-in services via modem. https://en.wikipedia.org/wiki/XS4ALL.
17. The Next 5 Minutes conference took place in Paradiso from 8 January to 10 January 1993 with the aim of exploring and discussing the role of independent media in networks and societies.

"I am an engineer and therefore a radical": an interview with Lee Felsenstein, from Free Speech Movement technician to Homebrew Computer Club moderator

Julie Momméja (iD)

ABSTRACT
The following interview delves into Lee Felsenstein's upbringing in a bohemian communist family and his path as an engineer and technologist in the San Francisco Bay Area. He discusses his role as technician of the Berkeley Free Speech Movement, co-creator of Community Memory and moderator of the Homebrew Computer Club. Felsenstein also shares his vision of "community", "convivial tools" as defined by Ivan Illich and technology as an "invisible force". He proves how his political activism has guided his technological creative process, making and sharing tools that will contribute to build convivial, open and informed communities.

Introduction and interview

In 1973, inside a Berkeley record store, the "doors to cyberspace" got opened by five young people who set up a teletype terminal linked by telephone to an SDS 940 computer through which students and customers would be able to leave messages and share information. Called "Community Memory", the project became the first public semi-virtual community, an intangible gathering of people using technology as a communication tool on a new "hospitable territory".

Lee Felsenstein, self-described as "an engineer and therefore a radical", was one of its founders. Born in Philadelphia in 1945, Felsenstein grew up in a bohemian communist household where DIY technological inventions were encouraged. That political and technological upbringing led him to study engineering at UC Berkeley where he was also able to take part in the 1964 Free Speech Movement, when thousands of students joined together to protest restrictions on political speech on campus, combining his radical ideals to his technological creations and thus contributing to the fight for freedom of expression. Felsenstein continued to experiment with the symbiosis between politics and technology, which materialized in various ways, especially as he became one of the co-founders of Community Memory and then moderator of the

Homebrew Computer Club (founded in 1975), two key "maker spaces" as we would say today that succeeded in placing computers at the center of their respective community, in Berkeley and Menlo Park.

The following interview was conducted at the Long Now Foundation in San Francisco on February 27th, 2017. It is part of a larger corpus of interviews recorded in the context of my PhD dissertation, "From *The Whole Earth Catalog* to the Long Now Foundation in the San Francisco Bay Area: co-evolution on the creative 'Frontier' (1955-2020)" defended at the Sorbonne Nouvelle University in March 2021.

This research focalizes on the notion of human-machine co-evolution, as theorized and put into practice by a certain number of communities and pioneers, Lee Felsenstein among them, who remained active during the sixty-five years considered. It proceeds to a historical division into three phases: the first phase of revolution (1955-1973) during which the Free Speech Movement occurred is followed by a phase of co-evolution (1974-1996) that saw the creation of Community Memory and the Homebrew Computer Club, a period which then leads to a post-co-evolution phase (1996-2020). The hypothesis developed is that co-evolution leans on the code and its infinite variations from a finite system (the alphabetical, the numerical and the genetic) and on communities of pioneers making and using tools, analogic then digital, that help reshape and reinvent the San Francisco Bay Area as an evolving creative "Frontier". Events such as the Free Speech Movement and communities formed around artefacts such as *The Whole Earth Catalog* (a catalog of tools founded by Stewart Brand in 1968 as a way to initially empower people living in remote back-to-the-land communes) and Community Memory contribute to build the analysis of this co-evolution.

Lee Felsenstein's path as a technologist is deeply rooted in the Bay Area dissent of the 1960s. Through an immersive research approach, the aims of this two-hour-long meeting were to delve into Lee Felsenstein's personal background and career path, chronologically, while highlighting specific themes such as "community" and "convivial tools" as defined by Ivan Illich (*Tools for Conviviality*, 1973), both envisioned as guiding processes at the core of the interviewee's projects. Questions were also asked regarding his connection to the local counterculture and the Free Speech Movement central organization, and his links to Stewart Brand and *The Whole Earth Catalog*. His participation in Community Memory and the Homebrew Computer Club were also discussed through the prism of his vision of technology as an invisible force, one that is able to transform positively communities and societies.

Throughout this interview, Lee Felsenstein embodies a visionary DIY technologist, from analog to digital and back, whose political activism has been central in shaping technological creations as "cool tools" made to serve the community, foster participation, conviviality and help sharing information freely, as demonstrated in my PhD research.

I would like to thank Lee Felsenstein for answering my questions and for agreeing to the publication of this interview.

--

Julie Momméja: [...] As I explained to you, I am really interested in themes such as "Community" and "Tools", and would like to hear more about how you were involved with these two concepts: how it all started, from your involvement with the Berkeley Free Speech Movement, the beginning of Community Memory and the Homebrew Computer Club.

Lee Felsenstein: Well, I came to Berkeley, in pursuit in part of the Beatnik culture and the political culture that came along with it, as a dissident. I came from a family that was, you'd have to call them, bohemian for their time in the 1930s and 40 s, when nobody dressed different from anyone else. But there were a lot of books in the house, for instance by Lewis Mumford, other names I can't even recall, people who were questioning the main culture. [...] My parents were in the bohemian culture such as it was in Philadelphia. My father was a commercial artist, and my mother had been raised in a very upper middle class family in Eastern Pennsylvania. Her father made a lot of money by inventing technology that improved the diesel engine operations to the point where it became visible, it could not fit in chips but in vehicles, railroad, locomotives and so forth, and so forth. She made it very clear that I needed to follow his path. [...]

JM: Growing up, you got interested in the Beat Generation. How did it all start?

LF: [...] I was always brought up to not follow the unique crowd, and to think for myself, I was given a copy of *Brave New World* by Aldous Huxley, when I was in high school. I can't quite remember who gave it to me, I was about 15 or 16. And my parents, they were activists in the Communist Party, and they never however attempted to indoctrinate me. On the other hand, my mother would take me along when she would work with the Women International League for Peace and Freedom, and I learnt how to run a mimeograph at that point. I was probably about 11 or 12. So my interest in technology and electronics and so forth started from age 11, me and my brother were definitely seriously encouraged in that direction.

JM: And you were already attracted to radical intellectuals and this led you to Berkeley and the Bay Area ...

LF: Yes ... When did I first know that the Bay Area was a hot place? ... Certainly in 1960 when there was the anti HUAC (House of Un-American Activities Committee) demonstrations, my parents had been submitted to appear before the Senate equivalent of that, the Senate Internal Security Subcommittee, as an attempt to try to suppress their community activity. In 1957. I was very aware of that kind of activity. When my parents were invited to leave the Communist Party in 1963 or 1964, we subscribed to the *National Guardian*, for non-communist communists or ex-communists, and so we always had this newspaper around where I would read articles and so forth, and sort of get educated on what was happening, so I knew about it, about the Red Hunt, the repression, and I read about the demonstrations in San Francisco in 1960, also in the regular press[1]. By 1962, it must have been, I was hanging around with a sort of group that were red diapers babies, and so their parents knew my parents, and so we would do things like take a bus down from San Mateo to Washington for the 1957 or 1958, Youth March for Integration[2]. As I recall Martin Luther King was a speaker there, this was a 20,000 people march - or demonstration - totally blacked out by the news media. So we sort of had practice in demonstrations and practice in seeing what was done in the press. About that time, I started reading a book called *The True Bohemian* which was about San Francisco, the Beatnik scene and the University of California, and this was kind of not quite the final event, but that was a really important one[3]. The final event was when I applied for university, I was accepted at Carnegie Tech, which is now Carnegie Mellon in Pittsburgh. I did not get a scholarship, though I was a finalist, so I applied to other universities, UC Berkeley among them, 'cause I would be able to afford that. And that's where I got accepted [...]. I arrived in September 1963, within a few weeks, by October, there was a visit by Madame Nhu[4], I think she was the sister-in-law of the [President] of South Vietnam.

JM: This is when the first anti-Vietnam war protest happened.

LF: Yes, the first one. I was there and walked to the picket line with Allen Ginsberg, who had just won a poetry award. I was hanging out with this little batch of about 100 people or so, who would be available for protest. I had been doing some Civil Rights protests in Philadelphia in 1961, picketing Woolworth, but I didn't even know who the sponsoring organizations were, I didn't care. So, my path to Berkeley was attracted by the bohemian culture and the political subculture, which I saw as connected.

JM: And your first community there turned out to be the Free Speech Movement one.

LF: Well ... yes, you might say. Now I did fortuitously, just because of its geographic location, was a part of Oxford Hall Student co-op. It was a part of the university student cooperative association [...]. That was really my first community, about a hundred boys - or men. So yes, that would be my first community, in perhaps the smallest sense of the word. And even to this day I consider that as being my Alma Mater, not the university. I got a job on campus doing electronic technician work with a Professor who was a refugee from Hitler, came through Australia ... And then I heard about the cooperative work study program in engineering and signed up with that and got hired into a job at NASA, flight research center, an Air Force space in Southern California. That was the Summer of 1964. [...] It was necessary to have the lowest level of security clearance confidential, it was a one page form you had to fill out, with such questions as: "Do you know any communist?" and so forth, and I said "no", because my parents had never told me they were members of the party! They had told my brother.

JM: But you didn't know ...

LF: No, I didn't! I was called into the security office and was given another form to fill out, listing everywhere I'd been and lived, [...] and asking for references, I'm sure that two of the references I gave were communists themselves, I didn't know that. [...] I ended up suspecting something was wrong, and they finally called me and they said: "You can't work here, we're going to recommend denial of security clearance. Here's what we recommend you do: we recommend you resign in order to return to school". And more or less off the record, a guy told me: "By the way, your parents were communists", and I absorbed that information without emotion. You know, actually, I had been subject to the communist propaganda, I had accepted a good deal of it, because I didn't think my parents were among them. So the emotional impact was pretty severe, I went down to the nearest paid phone, called my father and I asked him: "I need to know, where you a communist?", and he said: "I don't want to talk about that now" and I remember hanging up the phone and looking out the window and there was the Mojave desert and that was the desert I was being expelled to, outcast into the wilderness, and it was a serious emotional impact. I called my former employer [...] and he said: "Come on back and we'll put you to work".

JM: So, when are we now?

LF: I left on October 15, 1964. The Free Speech Movement had started, as you know, on September 30, with a - quote - "riot", a police car entrapment, that lasted till the 2nd I think[5]. And I really didn't have any knowledge about that. I was working on campus, no classes, and I was accepted by the co-op office and was able to attend rallies. It took me about a week to learn enough about it. When I left, the Southern security chief of the base told me: "You keep your nose clean for a year or so, you will have no trouble getting back in". Ok. So I had to weight that against not keeping my nose clean. It wasn't that much of a decision, but it was some, I gave it a week and decided I was not going to keep my nose clean, I'm gonna get involved 'cause this is right. That was my Huck Finn moment, you know, when he says: "I'll go to Hell".

JM: And when would you consider your epiphany moment to have taken place? That moment you discovered technology could be a tool to spread information, I read about your involvement at the Oakland protest against the draft in 1967.

LF: I was down on the front line. [...] I concentrated on audio, and analog electronics and when I left for college I had with me a very good tape recorder, a very good-quality one. I figured maybe I can make use of this, I did try to see if I could go into business running the use of the recorder for people to record, but I never pursued that particularly.

I went to the headquarters of the Free Speech Movement and tried to find out what I could do, I'd take the recorder or whatever they sent me to the Press Central and I tried to come up with an audio press release, they gave me a mimeograph there and I could help with that. At the central office, they had a phone room. There were two telephones, and a lot of papers tacked to the wall, so I thought: "These folks need a filing system". Card filing. There was a technology I tried to implement - I didn't go anywhere with it - but I wasn't really aware of what was going on, but slowly I learnt that this was not an officially run communication center with orders going out and information coming back in and everything being put in its place, it really was a cross-connection point among people who would call in with questions, with ideas, with offers of help, with needs. And other people would call in with the complement of that, this went up on the wall and the people who did that just knew about it, it was the prototype of what became later in the sixties the switchboard, an interested specific information referral system place, a contact point. And I say that: it was essentially the contact point of the Internet in terms of information structure. I saw that happening and I really was trying to have people tell me what I should do with my technological experience, there were a few people who had such experience, I started to know their names, they could set up amplifiers and things like that.

Then, the event called the "police radio incident" happened. Someone came running in the door, someone shouting the police had surrounded the campus - of course the campus is so large you couldn't do that, but that didn't matter. Objectively, what happened was that one person there, Marilyn Noble, who had come in and installed herself the house mother of the place - she was an applied sociology grad student - she apparently remembered something she had learnt from her father, and back then you could retune a regular radar receiver to receive police calls, so she said: "Quick, make us a police radio!". I - as everyone in the room turning to me as one, in unison, saying: "Quick, make us a police radio!" - I knew immediately that you could have done it in 1939 but you could not do it in 1964 for technical reasons, but how to explain this? I stumbled and said: "But you don't understand, it takes time!". Whereupon, subjectively, I heard everyone say in unison: "Never mind about that! Make us a police radio!"

And so, instantaneously, I understood my model was wrong, that waiting for people who were smarter than I were, than I was, to tell me what I should do, to take orders from them, was never going to work because they wouldn't know enough to give me any kind of intelligent request. It was my responsibility, if I wanted to help in this process, with technology, I had to go ahead of the need. The model that I used, the metaphor that I used was from tunneling ahead of the shield. I mean, in tunneling there is something called the Brunel's shield which is a structure that keeps the earth from collapsing, and they build the pacing of the tunnel within there which can actually retain, hold back the earth from the tunnel. And then you dig away at the front of it and expand and move the shield forward, it's kind of a pretty scary stuff, and people would go out ahead of the shield with nothing at all for protection: and that was my metaphor for where I had to be.

JM: That's when you realized you had to be a visionary and find the tool ahead of time.

LF: I saw that when they came to me the next time and said "Quick! Do this!". I would be able to say: "Well, you can't have that, but here's what you can have". And they couldn't argue with the fact that I would have it on the shelf by that time! So that's been my model ever since then, that I've been pursuing with some success. [...]

JM: At that time, did you consider you were also a part of the counterculture movement somehow?

LF: No, I simply considered myself to be, well, first and foremost an engineer. Someone who has been empowered by learning aspects of technology: that we can put things together and make them work and keep them working. Also, to me, when I was thrown out of the job at NASA, I was telling people the history and so forth and somebody thought I had left home because of my parents' communism, that I was rejecting it, and I said: "No, no, I'm a radical too, I consider that I am an engineer and therefore a radical". I said that at that point, at age 19. And I was not that interested, or that able, to join a community, I had to learn how to do that much later. So, I saw myself as an individual, as a member of a small set of individuals who were sort of a brotherhood - as it was all male - of technologists. The day I arrived at UC, I went up to the campus radio station and turned myself in: "I'm going to build things for you", that was sort of my community, much of geeks. And you can see in a picture of *1964 Blue & Gold*, which is the Campus Year Book, there's the listing of various extra curriculum activities and there is KAL, the campus radio station, there's a picture of me and some other geeks, dressed in my work clothes, my daily wear, very close cut. So I was part of this nerd-tech community.

JM: And then part of the FSM.

LF: I just continued to hang around and tried to be a technological resource. The first six months of 1965 were a time that was magical to me. I since concluded that I had been through a revolution, a defining revolution, a mass event that overthrew an existing order which in this case was a local apparatus, and which had consequences far beyond what was originally expected. I attended a seminar, or a meeting discussion, of what had happened and Marvin Garson - who was with the independent socialist club at that time, more or less a Trotskyist organization, and who had been a member of the FSM - talked about it. He said that, according to him, the barriers to communicate among the members of the campus community went down due to the crisis. It became acceptable to talk to strangers, and that has become the foundation for my thinking about communication and social medium. I had seen this happening with the phone room, I remember a sign after the sit-in that said "Haircut Central - if you need a haircut, call this number" which was obviously one of those things that could never be anticipated but when the offer came in, was posted, who knows how many people took advantage of it. In the aftermath of the FSM, we tried to set up a free student union and that's where I started being involved with computer games, somebody taught me how to use keypunch cards and there was a whole room filled of keypunch machines.

JM: Can you tell me more about what kind of information you were gathering on these cards?

LF: Keypunching was completely open and I worked on a questionnaire as we wanted to know where resources were and how to access them for the next event. We also tried to do a registration system for our local meetings, nobody attended the local meetings, we tried to keypunch that - which didn't really work. I was sorting out the cards, printing out records, so that was my first foray into - not really computers but digital technology as it assists for community or organization.

The critical observation I then made of the Free Speech Movement was - and in accordance with what Garson was saying - was that this batch of thousands, tens of thousands of isolated alienated individuals polymerized - he didn't use the term, that's my term - in order to form a community, there was a cross connection of inter-channels, basically not knowing who the other person was, and being able to meet people you didn't know, talk to them without barriers, made it possible for a community to form, and that's why we were able to win, it wasn't because we had the correct ideology or we had a big centralized structure. We did have a structure but the execu-tive committee of the FSM was really kind of a House of Representatives, because it drew from representatives to other organizations and the functionality of that was to bring information in from this community as it was forming and send information back out to explain what was going on. That sort of a root-structure was really critical. At a certain point in there, I came to understand that there were two types of media: broadcast and non-broadcast. After the sit-in, there was an effort to call everyone to the campus fund directory and tell them what was going on, get them to the rally and so we took one of the campus phone books and tore out pages and handed one to each person or volunteer to call everybody on the page, and I took it back to my shared apartment and monopolized the phone the whole evening and somebody was finally able to call in while I was hanging up and I realized that people wanted to use this phone too! I realized the phone system was there and functions to unable any one phone to call any other phone simultaneously, but we just don't have the right directories, so I began to think how we could change that, and of course the phone room of the FSM was a directory that could update itself dynamically. [...]

Now, in 1967, during the "Stop the Draft Week", I realized we needed amplifiers and I tried two different designs that didn't work really well, and later on in 1969, I did a third one that could have been networked - the technique I was using was very high-quality sound, not very high level. By that time, I had dropped out, I was working at Ampex special products doing design of audio, so I had all the tools. And I realized I'd like to be able to make the crowd talk back to the speaker, to respond.

JM: And as John Markoff writes in *What the Dormouse Said*, that's when you real-ized there was a power to invisibly transform political events, especially during the "Stop the Draft Week". That technology you were creating and using was invisible to police officers, could you tell me more about that invisible force?

LF: I was never trying to be terribly visible. My political status as an engineer allowed that. Seven people got arrested for conspiracy and organizing the "Stop the Draft Week" demonstration, I was not one of them. During that organizing time, we'd have this committee meeting with no other external support group, and I said: "Look, I can't contribute much politically, I'm here to do things and so you just tell me what you need done and I'll try to do it, but I'm a technician, I'm not a political person". I was not involved with any of the political discussions but helped as much as I could in getting things together: to do the radio squads and so forth. And I didn't get indicted, although the lawyer, in wrapping up, said: "Most of the testimonies that have been given have been about what Lee Felsenstein did, they should have indicted Lee Felsenstein".

So I began to understand [...] I had too short a wave length for the political struc-ture to see me, that's the metaphor I'm using here. More realistically, or less meta-phorically, that means that they indicted people, but they didn't come after me who had been doing much of the work. And I figured because I'm operating in a different play, they're operating in a political environment. And there it's a matter of who's known, who has what support, who says what and so forth. I'm operating in an envir-onment where it's what you do that counts, and they - the political structure - takes that for granted. When we want something done we'll just say: "Do it" and someone will do it: I'm one of those someones. And apparently, I should have been one of them, but for some reason I didn't exist in the stratum that the political power structure thought was the important stratum.

JM: Community Memory is still a few years ahead, but it seems that by 1967 you already know technology can be a weapon, am I right?

LF: By 1965, I was listening to radio reports from the South and things were pretty difficult for the Civil Rights movement there, like voter registration, and I began to think: "Is there such a thing as a non-violent weapon? What would it be?" And I came up with the idea that maybe if I can make a thing where if you take a ball point pen refill in it and a CO_2 gas cartridge, like they use in air pistols, and so you can squirt the ink at somebody attacking you, that stuff is almost impossible to get off, so you can identify someone. I never did anything about it but it was the idea of a non-violent weapon being an information weapon because what that would do is begin to convey information: that person had been marked as an attacker. That may or may not have helped anybody but we never got a chance to find out, thank God.

So yes, information weapons and the need for community, both as a means to political success let's say, and as they end result. Because in January 1965, it was nearly orgasmic to experience this "We're able to do anything we want to, anybody can do anything". I had decided then that I wanted to try to do what I could to get back to that point, all the time, I wanted all of life to be like that. The result being information technology is going to be necessary to allow for those barriers to go down for communication.

And I thought, the *Berkeley Barb*: "That's a community newspaper, there's a very small community at the outset". People were putting on ads that said: "Ken Spiker needs a place to live" - Ken Spiker was a folk musician, not a very big one - but people who were reading, they would know who Ken Spiker was, that's all it needed to say. Of course, as the *Barb* grew, the ads became sex ads, and so forth, a big source of revenue but they were not that community oriented at all. So, the success of the centralized media that was print media was its own undoing in fact, and it could not be a community relevant communication media, so I kept thinking about what would be. [...]

And there was an example of the connection mechanism happening in the midst of crisis. And it was probably in 1970 when the group called People's Architecture published what they called "The Plan for a Liberated Berkeley", published certainly in *The Berkeley Tribe*. And there was some technological thinking applied and one of the things they came up with was what they called a "life house", that would be like the front room of a house made available by the inhabitant, someone who wanted to be connected with the community and therefore made the room available for their community, not necessarily just everybody, as a communication center. And I understood you could have copiers there, mimeographs, pretty technology, and you could link them, certainly by phones. They'd have phones there, they'd know where the others are, they had a network that way. And as I went forward, I began to realize that networked computers would be the technology that would allow for this larger scale basis, the technology that would support the creation and recreation of community. That was occasioned by my being sent to learn the BASIC computer language, in those days, you had to go to the computer.

JM: And BASIC would allow you to create a non-hierarchical medium for everyone, everywhere, so you already had the idea of connecting people through a network

LF: Yes, the computer network would not be determined by geography, it could be everywhere and yet nowhere. And you could create communities of interest and have them kept organized, more or less, self-organized.

JM: That's where I can see, again, a parallel in between your vision and Stewart Brand's at the time with the *Whole Earth Catalog* and creating a community around it[6].

LF: I wanted to make it possible for everybody to form the communities they wanted to form, and to keep them reforming because communities need that. And I'm sure that was the same vision that Stewart Brand had, but I came to it my way and with a digital component to it and that sent me in the direction of Community Memory.

In 1970, I had a realization: "Where am I gonna get a computer?" By 1971, out on Telegraph Avenue, somebody ran out to me and said "Lee! That stuff you've been taking about, there are some people over in San Francisco, they have a computer to do it!" This guy was a crazy guy who I didn't really trust, but I went out to find out and it was true, and that was Resource One. And I joined with them and helped bring in others like Efrem Lipkin as assistant programmer. Basically, I brought in this idea of a kind of "life house"-based network, they had taken over the corporate structure of the San Francisco switchboard, which was very successful in the Haight Ashbury. They knew they wanted to provide a common filing system for switchboards, which would have been a good start. The trouble is they couldn't make contact with the switchboards that meant anything. But I was there with this idea that we could be a system, a tool, that people could use to create this basis of community, whether or not using switchboards, or whatever. So I can take some credit for the concept of Community Memory that way, the actual implementation, not so much. Like I said, Efrem Lipkin had the idea of actually putting a terminal on public because we had an empty information retrieval system and our librarian said: "It's like having a shelf without books, put some books on it and see what happens". I played a fundamental role there, but certainly not the entire role.

JM: I really enjoyed reading your memories of having all these people coming to Leopold's Records and your surprise as you were not expecting them to be interested in computers.

LF: Right, we expected they would be hostile: "How dare you bring a computer into this music counterculture place?". But because it was visually obvious and awaiting them putting their hands through the holes to use the keyboard, everybody was - with one exception we've known - delighted with the idea. And that was what I call opening the doors to cyberspace and discovering this was a hospitable territory.

So we opened up the terminal in Berkeley in 1973 and another one on the counter of the Mission branch of the San Francisco Public Library.

JM: And then one at the Whole Earth Access.

LF: Yes, a few months later on Shattuck Avenue, we moved the terminal from Leopold's to there. It became a CRT terminal, not a teletype, and that's when I began to understand that better technology was going to be needed for public access computer systems, and that started me on the path for personal computers.

JM: And at that time, were you reading the *Whole Earth Catalog*? Were you connected to that community?

LF: Oh yes, well I wasn't connected to it except I was reading it and was kind of thrilled by it and I know, I remember, in 1973, I was attending these potluck dinners at the Community Computer Center in Menlo Park. I would take the train down there and right there, adjacent to the train station, was the office where the *Whole Earth Catalog* was being published...

JM: Yes, the Portola Institute...

LF: [...] I remember thinking: "You know, I wish I could tell them what is going on!". They are the ones who know where everything is, they know where everything's at - as the proper phrase was - and I wanted very much to sort of bring them in on what this was but I couldn't figure out a way to do it, better I should concentrate on making it happen. So I saw the *Whole Earth Catalog* as doing something approximating what we were trying to do, they were using a core print technology, which had many limitations, and for that reason I figured: they'll do what they do, we'll do what we do, and there will be some change in coming together in the future. I know... well, it would have been later, 1977 or so, the New Games Tournament... [...]

JM: *Tools for Conviviality* by Ivan Illich was a source of inspiration for you, as it was for Stewart Brand...

LF: Oh was it? Ok, that's very good...

JM: Yes, and I'd be curious to hear more about it and how it did help you shape your conception of tools and design.

LF: Well, yes, in 1973, we decided to move the terminal from Leopold's Records to the Whole Earth Access store, we had rented a CRT terminal, and we had paid for a maintenance contract, so much a month. And I wasn't there but I heard the maintenance technician managed to take the inside of the keyboard out and dropped it and knocked the top off of one of the integrated circuits - they were built in such a way that that could happen. And when people said: "Well, shouldn't you do something about that?", he said: "No, it doesn't matter", which I knew otherwise. And when I heard about that, I figured we were not getting our money's worth from this maintenance contract and we shouldn't plan on it in the future, and beside the terminal cost a lot of money... At that point, by September 1973, there had been a TV typewriter article that had come out in the *Radio-Electronics* magazine, it raised an awful lot of interest — 10,000 paid responses, and people, within my little sort of computer under-ground society, were industriously trying to figure out how to use this to get for instance access to time sharing. Wozniak also did the same thing, he designed his own, and he was going to sell it to Core Computer, a time-sharing service that actually solicited hackers and certain computer underground people - and they might have been listed in the *Whole Earth Catalog*, they would have been.

So anyway, we were trying to figure out how we could make a terminal that could be used in public without supervision, without a maintenance contract, and how to make that happen. And my father, had become a New Ager, he took LSD, I never did. He called me out, unsolicited and said: "I've been reading this book by a guy named Ivan Illich, it's about convivial technology and this is not conviviality in the sense of having a party, you should read it." I don't know, he may have sent it to me, I think that's how I got it. And the book basically was a revelation to me, because it was so familiar to me: he was talking about how radio had spread in Central America, devel-oped and grew its own category of technicians. Two years after the radio arrived, peo-ple there knew how to fix it, they didn't come from outside, they were always there. They were there and they could learn the radio because the radio technology was suf-ficiently forgiving, that it didn't break immediately if you tried to open it up and do anything with it. So they could learn about fixing radios, because the radio technology was there for a convivial technology in an eulogist definition - he was counterposing convivial with industrial. And that reminded me of how I had learnt electronics start-ing from age 11, how I had been given a radio and television repairs correspondence course - which was a good start, but nonetheless, I sort of learnt it on my own with a friend, and I kind of groped my way to learning electronics, not in an institutional set-ting. It said to me that it should be possible to design a computer device, a computer terminal, so that it collects a group of people around itself, a computer club, and they are the ones who would keep it going and improve it if it were designed to encour-age that improvement. I set myself a goal of designing what would encourage that growth. We needed a terminal, it wasn't clear that microprocessors were ever going to be cheap enough to be little computers but we could allow for that. I designed the Tom Swift Terminal which started life as a terminal, and then could grow by plugging things in and then define the back plan structure, the interchange protocols. I never built it but was able to build something like it with the VDM-1[7].

JM: That was in 1975, am I right?

LF: VDM-1 was 1975, yes. I published up the specifications in 1974, I mimeo-graphed it myself and sold it for 25 cents within my little community, so it qualifies as a publication. And so the idea that in order for a computer device to survive in a pub-lic access environment it has to grow a computer club around itself, that's a concept that I credit Illich with.

JM: That's the idea you presented to the Homebrew Computer Club?

LF: Well, so the Homebrew Computer Club grew out of the Community Computer Center in Menlo Park. I didn't meet him at the time but Fred Moore was hanging around taking names and addresses and building a mailing list. For what, he was not terribly sure, but he was a pacifist activist, he thought he might want to do something, create a class to learn computer hardware. That's when the Altair came out and it really changed the game. There was this ad in *Popular Electronics* in January 1975 that Bob Marsh showed me, we were in the same student co-op and later reconnected through Community Memory. And Fred Moore met Gordon French, and the both of them started posting flyers inviting people to come to Gordon's garage to see the Altair: that's how the Homebrew Computer Club started in March 1975, with 30 people.

JM: And did you meet Steve Wozniak at that first meeting?

LF: Yes, he was there, with what he called a TV typewriter design. In the end, 23 companies originated from the Club, and Apple was one of them. And Steve Wozniak's design turned into the Apple I, which then became the Apple II. And the following year was the first computer fair ever in Atlantic City: the PC 76 Computer Fair. I was there helping and taking orders for the Processor Technology SOL-20, the computer I had designed, because Bob Marsh wanted something around a VDM display. Steve Wozniak, Steve Jobs and Daniel Kottke were also there, selling the Apple I at their booth. [...]

JM: I know we have to end this interview soon, which leads me to 1984 as the year of the release of *Hackers* by Steven Levy and the first Hackers' Conference. What can you tell me about that time?

LF: Yes, Steven Levy interviewed me for the book, and Stewart Brand asked me to come to the book release party in Sausalito, with other people interviewed by Levy. I then helped organize the first Hackers' Conference. We actually had Community Memory on display there.

JM: And what about your participation on the WELL? How did you see it?

LF: It had the same spirit as Community Memory. I was the third person to register on the WELL. There was Stewart Brand (sb), Matthew McClure (mmc), and then me (lee). Stewart asked me to run and host the Hackers Conference on the WELL, which I did for two years. [...]

Conclusion

The first Hackers' Conference organized in November 1984 and the creation of the WELL (Whole Earth 'Lectronic Link) as one of the first virtual communities by Stewart Brand and Larry Brilliant the following year, both in the San Francisco Bay Area, appear as extensions of what Community Memory and the Homebrew Computer Club accomplished during the previous decade. Through these various adventures, Lee Felsenstein's vision of technological tools got confirmed, one that foresaw computers not only as communication devices but as community creators where the free exchange of information, through words or codes, was key.

As creator, moderator or participant, Felsenstein embodies a radical engineer that keeps reinventing computers from the inside while reforming groups of people around them in a "convivial" way. The last decade shows he continues following the same logic as he has taken part in the creation of a hackerspace in Silicon Valley, Hacker Dojo, and designed a logic simulator board, called "State Machine Logic Demonstrator", to teach middle school students how to program computers. Through hands-on participation, he continues inspiring and providing "cool tools" to the next generation of engineers.

Notes

1. Throughout the 1940s and 1950s, the House Un-American Activities Committee (HUAC) inves-tigated American citizens suspected of having affiliations with the communist party. In May 1960, as the HUAC held hearings at the San Francisco City Hall and refused access to the general public, a protest started, mostly formed by Bay Area students.
2. The "Youth March for Integrated Schools" events happened on October 25th, 1958 and April 18th, 1959, the second one was the most attended one, and the one Lee Felsenstein is referring to.
3. The 1950s, with the opening of City Lights Bookstore by Lawrence Ferlinghetti in the North Beach neighborhood, confirmed San Francisco as an artistic and literary center. The bohemian community, then followed by the Beat generation writers and poets, gathered and created in the city and its region, inspiring a new generation of young people to move to the area and invent new ways of living outside of mainstream America.
4. Madame Nhu gave a speech to UC Berkeley students on October 29th, 1963.
5. Following the occupation of Sproul Hall the night before and because he was engaging in po-litical activism on campus, former UC Berkeley student Jack Weinberg was arrested for violating the University's rules on October 1st, 1964. The police car he was taken to was spontaneously surrounded by Free Speech Movement activists and students in an act of civil disobedience. The sit-in lasted for over thirty hours, interspersed by speeches given from the police car roof by activists such as Weinberg and Mario Savio, it symbolically marked the beginning of the student protest movement for freedom of expression and social justice. See Cohen, R. (2014). *Freedom's Orator: Mario Savio and the Radical Legacy of the 1960s*. Oxford University Press.
6. From 1968 to 1974, Stewart Brand managed to gather a real community of readers and review-ers of the tools presented in the pages of his catalog. From books on geodesic domes, nature or cooking to hand woodworking tools and wind generators, *The Whole Earth Catalog*, which first provided information and "access to tools" to back-to-the-land communes, became of interest to a wider DIY and technologist readership throughout the US. See Brand, S. (1968). *Whole Earth Catalog: Access to Tools*. Turner, F. (2006). *From Counterculture to Cyberculture: Stewart Brand, the Whole Earth Network, and the Rise of Digital Utopianism*. University of Chicago Press.
7. Video Display Module, later the inspiration for the display of personal computers.

Disclosure statement

No potential conflict of interest was reported by the authors.

ORCID

Julie Momméja ⓘ http://orcid.org/0000-0003-1148-2490

Interview with Aleksandra Kaminska

Maria Eriksson and Guillaume Heuguet

Aleksandra Kaminska is an Assistant Professor in the Department of Communication at the Université de Montréal, Canada, where she also co-directs the Artefact Lab and the Bricolab. Her research is based in media studies and aesthetics, and the history of technology. She is currently preparing *High-Tech Paper: Security Printing and the Aesthetics of Trust*, a monograph that examines the making of authentic paper for circulation in secure systems and infrastructures. She situates security printing within media and printing histories, but also as it intersects with art, craft, and design. Her work on authentication devices includes the production of *Nano-verses* (nano-verses.com), an art-sci collaboration that explored how the technology of nano-optical authentication can be rethought as artistic media. The articles discussed in the following interview are: "Storing Authenticity at the Surface and into the Depths: Securing Paper with Human- and Machine-Readable Devices" (*Intermédialités*, 2018); "'Don't Copy That': Security Printing and the Making of High-Tech Paper" (*Convergence*, 2019); and "The Intrinsic Value of Valuable Paper: On the Infrastructural Work of Authentication Devices" (*Theory, Culture & Society*, 2020). She recently co-edited an issue of *PUBLIC: Art/Culture/Ideas* on "Biometrics: Mediating Bodies" (2020), and is currently finalizing a co-edited volume of the *Canadian Journal of Communication* on the theme of "Materials and Media of Infrastructure." In 2020–2021 she is co-organizing the online series Paperology: A Reading and Activity Group on Knowing and Being with Paper.

Your work centers on efforts to secure the authenticity and identity of things and highlights how material standards contribute to the ordering of the world. In much of your writings, you place focus on techniques for identifying analog objects such as money and documents/valuable paper but we have also found your work to be highly stimulating for thinking about efforts to identify digital content like moving images and sounds.

In "Storing Authenticity at the Surface and into the Depths" you introduce the concept of "authentication devices" to discuss the role and function of identification techniques. Could you explain a bit more about what you mean by this concept and how/why you think it is useful for thinking about strategies of identification?

Thank you for the opportunity to talk to you about this work, and especially in this context that brings it in conversation with today's digital and online technologies. Let me start with some background on some of the concepts and questions that animate this research before delving into the details of the question.

"Authentication" is derived from the Greek word *authentikos*, meaning original, real, or genuine. In popular culture and speech, we tend to apply it to the idea of *being* authentic, as a manifestation of someone identity through appearance or performance for example. This is somewhat different or less precise than when we use notions of authenticity to assess or describe knockoff products, fake documents, and other counterfeited and forged material things. In these cases, there are physical qualities that materially define the "real" version, so that what become significant is the processes of authentication, or the way that authenticity is determined. What do we *do* when we authenticate? What is there *to* authenticate? How do evaluate, verify, validate? Authentication in these instances is this process of verifying an object's genuineness and legitimacy based on certain hallmarks and predetermined characteristics. This applies to things, but also to individuals when there is a need to verify an identity using documents and prove that the identifying information a person gives is accurate.

People have been authenticating before even thinking of it as such. The question or problem of how to distinguish fakes, forgeries, counterfeits and counterfeiters, and illicit reproductions of all kinds, has a long history in human culture. Today's digital environment provides new challenges as well as opportunities. The big problem of knowing "what is true" has become a question for those interested in content and information and well as those looking for material evidence, inscriptions, and traces. I'm interested primarily in the latter, and I tend to gravitate towards artefacts and things. Quickly my project developed a more historical perspective than I expected. I began with the sophisticated technologies of nano-optics (for the *Nanoverses* project), but it was clear that to understand what was happening and why—in terms of both the technology and how it was being used—I had to go back in time. And when I considered the variety of goods that circulate as real/fake, whether computer chips or medical supplies, I also ultimately ended up with the technologies that brought us the questions of copies and technological reproduction, printing and paper. So this is how I came to anchor this project around paper, but a paper that evolves and changes and becomes highly complex. The newest technologies to protect paper are used for banknotes and passports, but there is wide assortment of papers that must function with authority: mailing stamps, tax stamps, certificates of all kinds (including certificates of authenticity themselves), branding labels, bonds, identification documents, official documents, etc. We are surrounded by such papers even though we rarely stop to think about the technologies that they put to work. We could say that official structures and systems—whether of bureaucracies, states, institutions, industries—must continuously communicate, affirm, and reproduce their legitimacy, and they do so in part through the material things they produce.

There might be an impression that the materials problems of paper are of a different time. On the one hand there is the discourse of the paperless society, which tells us we should no longer have to worry about how authenticity is inscribed through paper (and paper-like things which co-exist alongside cellulose-based paper such as polymer-based paper), because paper itself is becoming obsolete. And there is no denying we have shifted many things outside of the realm of paper. But a paperless world is still largely one of the future. Yes, there are examples to the contrary, including the nearly cashless society in Sweden, the increase of cashless payments during the COVID-19 pandemic, or workers being implemented with chips so that they no longer have to physically punch in. But it is worth remembering that going cashless is an equity issue: 1.7 billion adults in the world are still unbanked, according the most recent report from the World Bank (Demirgüç-Kunt et al., 2018), which means they operate on cash. We also know that it is still essential to have an identification document like a passport to be recognized as a person—without such papers we are no one belonging nowhere (as is so well denoted in the French expression *les sans papiers*). Meanwhile, according to the Organisation for Economic Co-operation and Development, $509 billion, or about 3.3% of all trade worldwide, was based on counterfeit and pirated goods (OECD, 2019). All of this indicates that, at least for now, we still have to worry about how authenticity is inscribed in the physical world of things.

Coming from media studies, I started to question how we mediate authenticity, and as I mentioned, my interest in how we authenticate rapidly took on a historical scope. I noticed certain technical and aesthetic strategies used across time but, scanning my background, I recalled very few encounters with the topic and techniques of authentication. As I imagine is the case for many with a similar communications and media studies trajectory, the closest I came was trough Walter Benjamin's discussion of technological reproducibility and the aura, which does not really work once the object becomes a banknote rather than a painting, or even once the object becomes the painting's authentication certificate, rather than the painting itself. So I turned elsewhere: art history; theories of the copy; personal accounts of counterfeiters and those who tried to catch them; histories of printing, books, ephemera—and the list goes on. Also very helpful were historical accounts of figures and printers, which give us a wealth of information about how, why, and what it took to go from "mere" printer to *security* printer, or what was also called a printer of fine or luxury paper. Following the story of De La Rue (the world's largest security printer today) is a good example: the company began by printing a newspaper, in 1813, and gradually moved to the printing of playing cards, greeting cards, and eventually stamps, banknotes, and passports. The move came from an interest in printing well, with quality rather than quantity, and in developing new technologies and techniques—motivations which allow us to understand how making paper valuable, unique, and trustworthy became hallmarks for the production of authentic papers.

Ultimately the security printer develops a variety of devices that makes his paper "secure." As I noted, banknotes and passports are the most sophisticated objects produced by the industry of security printing and they are the ones for which we will develop, integrate, and introduce the newest techniques. Today these include advanced optical imaging using new forms of holography and nanotechnology, magnetic threads, or UV printing, on top of older strategies like microprinting, complex engravings, unique inks, watermarks, and substrates. So even though we don't tend to think of paper as a site of technological development (security printing itself is not an industry the general public knows much about), delving into the world of security printing is a real eye opener. Security printers for instance have their own R&D departments, which develop new features for their clients. I started thinking of these documents as "high-tech paper" to emphasize their perpetual technological newness, one which of course comes from the need to remain one step ahead of everyone else. Why is it that you and I can't reproduce our own passports or banknotes with our photocopier? We all know this to be the case—somehow we learn this early in childhood—and the reason is the material specificity of secure papers. So I started here, trying to understand what constitutes this specificity, and to then "translate" these technologies and the way they have been written about, for media scholarship. Using our histories, theories, and conceptual baggage, how do we, media scholars, address authentication, or what we could describe as the technologies and process of mediating authenticity from an institutional authority to a stored material inscription?

In the industry and labs that produce these technologies today, authenticating elements are commonly referred to as devices or features. A "feature" is a rather generic term, but a "device" describes a function and I thought could open up some more doors in terms of an analysis. I started working with this notion of the device primarily, even if I use it more broadly than a scientist might. One challenge however is that, interestingly, "device" (at least in English), has not been given the same pronounced analysis as other terms that refer to technologies—machine, tool, instrument, *dispositif,* apparatus, system, etc. What quickly became clear however is that the device is understood in relationship to its function, to what it *does,* and this made sense in the case I was interested in: the features are securing by assuring and mediating authenticity, trust, and value.

The concept of the device allows us to think about the many ways that authenticity is mediated. There are some techniques that are designed explicitly for this—microprinting for example. But if we think more broadly, an authentication device is also the *feel* of the paper that is used, the *quality* of the specimen. These are constituted through technologies of papermaking and printing. Historically the content has also been shown to play this role: for instance, in his recent *Banknotes and Shinplasters* (2020), Joshua Greenberg examines the thousands of specimen that circulated in the United States in the 19th C. He argues that one way that individuals could distinguish real notes from fake ones was through the images that were used: did an image make sense in the area that it was being used? For example, an image of Niagara Falls on a note produced in California makes little sense, and would trigger some suspicion. In such an instance, the choice of the image itself could work as an authenticating device. These days reproducing the content is not a reliable way of assessing veracity; what is however, is reproducing it *well,* with exactly the same techniques, tools, and skill. This is one way to explain the usually ornamental (i.e., complicated, finicky, fine) aesthetic produced by security printers, as is the layering or multiplicity of devices used on a singular document. It's worth noting here also that people today rarely bother *reading* the text in papers like banknotes, a point that was meant brilliantly by a recent case in Australia, where a note was released with a typo in the microprint that wasn't noticed for six months (BBC, 2019)!

In *Storing Authenticity at the Surface and into the Depths,* my aim was to present large categories of authentication devices based on how they can be read, or what we could call different layers of legibility. Devices that can be verified by a human reader are "at the surface," meaning that they can be fully assessed by the human senses. Devices with their authenticating information stored in such a way that it can only be read by a machine are "into the depths," which keeps authenticating information inaccessible or hidden to human senses. An example of this could be a biometric chip, like those found in some passports, which can be felt and maybe seen, but this sensory detection is not key to its function: rather, it works only when it is scanned and matched to a database entry, making convincing link. A third type of device works as a hybrid: information can be made sensible on the document itself to the human verifier, but only with the aid of a special reader. This is the case with UV printing, for example. Ultimately what this means is that authenticity is inscribed at many levels and layers, and unevenly accessible to different readers.

As well as becoming unevenly distributed, this process is also increasingly automated: when going to passport control, we are often now told to use a machine that will scan both our document and do a biometric reading. There are two things happening: the ID document is authenticated by the machine reader, and there is confirmation, through a biometric like the iris, that this passport belongs to this passport holder. This means that the passport could be authentic insofar as it is a genuine document produced by a state, but the person presenting the passport still has to prove, or identify, themself, as the rightful owner. The chip as authentication device thus works to both confirm the legitimacy of the passport and the passport holder, and is largely considered now as a decisive authentication device in passports. Devices like the chip also complicate the status of security papers as analog technologies: rather, we see that paper can be connected, inscribed with invisible and coded information, and digitally augmented.

The web is in part exciting because of the freedom people have there to be whoever they want to be, or choose to hide who they are, or change their persona from one day or site to the next. In many instances moments of identification are not tied up to any authenticating mechanism: at the surface at least, we can use a collection of avatars, usernames, and passwords for our pseudo-selves; fake names, birthdays, locations; and we know that is only the tip of the anonymous web's iceberg. Unfortunately, abuses to the system have often emphasized the dark side of anonymity with problems like trolling, catfishing, or deep fakes. Yes, these can be forensically discredited, but this kind of work is not accessible to the average web user. This is not to say that there are no authenticating mechanisms online: they are there, but not consistent: we could think of the verified accounts on Twitter or the requirement by Facebook to use our real name, secret questions, double-verification processes with an email or phone number, a connection to biometric information such as voice or fingerprint, or in official instances such as government sites, codes and confirmations sent to a physical address. Identity is so loose online, identification can only be meaningful if it is also authentication.

Your work highlights the transition from manual (humanly-readable/visual/tactile) to automated (computer-readable/covert/non-visual) identification techniques. How would you describe the cultural, political, and economical changes that this shift has brought about? What continuities and ruptures exist between analog and digital techniques for identifying content?

The automation of authentication—and by extension of identification—is part of the longer history of automation rooted in the technological shifts of modernity and Industrialization. It illustrates a desire for efficiency and expediency that underpins the logic and need for standardization and classification. It also illustrates our collective "decision" to trust machines, and not only that, to trust them more than we trust human judgment and the human senses, and thus each other. How do we assess the consequences of such a change? Does it matter that the things that used to mean something, like someone's word, have little value (or currency, to put it differently) today? Then again, as we usually tend to do, it is easy to make idealistic assumptions about the past, but there are more continuities than we might think.

One of the first texts I read that dealt with the history of banknotes and the problem of authenticating paper is "The Aesthetics of Authenticity: Printed Banknotes as Industrial Currency" by Frances Robertson, to which I have since returned many times. In it she writes about the moment of passage, in England, from metal coins to paper currency. The material and "public relations" challenge of paper was that, unlike coins, it was not perceived to have any intrinsic value (coins were in principle equivalent to their worth). Robertson goes on to analyze how value was created, and how, with the right techniques, paper currency would come to circulate legitimately and be recognized as such by the public. To make a long story short, one of the important techniques that was used, a hallmark of old currencies, was the geometric lathe pattern produced by the rose engine (these are the circular patterns that look like spirographs). Using a rose engine meant that patterns were made with "machine-like" precision, each one identical to the next. The ornate circles, which are still present on most currencies, had to be made by specific machines, and could not be produced otherwise. The result, Robertson argues, is that from this moment the public learns to shift their trust to the machine aesthetic (mechanically drawn and industrially reproduced)—the regularity of the machine-made form—replacing the trust once reserved for marks of individuals hands and craftsmanship. The expectation of precise repetition of forms allowed for comparison and evaluation, since noticing anomalies became an easier way to assess difference; with the handmade, anomalies made it impossible to evaluate whether the difference was within the accepted range of variation, or if it was evidence of an illicit reproduction. Identical copies beget standardized forms, which opens the door to automation.

Automated identification (through automated authentication of documents) has its consequences. For one, it leaves little room for abnormalities, circumstances that require a human sensibility, care, or empathy, and the possibility of making exceptions, or turning a blind eye. We have all been frustrated by bureaucratic systems, or bureaucrats themselves, that refuse to bend the rule, to open up a category, or to, we might think, use common sense or judgment. Automation doesn't care. Second, automation must be programmed, and programs like programmers, as we know, have biases. There are possibilities of discriminating "results" that, because they are produced by the "objective" machine, are hard to contest. This is being well documented these days in all the fantastic work on algorithmic bias. But to bring it back to the previous point, this is possible because of an ongoing "mechanical objectivity," as Peter Galison and Lorraine Daston memorably put it, a belief that machines are more trustworthy than human perception.

Secure papers use analog, digital, and hybrid authentication devices, and the distinctions are not always clear-cut. Even if they are experienced as analog (e.g. images that use nano-optical technologies have effects seen by the naked human eye), they are built using many digital machines and tools, their colour is produced very differently than printed images or holographs, and this is revealed, notably, when they are magnified. As this example shows, when dealing with paper thinking the differences between analog and digital devices in terms of categorical ruptures is tricky. I'm less interested in sorting devices as either analog or digital, than in discerning the continuities of the aesthetic logics of authentication devices across devices and through time: what are the overarching features of secure papers? What formal and aesthetic ideas have we been consistently working on and perfecting? Are these mutating or disappearing in digital environments? What are the material traits we invariably if unconsciously associate with "officialdom" and particularly official documents"? What insights can we glean from security printing that might apply to the challenges of digital security?

One such overarching principle I briefly noted already is ornamentation, or the ornamental quality that has long characterized official papers. While there are exceptions (such as the notable minimalism of Norway's 2017 banknote series), security printing has for the most part retained a 19th century aesthetic, what Finn Brunton describes as a "deliberate archaism of banknotes" (2019, p. 22). There are various ways to explain this, whether as a call back to the authority of history or an appeal to what is familiar—in any case, it is not worth undoing. Indeed, since individuals must know what a true document looks and feels like, it is useful to be able to draw on some longstanding characteristics. This is why, for example, American bills have always been printed on the same paper produced by the same papermaker. This paper is no longer the most sophisticated, but it is so recognizable, and so much associated with the "greenback" that no one dare change it … It just wouldn't feel right. The same goes for the particular green ink.

Another principle would be the camouflaging of information. This can happen in many ways, by making small or invisible. At the surface examples include microprinting (e.g., microtext or micro dots) or watermarks. A more recent hybrid device would include UV inks or some nano-optical features. Digital devices and encoded information are in a way all about hiding, so much so in fact that our human senses cannot reach the information. We can also note the strategies of matching halves and the cut, which are sometimes used together, but not always. This includes artefacts like indentured contracts and carbon copies, but also unofficial paper currencies that cut a designated paper. This was done with playing cards in the 17th century as a way to prove a transaction, and it continues to be a method communities draw on today. For instance, in the Gaspé region of Quebec, an unofficial currency called "la demi" ("the half") cuts in half official Canadian banknotes (halving their value by the sake token). These halves have no value outside of the communities that recognized "a half" as currency, those assuring that money circulated within, rather than out of, the local economy.

The signature is a good example of a device that teeters ambiguously across the analog-digital divide, and one that we still use widely to mark documents. It is a device that is or looks like the handwritten, and it generally accepted as an individual's marker and sign, even though a signature can be quite irregular in practice. The resilience of the signature as a trustworthy inscription is actually very impressive if we consider how unsecure it is: a forgery might not pass a forensic text, but probably neither would the signature we quickly squiggle on touchscreens, to name just one flagrant instance of common signature-distortion. There is much to be said on the signature, but let me just leave it here by noting that we still use unverified signatures in the digital realm even though we could use much more secure methods.

What we do know is that the human body, rather than, for instance, someone's word, has come to speak for us, and continues to do so, at times despite our own will. We can see this today in all the uses of biometric identification systems: whether it is using the fingerprint, iris, face, voice, gait, heartbeat—it is the body that identifies. This then can be used by states and institutions as a tight link, a guaranteed authentication mechanism between a body and the document it carries, but even more broadly, between a body and the data stored about that body. This is probably one of the main differences with machine-read information and assessment: that we do not necessarily know what information is stored about us and by whom. My bank, for example, now uses my voice to identify/authenticate me, yet I don't have a recollection of clearly consenting to this: one day I called and no longer had to go through the interminable identification process based on a series of questions. Rather, I was "benefitting" from the expediency of the voice recognition programme. But there are many ethical and legal questions raised by these tools, and we are only beginning to scratch the surface: what happens if my voice is deep-faked? Or if it used to determine I have a medical condition, which is then communicated to my insurance and my employer, among others? Or if it is manipulated in such a way to fake a condition? These aren't farfetched scenarios. A recent story on a biometric shoe insole that could be used to "record an individual's unique way of standing, walking, running, or gait" and then link this to their identity was described as potentially useful for "Health Insurance and Health Care providers, Corporate Security providers, Banking Service providers, Government and Military, as well as individuals and athletes" (Pivcevic, 2020; style in original). But why exactly would my bank want information about my gait? My body speaks for itself, but it might say more about me than I would like, and that, often, I am legally allowed to keep private. So if the body can't be trusted, and its data is used in illegitimate ways, how to maintain control over our identity and ourselves?

What would you say are the biggest political consequences of the shift from manual to automated ways of securing authenticity? What is at stake in the increased reliance on algorithmic and machine-assisted strategies of identification?

It is true that some automated forms of authentication are becoming increasingly important. The biometric chip in a passport is one such example. But it would not be entirely accurate to speak of a complete shift from manual to automated because the two continue to co-exist. In everyday life, most ID cards are not biometrically-augmented, but rather rely on human judgment. A store clerk might ask himself whether the photograph looks like the person standing in front of them, if they look to be the age indicated, if the card itself is a legitimate card, and all of this in a matter of seconds. There is a person making the decision, and this person could bend the rules or make mistakes, make things easier or more difficult. What machine-reading offers—for better or worse—is consistency, and this is in part why machines are "trustworthy". We can trust they will give us the same result each time since they are simply executing a protocol (more would have to be said for machine intelligences, but we will leave that for another discussion). Since there is still a public perception that information provided by machine-reading is neutral, impartial, and free of the machinations of human politics, we could say then that at stake in machine-automated identification is that the impression of consistency masks the humanness of a system that is written by people, using information they obtained, classified, deemed important, *etc.*, with all of their biases and subjective motivations, and within specific historical contexts and ideological frameworks. One dangerous outcome is that we lose the capacity to argue, evaluate, or assess outside of machine-based results, ultimately rendering us powerless in the face of the "judgment" provided by the machine. What if a machine hasn't been updated? What if there's a bug? What if it can't read me for whatever reason? What if it's mistaking me for someone else but I can't prove it? Rendering a decision is one thing but proving it is still another. Being able to prove or disprove who we are, to argue, explain, point out discrepancies, argue (in the sense of applying a logical argument) or appeal to human sensibility or empathy, these are perhaps some or the things at stake when we leave things up to automation.

In *Don't Copy That: Security Printing and the Making of High-Tech Paper* you argue for the need to study media technologies that "work to maintain and secure (social, political, economic) order." Elsewhere, you have also located authentication and identification techniques within the history of governance, management, and administrative logics. Could you expand on how you conceive the relation between identification technologies and administrative/bureaucratic rationalities? How do authentication devices tie in with broader historical efforts to organize, supervise, and index things/information?

The arguments I make around this build on the invaluable existing research that has mapped the co-evolution of identification practices and techniques with those of governance, management, and administrative logics. While identification documents are just one type of document I'm looking at, they function in a particular way, and one that, as we just mentioned, eventually leads to today's deployment of biometric devices. The important thing for me is not to rewrite or retell this story, but to understand it within the changing practices of authentication, and specifically in relation to the development of devices that are used to inscribe and communicate trust, value, and authenticity.

The story of Alphonse Bertillon is probably familiar to many of readers, but it is still worth mentioning here since it is an important contribution. Briefly, working as a clerk in a Paris police station at the turn of the 20th C, Bertillon developed a systematic way of identifying persons based on the anthropometrics, or the measurements, of their body. As Simon Cole recounts in his book on fingerprinting *Suspect Identities* (2002), Bertillon was trying to solve an administrative problem: in a world that has yet to issue identification documents to all of its citizens, how do we keep track of prisoners, and especially recidivists? The system in place at the time was to organise prisoners' files by name, but names are changed on a whim if there is no document to prove otherwise. The result was the same individuals kept coming back, creating a new name, and thus requiring a new file, each time. Bertillon's idea to link the identity to the body would characterize an individual based on a set of data that could be compared against the data of all those on record. This is a very managerial way of understanding and classifying individuals, around a certain set of measurable facts, and it is the same logic that is used today. Bureaucracies need efficient, standardized, and preferably automated modes of verification: things like narratives, family connections, or someone's word require time and a case-by-case approach, all in a technological environment that precisely seeks to eliminate human judgement and assessment. With time, we have become used to being identified by numbers, and to being treated accordingly. Having chips embedded in our bodies by our employer is becoming an increasingly small leap to make. And this is just one example of how we have completely bought into a desire for efficiency, especially when tied to productivity.

We know, however, that the administrative world can also be frustratingly inefficient, and this often correlates with paper-based systems. It would seem few professions have clung to paper and the human signature as much as law and real estate (Graham, 2020). Sign here, initialize there, and please do so in triple sets, each original copies, etc. So we live very much in a hybrid world, one where we can pay our taxes online, and have our faces scanned at airports, but also where, as we saw recently in the US, we must sign a mail-in voting ballot, or physically go to a notary to sign paper documents.

There are also many, many, other kinds of organizational systems that rely on identification and authentication technologies. Infrastructures of global circulation monitor the movement of goods from point A to point B, from seller to buyer, so that the right things arrive at the right place. Goods particularly affected by counterfeiting such as medical supplies, brand name luxury products, cigarettes, or electronics, need to maintain the value of their products. As they pass through verification points such as ports, which are part of the logistical systems of global shipping, containers with goods are scanned to check their contents, or a tag might be scanned to check the history of all previous verification/scan points, thus being able to verify that this container has indeed followed the rightful trajectory. Ultimately the goal is to make sure that the container is not full of dupes.

In *Storing Authenticity at the Surface and into the Depths,* you talk about the importance of "biographical pedigree" that are included in devices such as RFID tags. Do you see pedigree as being a more current, maybe more and more dominant, criterion for authenticity? How would you locate emergent technologies such as blockchain projects within the longer genealogy of authentication devices?

It's interesting that you phrase your question around an idea of pedigree being potentially more current. In the sense that I used the term I had in mind rather the modern European towns and villages Valentin Groebner writes about this in his fantastic book *Who Are You?: Identification, Deception, and Surveillance in Early Modern Europe* (2007), which would have us think the pedigree as a return to something past. As he points out, in such settings a person's identity could be vouched by someone already known to the community, or they could be identified as someone's family member. This was proof enough. But as one travelled and needed to be granted passage through each village, they had to show documents which would identify them and justify their trip. Only once this was approved would they be granted passage (this could take the form of a letter that itself communicated authenticity—the precursor of the passport).

In the context of a village, then, people could know who everyone is, or at least know who was in which family. Someone's profession could also play such an identifying role—Groebner for instance notes that people's clothes could be more pertinent than their face since this is what identified them as merchants or tradespersons of specific goods, and this is what was considered the most significant identifying information. So by biographical pedigree I have in mind this information about someone's life that becomes used to make sense of who they are—their relations, where they are from, what they did or do—in a way that, in a given moment in time, was considered identification enough.

If we were to place blockchains as part of an overarching strategy of authentication, perhaps they could be thought, in a broad sense, as also constituted and vetted through their past or "life story," in the sense of being built and affirmed with each recorded transaction. This is not unlike a notion of pedigree, where the record of ancestry provides credibility. These constitutive records that depend on each other are perhaps analogous to our families, neighbours, or communities vetting for us. In other words, in such systems we are entangled with others and become less trustworthy when we are free agents.

You show that authentication devices have to be secretive and partly situated outside of public scrutiny to be efficient, yet at the same time there needs to be a global trust without which they can't fulfil their mission. How do you think the production of trust has evolved with the materiality of authentication devices? And is there a space for an ethnographic study of the production of trust through technology?

That's a very interesting question. Trust is, as we've been mentioning, essential in the enterprise of identifying and authenticating. If we return to the beginning, surface devices allow each person to evaluate what is passing through their hands. This is what is called the "first level assessment"—the public's ability to assess whether the authenticating device is legitimate. With time, as counterfeiters catch up with techniques, issuers of secure papers have had to introduce new devices and educate the public accordingly. If we consider trust as an outcome of the material qualities of secure paper, then the public needs to understand the authentication devices used in these papers and how to assess them.

For banknotes and passports, it is the government's job to teach us about new devices and how to evaluate them. They produce brochures and websites that teach us what to look for. Importantly though, only a small subset of devices is revealed to the public, while the rest is meant for specific readers. Some devices are made known only to particular evaluators—bank tellers, or passport control officers, for example. There are also devices that are just for the issuers themselves. This is the layer that is difficult to research in real time. If we return to the discussion on machine reading however, we are already aware that certain elements are no longer fully known to us, and this in itself perhaps fuels mistrust: not mistrust in the authenticity of the document, but mistrust in the institution itself.

How do we study, and can we even study, the production of trust through technology? Turning back to documents provides some historical clues about how trust was built to begin with. Security printing indeed emerged from a need to create paper that would be trusted by the public, that would be considered valuable. As we shifted from coins to paper in the 19th century, people had to be convinced a material they considered to be flimsy, quotidian, banal—paper—could be worth something. Out of this need offshoots a whole branch of the printing industry, one interested in creating perfect, genuine, and innovative paper things. These were the qualities that came to stand in for trustworthy, official paper. This was "fine" paper that was materially and sensorially *different* than the newspaper or the paper used to wrap groceries. A historical approach brings out the ongoing principles or logics that are used by security printers to produce trust. I mentioned a few examples here with principles like quality and material specificity, and strategies like ornamentation, concealment, cuts, and halves. To what extent to these continue to function as authenticating mechanisms, in and outside of the paper realm?

There are limits to what we can access about the present of security printing, but this does not make it impossible to study. The industry is secretive, but it still has a presence. Some security printers have websites that provide a wealth of information, not because they giveaway their technical secrets, but because they present a world of concerns that has been largely under-examined in media scholarship. Through these sites we can enter into the discourse of security printing and we immediately get a sense of the challenges and objectives that have to be met. We see how devices are being positioned and marketed, the rhetoric that is used, where emphasis is given—and the whole purpose of this messaging is to convince the reader that the end-result are technologies of trust and security. This is of course just one kind of work that can be done, and scholars from a number of disciplines are looking at how official documents are made to function authoritatively. I also highly recommend Anna Weichselbraun's work on the production of trust. As an anthropologist she did indeed do a year-long ethnography at the International Atomic Energy Agency as an intern in the Department of Safeguards. She examines the security seals, the inspector's manual, and other documents that outline protocol to understand how security, trust, knowledge, and expertise are configured across relationships between people and things (2019). These are just a few examples, but they do indicate I hope that there are ways to research the production of trust through technologies, even though this often occurs in ways and places that are opaque. Perhaps this is precisely why we should find ways to examine and think about the things that we trust.

In *The Intrinsic Value of Valuable Paper* you discuss how authentication devices are not just defined by what they can do (monitoring and securing identities etc.) but also by how they are *used* and integrated into circulatory systems (and used to safeguard law, for example). Are uses of authentication devices always related to the state apparatus or do you also observe other groups or institutions utilizing them? There is of course the case being made for markets of "surveillance capitalism," but is there also a space to think about more decentralized or grassroots initiatives trying to harness security and/or identification tools?

The need for authentication goes well beyond the state. Branding, especially for luxury goods and sports apparel, is the biggest source of counterfeiting. Medical supplies, electronic products, and in general consumer goods or production parts are all major targets for counterfeiters. Cities like Shenzhen have become famous for their ability to produce fakes, so it is no surprise that brand protection—and the quality, standards, and reputation that go with it—is a big area for security printers. Authentication devices are also used in official documents not issued by states. Certificates fall into this category, and include everything from education degrees to authentication certificates for sports memorabilia or artworks. In these cases, not entirely differently than the passport, the document that authenticates exists as separate from its object, and it must be able to validate itself, as well as the particular object to which it refers. This is by no mean a failproof method, and there is perhaps a future for authentication devices embedded in objects themselves, just as we do with biometrics. Perhaps we will have authenticating threads within the very canvas of a painting: we wouldn't need to analyze the work forensically or to rely on a certificate, because a quick machine read of the device, integrated into the material composition of the work, would provide the proof and information needed. This is entirely speculative, but not impossible!

Real security printing, with the most current technology, is an expensive endeavour probably inaccessible to most grassroots initiatives. But this does not mean the same basic strategies of authentication cannot be applied. If we look at communities that develop their own currency, as I mentioned above, we see how they come to produce *something* that can be circulated with trust. At the heart of this is an agreement. And this could be anything. This is true of everything I've discussed: we as a community or a society decide what it is that we trust and what it is we consider authentic—it starts with an agreement.

Disclosure statement

No potential conflict of interest was reported by the authors.

References

BBC News. (2019, May 9). *Typo on millions of Australian bank notes*. https://www.bbc.com/news/world-australia-48210733

Brunton, F. (2019). *Digital cash: The unknown history of the anarchists, utopians, and technologists who created cryptocurrency*. Princeton University Press.

Cole, S. A. (2002). *Suspect identities: A history of fingerprinting and criminal identification*. Harvard University Press.

Demirgüç-Kunt, A., Klapper, L., Singer, D., Ansar, S., & Hess, J. (2018). *The global findex database 2017: Measuring financial inclusion and the fin-tech revolution*. World Bank. https://doi.org/10.1596/978-1-4648-1259-0

Graham, D. A. (2020, October 21). Signed, sealed, delivered—Then discarded. *The Atlantic*. https://www.theatlantic.com/ideas/archive/2020/10/signature-matching-is-the-phrenology-of-elections/616790/

Groebner, V. (2007). *Who are you?: Identification, deception, and surveillance in Early Modern Europe*. M. Kyburz & J. Peck (Trans.). Zone Books.

OECD. (2019, March 18). Trade in fake goods is now 3.3% of world trade and rising. *OECD Newsroom*. https://www.oecd.org/newsroom/trade-in-fake-goods-is-now-33-of-world-trade-and-rising.htm

Pivcevic, K. (2020, December 11). Biometric shoe insole provides new way to measure health-insights. *Biometric Update*. https://www.biometricupdate.com/202012/biometric-shoe-insole-provides-new-way-to-measure-health-insights

Weichselbraun, A. (2019). Of broken seals and broken promises: Attributing intention at the IAEA. *Cultural Anthropology*, *34*(4), 503–528. https://doi.org/10.14506/ca34.4.02

Section IV

Methods

The historical trajectories of algorithmic techniques: an interview with Bernhard Rieder

Michael Stevenson and Anne Helmond

ABSTRACT
Bernhard Rieder is Associate Professor of New Media and Digital Culture at the University of Amsterdam and a collaborator with the Digital Methods Initiative. His research focuses on the history, theory and politics of software and in particular on the role algorithms play in social processes and in the production of knowledge and culture. This includes work on the analysis, development, and application of computational research methods as well as investigation into the political and economic challenges posed by large online platform. In this interview, Michael Stevenson (MS) and Anne Helmond (AH) talk to Bernhard Rieder (BR) about his forthcoming book entitled *Engines of Order: A Mechanology of Algorithmic Techniques* (University of Amsterdam Press, 2020). In particular, Rieder discusses how the practice of software-making is "constantly faced with the 'legacies' of previous work" and how the past continues to operate into present algorithmic techniques.

Bernhard Rieder is Associate Professor of New Media and Digital Culture at the University of Amsterdam and a collaborator with the Digital Methods Initiative.[1] His research focuses on the history, theory and politics of software and in particular on the role algorithms play in social processes and in the production of knowledge and culture. This includes work on the analysis, development, and application of computational research methods as well as investigation into the political and economic challenges posed by large online platform. In this interview,[2] Michael Stevenson (MS) and Anne Helmond (AH) talk to Bernhard Rieder (BR) about his forthcoming book entitled *Engines of Order: A Mechanology of Algorithmic Techniques* (University of Amsterdam Press, 2020). In particular, Rieder discusses how the practice of software-making is "constantly faced with the 'legacies' of previous work" and how the past continues to operate into present algorithmic techniques.

MS & AH: First of all, congratulations on completing your book! If the pre-publication buzz on Twitter is any indication, this book will certainly find a large audience in Media Studies and beyond, and deservedly so. The book is also of particular interest to readers of *Internet Histories*, as it historicizes the various recommendation systems and other information ordering devices that are so central to Internet culture and the impact of new media and computational systems on society.

Importantly, the book focuses on a class of objects that you call "algorithmic techniques," which is distinguished from, say, specific ranking algorithms used for a search engine or social media platform. Before we turn to the connections between the book and our special issue on "Legacy Systems," could you walk us through this concept and discuss why it represents an important object for media scholars (and in particular historians of media and technology) to address? Could you tell us how this perspective is both different from contemporary critiques of "algorithmic bias" and can perhaps inform these debates from a different angle?

BR: Thanks! And yes, the concept of "algorithmic technique" is really central to the book and an attempt to find a way to deal with the increasingly sophisticated technologies that surround us. Let's face it, computers and software are incredibly complex, but we need some way of achieving a robust critical understanding of how something like Google's search engine or Facebook's newsfeed actually works. We can go some way towards this by scrutinizing their results for bias or by critically assessing how these mechanisms reflect the balancing acts these companies must play as "platforms" that mediate between users, content producers, and advertisers. But the technical principles at work should not be ignored and that is where the concept of algorithmic technique comes in. It takes some of its cues from Simondon's work and starts from the question how to conceive the "substance" of technology and, in particular, its "units". This sounds a bit complicated, but in the end, it is an attempt to find a middle ground between very broad categories such as computation or artificial intelligence on the one side and concrete programs or systems on the other.

The concept also aligns itself with technical practice and the relationship between technical knowledge and concrete material artifacts: if you open a textbook on machine learning or look at a programming library like Python's scikit-learn, what you will find is not some singular principle, but a whole range of techniques – from Bayes classifiers to neural nets – that do broadly similar things but which have their own "character", advantages and disadvantages, performance characteristics, and so forth. These techniques often have their own histories and draw on different heuristics and concepts. They have been laid out in scientific papers, studied, improved upon, tested, measured, and dissected. But they are still "broad" in the sense that there are variations, parameters, different ways to prepare inputs and outputs, and so forth. When a developer builds an actual system – and this is very much the situation the book thinks about – they will draw on existing techniques and associated knowledge, but they will then embed them within a working system, adapt and tune them, surround them with many other components that draw on their own historical lineages.

I hope that thinking about algorithmic techniques, their historical trajectories, and central characteristics helps media scholars take a step closer to what information and computer scientists are actually putting into the world, without having to fully engage the extremely detailed and specialized meanderings of the full research landscape. There are thousands of research papers dedicated to describing, prodding, or extending the Bayes classifier, a simple machine learning technique that has been around for almost 60 years, and there are thousands of implementations that are used in all kinds of settings (see Rieder, 2017). It would be hard to engage all of this in detail, but there are certain basic characteristics that allow us to develop an understanding of what actually hides behind a loaded term like "artificial intelligence" in a way that is not a caricature. And from there we can develop a more nuanced appreciation of what something like "algorithmic bias" could look like and what kinds of effects it could have as part of a larger system. Simondon had the idea that machines "signify" by what they do (Simondon 2017), that they have meaning through their function or operation and the notion of algorithmic technique is maybe first and foremost an attempt to make that more broadly readable, to develop a conceptual vocabulary to talk more concretely about what machines do and how they do it.

MS & AH: How is the study of algorithmic techniques, in combination with Simondon's philosophy, distinguished from the search for basic or even universal principles of computation that give us a broad understanding of its effects, an effort that seems to stem from formalist media theory a la McLuhan? For example, your book could be understood in some sense as a critical response to the likes of Lev Manovich's earlier work on *The Language of New Media* (Manovich 2001), while closely aligning with Manovich's later work *Software Takes Command* (Manovich 2013). Perhaps this question can also be seen as an invitation to elaborate on how you build on the concept of "cultural techniques" (Siegert, 2013)?

BR: In a certain sense, Simondon's idea of functional meaning that I just laid out is kind of a "the medium is the message"-style call to pay attention to the material properties of contemporary technology, even if social effects are certainly not its main concern – also because technology is seen as a constitutive part of the human adventure, a type of expression rather than some kind of outside force that operates through "effects". And crucial to that idea is that technology is a constructive and cumulate affair rather than a singular logic or *techne*. It is not a tree that splits into branches, but a forest that has many different trees, some thin, some thick, some small and bushy, others growing on top of other trees. When we look at the sprawling landscape of algorithmic techniques – and the book only discusses a small selection from the subfield of information ordering – we can appreciate that all of this is made possible by the very fact that mechanical computation exists, while recognizing that there is no way to bind everything that has been happening in computing over the last 70+ years to that basic fact. Proust's *À la recherche du temps perdu* cannot be explained by the existence of the French language. And I think that the realization that looking at computational foundations is useful but ultimately far too little to understand what has been built out of it has always been a central part of Manovich's work. For the technical practitioner – and he is one – it is almost impossible not to marvel at the vast reservoirs of *stuff* that have been built by millions of people on top of computation. His earlier work is certainly still a more classic inventory of interface forms and key principles and, in that sense, less clearly marked by a resistance to foundationalism than his more recent writings. But there has always been an attention to variation, I believe, and a desire to think about what makes the forms and functions we see on the screen possible. *Software Takes Command* (2013) indeed looks at a more demarcated space – what Manovich calls "cultural software" and no longer just "new media" – and the inventory of forms and principles necessarily becomes more detailed and specific. Simondon's long passages on the particularities of diodes and triodes come to mind, but indeed also the German cultural techniques tradition, which has always been interested in the many procedures and technicities that run through everyday life. What connects all of these efforts, my own included, is what Siegert calls a preference for "empirical historical objects" over "philosophical idealization" (Siegert, 2013, p.10). Again with an eye on Simondon, one could say that this locates the "substance" of both culture and technology not in some underlying principles, but in the massive webs of relationality that have been spun on top of whatever base layer of being there may be. Anti-platonism is one way to label this, but within media theory it basically means that we exchange McLuhan's classic inventory of media "verticals" for a transversal and increasingly integrated media landscape where all kinds of techniques produce all kinds of visible and invisible forms and functions, and software developers build new things out of old stuff, new stuff gets invented, and so forth.

MS & AH: We often conflate today's "engines of order" with a kind of neo-Enlightenment: the history of digital culture is littered with objects and ideas that carry more than a whiff of the "Universal Language" that Borges (2000) famously lampooned and Florian Cramer (2007) identified as a tendency in certain semantic web search initiatives. In addition to Ted Nelson's Xanadu, we could think of Wikipedia or even Julian Assange's notion of "scientific journalism" as interesting real and imagined examples of how digital culture extends the political liberalism and positivist epistemology associated with the Enlightenment. However your book – in addition to being much more careful in its historiography than this short interview format allows – shows us that this conflation obscures a very different epistemology operating within the research labs of today's search and social media companies. Could you talk about your specific interest in "information ordering" as a set of algorithmic techniques that developed outside of public libraries and how this relates to the rise of a different set of epistemological commitments, one that underlies much of the infrastructure for the data-intensive, algorithmic media we use today?

BR: Yes, this is spot on and a really important problem, I think. One of the points I am trying to make in the book is indeed that there are all kinds of epistemological stances and commitments within the information ordering space and computing in general. Conceptually, I am drawing quite a bit on well-known work, here: Hacking (1990) talks about different "styles of reasoning" in science, Desrosières (2001) lists four possible "attitudes" toward the "reality" of statistics, and Hjørland (2011) argues that we can distinguish rationalist, empiricist, hermeneutical, or critical "theories of knowledge" in information science, even if these positions are not often clearly fleshed out. These authors do not necessarily talk about the same things, but they are all sensitive to the variety of epistemological commitments we can find in technical or scientific disciplines. In the book, I dedicate much space to early information retrieval and its pretty fundamental opposition to the library tradition. Interestingly, this story does not pit "literary librarians" against "positivist scientists", but rather the universalist positivism of the public library, very much tied to the Enlightenment tradition, against what you could call an empiricist perspectivism that eschews universalism and installs efficient decision-making in its stead. Practically, this means that early information retrieval techniques based on simple boolean keyword matching, such as coordinate indexing, are not evaluated in terms of whether they correspond to some universalist ideal, but rather through empirical tests and competitions that measures some kind of "retrieval performance" against other systems and human experts. If you look at sites like Kaggle (bought by Google in 2017), you can easily see that this basic evaluative setup – as well as measures like recall and precision – continue to structure the wider information ordering field. If one wants to describe this as "rationalist" or "positivist", why not, but it is not a Chomsky-style rationalism based on some logic-driven univer-salist ontology. People like Stephen Wolfram certainly fit that description, but I would argue that fields like information retrieval and machine learning have been dominated by output- and performance-driven thinking that has (maybe) surprisingly little interest in ontological concerns.

Whether Google's machine translation system "understands" human language is simply much less relevant than the various measures of user "satisfaction" the company can derive from its interface and other forms of practical evaluation. I think that we really underappreciate how important that difference is. I still often read that informing all of these efforts is some kind of Laplacian determinism that imagines a computational universe where everything can be known and predicted given the right technique. I would guess that very few people in the field actually think that way, but in the end, it is really not very relevant. What is much more important is that the prevalence of computational infrastructures – think online platforms – make it easy to submit every algorithmic decision, from ranking to recommendation to price modula-tion, to some kind of empirical test. Do users click on the ad I put on the screen? Do they buy the product? Do they pay back the loan? Again, there are different epistemo-logical strands running through computing and stuff like the Semantic Web could indeed be seen as a continuation of the library project; but what Desrosières calls "accounting realism" (2001), where truth is simply a function of performance, seems to be what is really dominating at the moment. It is all about practical outcomes, "solving problems", and so forth, pretty much in line with the morally and intellectually unambitious utilitarianism we have come to know so well.

MS & AH: For this special issue we have taken the concept of "legacy systems" out-side of its industry and computer science contexts to try and think through the inter-section of key themes in Internet histories research – continuity and discontinuity, the materiality of ostensibly immaterial digital production, the productive and creative practices enabled by "old" systems and the way these systems may also constrain future action, the question of how disappeared technologies continue to operate into the future at a cultural, economic, and social level, and so on. We would like to invite you to play with this concept – in particular we wonder how you might theorize or redefine legacy systems (from its original technical sense) within the framework you offer in your book. How does the concept relate to the kinds of accumulation and concretization of software technologies that you discuss? It seems that the hybrid systems you describe at times (e.g., that combine traditional library cataloging and information retrieval) could also offer a perspective. And much more speculatively, could you imagine a situation in which the information ordering techniques that you analyze themselves become legacy systems? What does history tell us about the possibility for some new schema that makes us reassess or doubt the value of the various algorithmic techniques at the center of your book?

BR: This question can be approached from different directions, but one way would be to start with the notion of "abstraction". In a software context, it basically means building function on top of function, like when higher level programming languages package a series of underlying operations into a single command. For example, most programming languages already come with the capacity to retrieve data from a remote server quickly and easily, "hiding" a lot of complicated network stuff from the programmer. One can lament, à la Kittler (1997), the loss of direct access to the underlying "hard stuff", but the fact is that modern development environments make it possible to do a lot of things very quickly, because of the layers of abstraction – or accumulated functionality – they sit on top of. Almost every piece of software is already a hybrid in that sense, tying together various elements that each have their own temporal trajectories.

Software-making is thus constantly faced with the "legacies" of previous work: since we necessarily build on top of other things, our space of expression is both *widened* and *structured* by what came before. Widened, because we can rely on other people's work, which is not just convenient, but allows us to integrate function that we would not be able to program ourselves – think about complex "mathy" stuff like machine learning, but also heavy "plumbing" like operating systems, network stacks, or database management systems. Structured, because all of that stuff we build upon comes with its own capabilities, idiosyncrasies, and ways of doing. I spend so much time on the book on these questions, because the information ordering techniques I discuss in the second part *have already become* hugely important legacies in that sense. The relational database model, for example, is still the standard way of thinking about data organization and access not just because it's a pretty powerful idea, but because the systems that implement it – from Oracle to Postgres – are everywhere. Every webhoster includes some MySQL storage in even the most basic bundle, every WordPress installation runs on top of it, every web developer knows how to use it, and so forth. Sure, there is new stuff around the margins, e.g., NoSQL databases that trade query power and consistency for speed, but so much of the technology we build upon today is really old, despite the constant improvements and enhancements Simondon calls "concretization" (Simondon 2017). Every new version of a programming language brings some new features, some performance enhancements, and maybe some stuff breaks somewhere down the line. And because some of that stuff is so ingrained, it can be hard to steer away – the concept of path dependence, which holds that past choices continue to structure future possibilities, applies particularly well to computing. This does not mean that things that were broadly adopted at one point never disappear, but most often it is some kind of rotting away as the version numbers climb.

HTML and JavaScript, for example, kind of trod along, newer pages starting to break on older browsers and vice versa. Flash would still be with us if Apple had not decided to kill it. But only megacorps like Apple, Google, or Microsoft have the power to intervene that hard in what is generally a rather steady stream, despite the constant buzzing at the margins. But make no mistake, these companies are certainly trying to pull that stream into their direction.

But there is really no regularity to these processes and this makes historical work so important: continuity and discontinuity emerge in complicated ways that sometimes have technological reasons, sometimes economic ones, and sometimes they come out of the haphazard work of some standards committee or some freak coincidence. But once established, technologies can echo through the decades and in computing almost everything is at least in part a legacy system.

MS & AH: In your book you take a software-building view to write a history of important software-making practices that have defined contemporary Internet-enabled services. If indeed "software is eating the world" (Andreessen, 2011) you ask the important question of how this software has been developed and which fundamental ideas and techniques have been built into it. You argue that a key starting point to explore this is to understand "software as historically accumulated archive of technical possibilities and of software-making as technical creation" (Rieder, 2020: p. 37). Software is seen as an assemblage of techniques and of old and new building blocks and ideas. A central tool in current web and app development is the employment of so-called software development kits (SDKs) which consist of reusable development tools libraries and as such provide predefined ways to develop applications. If most of such tools for building mobile apps or apps for social media platforms are offered by a single company (e.g., Facebook, Twitter, Google, Apple), then are we experiencing the platformization of app production? Additionally, as these companies retain control over when and how apps should be updated, are we witnessing an update culture where legacy systems and techniques have become impossible?

BR: In one way, this is not really new. Big companies – IBM and Microsoft in particular – have always exerted some level of control over what runs on their systems and stuff regularly stopped working for one reason or another. But the last ten years have certainly exacerbated the situation considerably and in new ways. As I said, making software always means relying on other people's work and that is not necessarily a bad thing. But the companies you mention now indeed provide building blocks that bind programs, integrating them into close and continuous relationships that can be severed at any time. These relationships certainly include technical provisions like SDKs, but the main element is platform access and how it is controlled. In the case of Facebook (excluding Oculus) and Twitter, this mostly concerns the possibility to tap into their social graphs in one way or another and the point of control are the web APIs and the legal frameworks that surround them. If you built a social game on Facebook's infrastructure some years ago and the company decided that it wants to move into another direction, that is it. That stuff is gone. In the case of Android and iOS (and Oculus), it is even more complicated since we are talking about full-fledged operating systems that are tied to both hardware and the app store model in complicated ways. The first problem is that it is pretty hard to just install a different operating system on these devices. You have alternative Android distributions, sure, but real top-to-bottom alternatives like Sailfish OS are hard to install and pretty limited. Huawei's HarmonyOS is a wildcard, but China always is.

Going back to the previous questions, we can say that in the context of smartphones, what developers can technically build on is provided and controlled by two companies. One is locked down further than the other, but building an alternative SDK for Android – which would be possible to an extent – is not trivial at all. And then we have the distribution model, the app store. For Android, you again have some more choice, F-Droid for example, but in both cases, there is a dominant way to get software on the device and this is not just coercion. These stores hide distribution and payment behind an abstraction layer and provide access to huge markets. So what these companies offer – and both MacOS and Windows are moving in the same direction – is a combination of carrot and stick that is hard to pass on. The consequence is what you point out: a fundamentally asymmetric relationship, where software-makers have to constantly adapt to technical changes, but also to changes in legal arrangements, in "norms" concerning e.g., sexuality or special provisions for kids, in marketing practices and visibility on the app store, and so forth. In that situation, a lot of stuff is just going to stop working for one reason or another.

Maybe what is needed is a new form of "unbundling" – that term refers to the 1960s, when IBM, under investigation from regulators, started to charge separately for hardware and software, creating a space for an emerging software industry. But given the size of these companies and the current climate of eroding international cooperation, it is hard to imagine how this could be pushed through. At the same time, there seems to be a growing willingness to consider these issues in thinking about antitrust measures and this is a reason to be at least a little optimistic.

From a preservation perspective concerned with "future histories", there is no one-size-fits-all solution to these problems. In some cases, keeping the old hardware around will work and emulation has certainly come a far way – this could even keep iOS software running when it is no longer available on the app store. But what about software that has a social component or runs on some proprietary network architecture? Walkthrough videos, screenshots, oral history projects, or data dumps like Twitter's (shaky) agreement with the Library of Congress may be the best to hope for here. Research papers dealing with the present will become sources for future generations. Historians have always dealt with imperfect archives and the ravages of time and, at the risk of sounding callous, what a society cares to preserve and what not is a first finding.

MS & AH: At the beginning and end of the book you discuss Simondon's argument that as societies we must prioritize "technical culture" more than we currently do, and you also call for a "widening of technical imagination." It seems these are points on which a broad set of histories of computing and digital culture can really build on your work.

BR: Yes, the related concepts of technical culture and technical imagination have been really inspirational. Just to be clear, this is not the "digital skills" type of thinking and certainly not limited to the push for programming education we are currently seeing in many different areas. These efforts are not detrimental either, but what

Simondon imagines when he talks about technical culture is a much broader consideration of technology as a central part of human life. This is very much a debate about the general knowledge – *culture générale* in French – a technological society needs to govern itself democratically. A broad understanding of technical principles and how they connect to the spaces and things around them is more important here than the "how-to" component. If you take something like a smartphone, there are many different elements to take into account, including the hardware and the different sensors that define the basic computational capacities, the layering of software, the networking capabilities and how they enable the myriad data flows that go in and out of the device at any second. But also things like the app store logic, the role of advertisement, and the data collection that informs business models. And not to forget the many life-cycle aspects that range from rare earth mining to energy use, waste production, and the planned obsolescence that remains prevalent in the industry. A sensitivity for potential social and environmental effects are part of this as well. Technical imagination is then the capacity to think creatively in these spaces, to come up with new ideas, but also to think about alternatives, limitations, and different ways of looking at things. Free software (and hardware) and civic technology are examples for areas where these sensitivities are given room, but ecological movements such as zero waste, circular economy, off-grid living, or even tiny houses also cultivate relationships with technology that are very attentive to the many connections between technical principles, modes of living, and systematic effects. I am not saying that these movements are going to solve the ecological catastrophes we are facing, but they show pathways towards fighting the alienation that comes from living surrounded by technical objects and systems that we neither control nor understand.

One of the things I emphasize in the book is technological pluralism and that not only means highlighting the differences in epistemological stances or commitments observable in computing, but also to plead for broader forms of education or, more generally, a clearer recognition that different approaches to computing are both possible and desirable. And this is where historiography comes in. Looking at the complex and often weird histories that have been unfolding around computing and other "digital" stuff not only sharpens our sense for contingency, but is also a pretty interesting way to learn about the substance and relational embedding of technologies. Writing a history of HTML, HTTP cookies, or Flash, for example, requires quite a bit of technical understanding and readers of such works inevitably learn about the technical underpinnings of the web, about the different forces that shaped them, and about the spaces of variation that opened and closed. Historiographical work that is attentive to technical principles is, in my view, both an example and a vehicle for technical culture.

Notes

1. More about Bernhard Rieder's publications and work can be found at: http://the-politicsofsystems.net/ and https://www.uva.nl/profiel/r/i/b.rieder/b.rieder.html.
2. The interview was conducted between December 2019 and January 2020.

Disclosure statement

No potential conflict of interest was reported by the authors.

Funding

This work is part of the research programme Innovational Research Incentives Scheme Veni with project numbers 275-45-006 and 275-45-009, which are (partly) financed by the Dutch Research Council (NWO).

References

Andreessen, M. (2011, August 20). Why software is eating the world. *The Wall Street Journal.* http://online.wsj.com/news/articles/SB10001424053111903480904576512250915629460.

Borges, J. L. (2000). John Wilkins' analytical language. In E. Weinberger (Ed.), E. Allen & S. J. Levine (Trans.), Selected non-fictions, (pp. 229–231). New York, NY: Penguin.

Cramer, F. (2007, December 18). Critique of the "semantic web". Retrieved from http://www. nettime.org/Lists-Archives/nettime-l-0712/msg00043.html

Desrosières, A. (2001). How real are statistics? Four possible attitudes. *Social Research, 68*(2), 339–355.

Hacking, I. (1990). *The taming of chance.* Cambridge, UK: Cambridge University Press. doi:10. 1086/ahr/97.1.157

Hjørland, B. (2011). The importance of theories of knowledge: Indexing and information retrieval as an example. *Journal of the American Society for Information Science and Technology, 62*(1), 72–77. doi:10.1002/asi.21451

Kittler, F. A. (1997). There is no software. In J. Johnston (Ed.), *Literature, media, information systems: essays* (pp. 147–155). Amsterdam: Overseas Publishers Association.

Manovich, L. (2001). *The language of new media.* Cambridge, MA: MIT Press.

Manovich, L. (2013). *Software takes command.* New York, NY: Bloomsbury Academic.

Rieder, B. (2017). Scrutinizing an algorithmic technique: The Bayes classifier as interested reading of reality. *Information, Communication & Society, 20*(1), 100–117. doi:10.1080/1369118X.2016.1181195

Rieder, B. (2020). *Engines of order: A mechanology of algorithmic techniques.* Amsterdam: University of Amsterdam Press.

Siegert, B. (2013). Cultural techniques: Or the end of the intellectual postwar era in German media theory. *Theory, Culture & Society, 30*(6), 48–65. doi:10.1177/0263276413488963

Simondon, G. (2017). *On the mode of existence of technical objects* (C. Malaspina and J. Rogove, Trans). Minneapolis: Univocal Publishing.

Internet histories and computational methods: a "round-doc" discussion

Niels Brügger, Ian Milligan, Anat Ben-David, Sophie Gebeil, Federico Nanni, Richard Rogers, William J. Turkel, Matthew S. Weber and Peter Webster

ABSTRACT

This conversation brings together leading experts within the field of computational methods. Participants were invited to discuss "Internet histories and computational methods", and the debate focused on issues such as why scholars of internet histories should consider using computational methods, what scholars should be looking out for when they use these methods, how the process of collecting influences computational research, what impedes the use of computational methods, to what an extent internet historians should learn to code (or conversely, if developers should learn about historical methods), what are the most defining moments in the history of computational methods, and, finally, the future of using computational methods for historical studies of the internet.

As editors of the "Internet histories and computational methods" special issue of *Internet Histories*, we wanted to bring together leading experts to participate in a roundtable discussion. Yet the difficulty of physically bringing together people was considerable, and we decided that it would be timely and appropriate to use the affordances of the internet: the ability to collaborate remotely! Experts were thus invited to participate in what we called a "Round-Doc" discussion, i.e. a roundtable conversation taking "place" not in a physical room, but rather in a shared Google document.

Although perhaps less ambitious, our intent was directly linked to one of the first collaborative writing experiments which took place on a computer network, namely the "Epreuves d'écriture", "Writing Samples", that were part of the exhibition *Les Immatériaux*, organised by French philosophers Jean-François Lyotard and Thierry Chaput in 1985 at Centre Georges Pompidou in Paris. For the exhibition, the organisers invited around 30 authors, writers, scientists, artists, philosophers and linguists to comment on a list of 50 words related to the topic of the exhibition, the immaterial(s). As this was in the very early days of computer networks, the organisers had to supply sponsored micro-computers and networks (cf. Lyotard & Chaput, 1985).

Much has happened with the internet since 1985, and we are now able to make a similar, yet much smaller, collective writing experience in a much easier way. The topic of our discussion here is "Internet histories and computational methods", and the process took place in the following way. First, we posed seven questions and seven scholars with a strong track record within the field were invited to respond. Then the document was opened for comments from two scholars each for one week, and after one week it was closed for these participants and opened up for two other contributors. Once all contributors had participated the document was open to all for two weeks. During this last stage, a couple of new questions were added. Finally, the document was edited.

The initial questions were as follows:

- Why should scholars consider using computational methods when they study the many forms of the internet, including the web and social media? Can you illustrate this by one or more examples?
- What should scholars be looking out for when they use these methods? What are the possible pitfalls and challenges?
- To use computational methods, the object of study needs to be in digital form. Do you have any thoughts about to what extent the process of collecting influences computational research? Are the right sources collected? In the right format? By the right institutions?
- Is there anything that in your mind impedes the use of computational methods in studies of the history of the internet? Are source collections not "researcher-friendly?" Is there a lack of adequate methods and tools? Are there other obstacles?
- How do you see the relation between subject-matter experts like historians and new media scholars and developers (from systems librarians to programmers)? Should internet historians learn to code, or conversely, is the onus on developers to learn about historical methods?
- The use of computational methods in historical study has a history of its own. What are the most defining moments in the history of computational methods?
- How do you see the future of using computational methods for historical studies of the internet? What are the biggest challenges? The biggest opportunities or most exciting projects today? Which type of methods and tools would you like to see developed?

The following scholars participated in the conversation:

- Anat Ben-David, Ph.D., senior lecturer in the Department of Sociology, Political Science and Communication at the Open University of Israel.
- Sophie Gebeil, Ph.D., senior lecturer in contemporary history at the Telemme Laboratory, Aix-Marseille University.
- Federico Nanni, Ph.D., Postdoctoral Researcher, Data and Web Science Group, University of Mannheim.

- Richard Rogers, Ph.D., Professor, Chair in New Media & Digital Culture, University of Amsterdam.
- William J. Turkel, Ph.D., Professor of History at The University of Western Ontario.
- Matthew Weber, Ph.D., Associate Professor, Hubbard School of Journalism and Mass Communication, University of Minnesota.
- Peter Webster, Ph.D., independent scholar and consultant, Webster Research and Consulting Ltd, UK.

We hope you enjoy this "round-doc" as much as we had convening it!

*

Niels Brügger and Ian Milligan: Why should scholars consider using computational methods when they study the many forms of the internet, including the web and social media? Can you illustrate this by one or more examples?

Sophie Gebeil: As a historian, I focus on how internet users deal with the past, memory, or heritage in general in the 2000s. As such, the traces of the web are considered as born-digital material, stabilised thanks to the process of archiving the web (reborn digital material). Even if in my research, I have favoured a micro-historical and qualitative approach, I think that as a historian who exploits online sources, we cannot ignore the question of computational methods. It intervenes at different stages of the research. When the corpus is compiled, they make it possible to identify dynamics and trends through data analysis. When analysing the corpus once it has been circumscribed: even working from the different archived versions of a single website such as histoire-immigration.fr, the amount of data available exceeds the researcher's capacity. However, the digital nature of Web traces makes it possible to begin to explore certain issues such as the evolution of the lexicon mobilised on the site (plain text) or the outgoing URLs in the different versions. For instance, in case of the history-immigration.fr host, we can see the data available for the period 2003–2019 on the Internet Archive.[1] This offers potential for analysis that is complementary to traditional historiographical methods.

Anat Ben-David: The internet is a computational medium, so it is rather tempting to apply computational methods in internet research, for there seems to be a convenient "structural fit" between medium and method. In particular, computational methods are helpful when researchers are interested in processing and analysing large quantities of data that cannot be processed manually or qualitatively. For example, it would be useful to use computational methods if one is interested in studying the evolution of hyperlink networks over time, or in analysing millions of tweets around a certain event; in finding patterns in internet traffic data, or in comparing user profiles across social media platforms. However the temptation to use computational methods in internet research just because of the "structural fit" might be misleading, as these methods may be helpful in answering certain research questions, but not others. For example, in Web history, computational methods are very useful in extending the scope of analysis that is often limited by interfaces to web archives, allowing to perform "distant reading" of entire national webs. However these meta-level analyses are useful in describing the structure of networks, or in detecting patterns in content, but they might fail to answer historical questions about user experiences and motivations, or in describing historical narratives in detail.

Federico Nanni: I think your point about a "structural fit" is a central point, using (especially shiny advanced) computational methods is often tempting, but our research should be guided by a specific question, not by a fascinating methodological application.

William J. Turkel: To take the opposite perspective on what guides our research, I think that many interesting questions can emerge when you start with a particular computational method or approach and think of ways to apply it to historical sources. For example, someone who is broadly interested in geospatial phenomena may decide to learn GIS. As their knowledge deepens they begin to find uses for techniques that they did not originally know about. They become able to read literature that was previously inaccessible, thus becoming acquainted with new research questions. This is one established career path in science, engineering or applied math: become an expert in digital signal processing, or nonlinear optimisation, or differential equations, then work on problems that suit your tools. At the most general level, I would argue that learning how to program is a similar strategy. In the case of working with born-digital sources, you can be confident your programming skills will not go to waste, even if you do not start with a specific set of questions that you know you will be able to answer.

Federico Nanni: I agree with what is said above by Sophie and Anat, but at the same time, I think it's necessary to distinguish between the use of computational methods in two different broad areas, the first related to the retrieval of information and the second to the quantification of information. While they are clearly interconnected (an information retrieval tool, for instance, based upon query-likelihood, relies on quantitative assumptions) the researcher's final goals are different. Dealing with large-scale web collections, information retrieval tools are almost always needed, at least as an access point, even when we plan to conduct a specifically focused qualitative analysis. It is therefore important that researchers understand what type of results such tools provide (and especially not provide) when we enter a query, starting from the basic fact that when employing many of these tools (e.g. Twitter search), results are tailored around our interests, location, previous interactions, etc.

Conversely, when researchers adopt computational methods for capturing and modeling a quantitative property of the data under study, they are entering into a very different framework of analysis, strongly aligned with social science approaches.[2] If we consider for instance conducting a diachronic sentiment analysis of a political campaign from social media data, researchers should work under the assumption that a specific tweet collection is a representative sample of the population under study, that a particular phenomenon (stating a positive/negative opinion towards a candidate) can be objectively measured and precisely captured with a computational approach (e.g. a dictionary-based sentiment classifier), that this can be used as a proxy for a real-world behaviour (e.g. being pro/against a candidate), and so on.

Richard Rogers: Instead of thinking of methods as toolboxes to be trucked to the next field of inquiry, no matter its distance, one could argue that media historically have had their classic methods for their study such as how studies of television prefer reception and film spectatorship. In European media studies, screen studies may be imported fruitfully into internet studies (such as encoding and decoding), but the internet could be said to be (among others) a medium of algorithmic recommendation. It would follow from a "methods of the medium" outlook to consider both critically unboxing these systems as well as applying them for the study of the workings of the internet. Interrogations into polarisation, the filter bubble, so-called fake news and other recent preoccupations in internet studies would benefit from capturing the hierarchies of people, stories and sources created to order media objects for the user. Studying how principles of homophily often override heterophily when understanding user preference presupposes an inquiry into how machines are trained to learn. In both these instances, one employs computational techniques but is not restricting method to the computational; rather the computational is part of the critical repertoire.

Matthew Weber: My colleagues have raised a number of important points in thinking about why scholars should use computational methods when studying questions pertaining to the internet, the web and social media. Computational methods are central in my research as a scholar focusing on digital technology and studying processes of technology evolution and change. I agree with much of what has been said; different domains of research have different traditions with regard to methods, information retrieval and quantification both often call for computational methods in this space, and often there is a structural fit.

That said, when I speak to graduate students and others who are just working their way into this space, I first ask about their research questions and the theory guiding their work. I rarely think the selection of the method should drive the research; William raises some important points about the power of computational methods to guide exploration, but from a social science perspective the structural fit of the method will generally trump exploration. To that end, I generally believe research questions should be derived from prior research, from personal motivations, and from an exploration of emerging patterns and new trends in society.

In the context of internet studies and historical studies, it is increasingly the case that questions focused on the web require the researcher to sift through data on a scale not seen in prior generations. Thus, this research questions in this domain often push scholars to work with computational methods. Personally, I came into this domain of research wanting to study how news media organisations were adapting to web technology in the early 2000s. I had read enough small-scale case studies to know that I wanted to understand broader patterns; my research questions, grounded in organisational studies, led me to computational methods because of the scope and scale of the questions that I was asking.

Peter Webster: One of the more sterile tropes of much of the discussion about the digital humanities is an opposing of "traditional" and "digital" methods, as if it were necessary that one of the two should be all-sufficient. This has much to do with scholarly politics and speculation about where the next piece of research funding will most likely be directed, but it is clear to me that digital methods in general add possibility – to answer the questions that could not feasibly be approached before – and that there is no reason to suppose that traditional historical method is thereby somehow under threat of extinction. Nothing in the fact of distant reading prevents me from also reading closely. As such, if a scholar sees a research question that can only be answered by the adoption of a computational approach, then that is the approach to take. That should not stop the deployment of traditional methods alongside it, and (as has often been the case in my own work) what tends to occur is a tracking back and forward between methods as the inquiry possesses. My computational processing of link graphs has often begun with a small number of known domains, and leads to the close reading of others, and then in turn to more interrogation of the graph. It is this integration at which we should be aiming.

Picking up the question of which comes first, method or question, it is surely the case that both are true. I could hardly even fire up a particular application without having some initial question to ask. Over time, my research question will evolve as the work progresses. And (as William suggests) I will most likely emerge at the end with new questions to pursue, some of which have only occurred to me as a result of coming to know more about the method. The two cannot meaningfully be untangled.

Niels Brügger and Ian Milligan: What should scholars be looking out for when they use these methods? What are the possible pitfalls and challenges?

Sophie Gebeil: There are many traps, individually and collectively. This depends a lot on the researcher's discipline and their own computer skills. In the case of historians, their computer skills are mostly underdeveloped in initial training. In this case, I identify two pitfalls related to their relationship to technology. First, historians' fascination with the belief that the computational tool is inherently objective, thus reconnecting with the myths of quantitative history and abandoning disciplinary hermeneutics by reducing the understanding of human societies to data alone. Second, the lack of interest that would amount to entrusting the application of the method to a data scientist without taking into account calculation biases in the analysis. On the other hand, by participating and cooperating in the choice and development of the analytical method, there are many possibilities. What interests me most is the possibility of monitoring the evolution of online content over time, which implies designing tools dedicated to web archives.

Anat Ben-David: In my view, a useful guiding question could be whether or not there is added value in introducing computation to the analysis. For example, when conducting content analysis of large volumes of text, researchers often use off-the-shelf methods, tools and scripts such as sentiment analysis, or topic modelling, that provide statistically based summarisation and classification of text. As these off-the-shelf methods gain popularity, they tend to become black-boxed (in that the user doesn't understand the theoretical justifications, histories and limits of the underlying method) and lose their critical edge. However, when computational tools and methods are critically devised and specifically tailored to answer specific research questions, they open up a variety of exciting new ways of thinking about research questions, and of answering them creatively, reflexively and critically.

An anecdote from one of my previous research projects illustrates both the potential and limits of the computational approach to internet research. My colleagues and

I were interested in characterising the typical colors of national webs, and to measure the "distance" between the average pallet of web pages from the color of the national flag (Ben-David, Amram, & Bekkerman, 2018). We used an off-the-shelf technique called K-means clustering to create average monthly color histograms of the entire national web of the former Yugoslavia. We found that the similarity of the domain's colors to the colors of the Yugoslav national flag decreases over time. However, qualitative analysis of a sample of the analysed images revealed that many of them displayed a tiny flag at the corner of the image. While the computational method allowed us to summarise the colors of about 40,000 Web pages, it was blind to the symbolic presence of these miniature flags.

William J. Turkel: One of the most valuable outcomes of working with specifically tailored tools is that they not only provide the kind of results that Anat describes, but that they often draw attention to their own limitations. Even when black-boxed versions of tools are available, I often encourage students to try to create their own.

Federico Nanni: I would like to further remark on the previous reference concerning tools as black-boxes. On the one hand, computational methods such as LDA topic models are based on specific assumptions, for instance, the fact that documents are generated by a distribution over latent topics, where each topic is characterised by a distribution over all the words in the corpus (cf. Graham, Weingart, & Milligan, 2012). This is the "idea" of what a topic "is", upon which the algorithm is built. If we disagree with such definition, we should not employ LDA in our study to capture "topics". On the other hand, it is true that in the last 10 years LDA has been used many times for explorative/serendipitous analyses, but I would argue that other techniques, which are often simpler to use, faster to run and rely on simpler assumptions could also be very useful, starting from key-phrase extraction (Moretti, Sprugnoli, & Tonelli, 2015).[3] So, in my opinion, researchers should not employ a computational tool because it is widely adopted in the community, on the opposite they should critically question it, especially because it is so widely used.

William J. Turkel: Strongly agree with Federico on this point. I might even say that the more widely adopted a tool is within a community, the less useful it becomes. This is another case where learning new computational techniques can lead to new questions. If one searches through the literature for alternatives to, say, LDA topic models, one not only learns new computational techniques but begins to see the advantages and disadvantages to various approaches.

Niels Brügger and Ian Milligan: If we may quickly interject here – the "more widely adopted a tool is within a community, the less useful it becomes" point that Turkel and Nanni are making is we think worth pausing on. Some work has been trying to coalesce around a standard stack of text analysis tools (i.e. let's make sure all scholars can do X, Y and Z), but now you're making us wonder if this is misguided?

William J.Turkel: When we come up with lists of things that all scholars should be able to do, the key thing is to focus on giving them skills to create tools, rather than giving them tools per se. To use an analogy from basic statistics, the mean is a useful operation for some datasets but it is not robust because it is sensitive to outliers. If we give everyone in the community a calculator with a button to compute the mean, we soon end up with a situation where the tool gets misused from time-to-time. It is a black box. A better tool would compute the mean while providing the user with some indication of whether it was appropriate or not. But best of all would be a standard of training that allowed people to build and test their own tools, or to verify that the tools of others were working properly and appropriate to the task at hand.

Federico Nanni: I completely agree with William. I recently organised a workshop on tool criticism, where we wrote a dictionary-based approach for sentiment analysis and plot trajectory from scratch (similar to Syuzhet) (Jockers, 2017). By doing so, the participants noticed how many little assumptions are already embedded in just a few lines of code and how by simply changing them, you could drastically modify the final results.

Richard Rogers: There is a series of contemporary critiques associated with the computational approach to the study of digital media, especially given the Cambridge Analytica scandal and the fake news debacle. In the one, a big data approach to studying people's preferences from social media data was unethically repurposed into a right-wing amplification project targeted at keyword publics, and in the other, platforms for participatory culture were reused for influence campaigning and astroturfing. Both of these campaign projects benefited from the knowledge of medium specificity as well as "web- and platform-native" techniques, and have led increasingly to "locked platforms" with social media data becoming scarcer rather than "bigger". There are now calls for "post-API" research, which in a sense is also an invitation to return to small data, ethnographic, and interface methods, including scraping. But web and social media companies actively work against data collection techniques (as well as apps) that they have not approved. For example, researchers who scrape are treated like any other "spammy" actor, and also could compromise themselves by becoming banned or suspended when striving to make a more robust dataset. Instead of allowing data collection through the APIs, social media companies are now furnishing datasets (e.g. in the case of Facebook's Social Science One initiative or in Twitter's sets of Russian and Iranian trolls) but these are "company-curated" and may be critiqued as such. This company-driven research also may lead to particular types of data and analytical practices, e.g. in the Social Science One initiative at one's disposal are all web URLs that have been posted on Facebook in the past year; these may be analysed remotely only on Facebook's infrastructure, with aggregates as outputs. These are big data for computational techniques. Qualitative and mixed methods researchers are not necessarily the envisaged users.

William J. Turkel: On this point, see Eriksson, Vonderau, Snickars, and Fleischer (2019). The authors explicitly engaged in covert and experimental methods (that violated the company's Terms of Use) to explore the "back end" of the streaming music service Spotify.

Matthew Weber: The point about black boxing of the methods cannot be understated. It is important to understand what the inherent assumptions of a methodology are but also to understand black box issues associated with the data. For instance, I frequently work with social network analysis, and I often see scholars presenting social network diagrams of large datasets without thinking about the algorithm used to generate the diagram. For instance, the popular Fruchterman Reingold algorithm is a force-directed layout that can be quite useful for visualisation, but with large datasets, it struggles to capture differences within subclusters in the data. Always be aware of the limitations and restrictions of an approach. With regard to data, I often work with archived internet data. Archived internet data provide a rich and robust record of web activity and web page content. On the other hand, archived internet data rarely provide accurate summaries of how the data were collected, and what the scoping and limitations are associated with the data. In one recent study, I conducted looking at archived internet data mapping US Congressional webpages, we found that up to 60% of the webpages linked to by Congressional webpages were not present in the dataset. This is not an uncommon problem, but it means that when you are using computational methods in the context of internet data you need to know the limitations of your data. The same is true when you are using pre-existing data such as Twitter and Facebook data, or if you are collecting and scraping your own data. These limitations are fatal flaws; they are often to be expected. But researchers have an obligation to be clear and transparent about these limitations and to provide access to their data where possible so that others can replicate and validate their work.

Sophie Gebeil: I fully agree with the critical and transparent perspective that the social scientist must build on the computational tools they use and the data on which these tools are applied.

On the issue of the "democratisation" of certain tools in communities that could undermine their usefulness, I identify two levels. The first is the need to create tools adapted to new research questions that will inevitably be specific and will also allow innovative methods and results. But at a second level, researchers who have a good knowledge of the tools and their limitations can also help to improve the development of internet studies among beginner researchers in computational methods. To use the case of web archives, I am currently working with engineers from the National audiovisual institute (Ina) on the WebTV collection. The idea is to design an extraction tool to explore this fragmented video corpus according to my questions about the memories of social movements. But there is also the will, or even the requirement for Ina, to propose a standardised tool, which any beginner researcher can use to explore corpora in the Ina archives, while being mindful of the limitations of the tool and these data.

Niels Brügger and Ian Milligan: To use computational methods, the object of study needs to be in digital form. Do you have any thoughts about to what extent the process of collecting influences computational research? Are the right sources collected? In the right format? By the right institutions?

Sophie Gebeil: In case of the web archiving process in France, two Institutions (the Ina, National audiovisual institute and the BnF, French national library) collect the web within the legal framework set by legal deposit. In my opinion, this is an opportunity because it gives a solid framework for collection institutions and gives web sources the status of a common heritage even if this results in a territorialisation of the web. The Ina and the BnF are obliged to communicate on how data are collected, structured and stored. Moreover, as Valérie Schafer and Francesca Musiani have argued, several pieces of information are missing from the collection process (Musiani, Paloque-Bergès, Schafer, & Thierry, 2019). In return, this also makes it more difficult for computer scientists to use the data, who must necessarily be part of a state-funded research project. Finally, the question of formats is crucial. In France, the BnF uses the WARC format and the Ina has its own internally developed DAFF format. This means that a project to develop computational methods for French web archives should adapt to these two distinct formats, without necessarily being able to cross-reference the results.

Anat Ben-David: I think that several years after what has been termed "the computational turn" in Digital Humanities, or the hype around "Computational Social Sciences", there is already wide acknowledgement among researchers that data collection practices are never neutral, and that constraints on access and on the ability to use various data pose significant challenges to the types of research that can be done with them.

Federico Nanni: The use of computational methods for internet research and the study of our present times is tightly interconnected with the availability of big data to be analysed by the community, from collections of news articles to tweet corpora up to national web archives. An aspect that is, however, not very often discussed is the complexity of obtaining access to such collections, especially for a scholar who is not affiliated with a national library or directly involved in an international project on the topic.

In my doctoral research, I examined the difficulties of reconstructing the history of the University of Bologna website (Nanni, 2017), which was excluded from the Internet Archive's Wayback Machine and at the same time was not archived by the Italian Central Library, as Italy does not systematically archive its national web sphere. The same issue can emerge again when the intention is to retrieve data from social media platforms (e.g. all tweets posted during the first week of Occupy Wall Street) or when we aim to study a specific sub-collection of a web archive (e.g. all personal blogs preserved by the UK Web Archive mentioning the Brexit referendum); in many cases, obtaining these data is at the same time not straightforward and not cheap.[4] This is due to many different reasons, from privacy and copyright constraints to the too often underestimated computational difficulties in retrieving such materials, up to economic interests of the "data-owner", especially when this is not a public institution.

Richard Rogers: In recent years, web data have become "cleaner" in the sense of being pre-structured and well-formatted. Web data are now a far cry from the messiness associated with incomplete crawling, folksonomic labeling and multifarious styles of engine querying. But the "editing" that has resulted in the new cleanliness is also different from how human editors classified websites to make web directories or

Wikipedians removed vandalism or handled troll contributions. From the Wayback Machine of the Internet Archive and Wikipedia to social media companies, data are preferably delivered through APIs, meaning there are available fields in the database as well as query routines. The APIs are designed with particular use cases (or "business cases") in mind, but also are interfaces to back-ends when researchers may have been more familiar with front-ends. When one begins building software that explores the API or wishes to make use of its data for specific research purposes, one also enters the realm of computational and developer culture.

William J. Turkel: On the one hand, there are the institutions like the ones that Richard mentioned which provide APIs and access to masses of downloadable, structured data. On the other hand, it continually becomes easier for individual researchers or small teams to crawl and index significant portions of the web by themselves if they have scripting skills. The datasets that one obtains with the latter method tend not to be clean, and intellectual property considerations preclude sharing them. For one of my research projects, I collected on the order of a few million documents relating to the history of electronics from the open web. The crawling took a few months using nothing more than a laptop and external hard drive. I would not share the dataset publicly, however, because I have no metadata associating each item with its copyright status.

Matthew Weber: Social media are a bit more straightforward when it comes to the sources and format, as well as the institutions. The structure of the content leads to a somewhat common pattern of data storage; for instance, most Twitter data contain certain key data points about the user and the content of tweets. Data today are often cleaner in terms of the formats; we have better standards for data structure than we did a decade ago, and we have a better awareness of those standards. At the same time, there are so many different types of data, and different standards, that the problem of data format remains complex. Web archiving is a great example; the web archive (WARC) file format is a standard for storing archived web pages, and yet different institutions use the WARC in different ways (populating some fields, and not others, and specifying provenance in a variety of ways). Data shared by the Internet Archive often differ from data shared by the Library of Congress or the BnF, and access varies widely as well. To Federico's point, access is often an issue as well. Twitter is a great example of access issues; the degree of access (and the percent of data you are able to view) varies widely based on access to funding, access to the data firehose (or API), and existing relationships with researchers at Twitter.

Niels Brügger and Ian Milligan: Is there anything that in your mind impedes the use of computational methods in studies of the history of the internet? Are source collections not "researcher-friendly"? Is there a lack of adequate methods and tools? Are there other obstacles?

Sophie Gebeil: As I have worked with web archives since 2011, I am finding that the modes of access have diversified. Of course, there is still a lack of tools that would allow us to quickly identify some characteristics from a corpus: hyperlink dynamics, textual analyses or even image analysis. It is difficult because of the specificities of the web archives but it is a new and exciting field. In my opinion, it is also the role of researchers in human and social sciences to contribute to the design of this type of tool. There are more and more historians who are interested in digital sources or digital humanities. There are also reticences that come primarily from a lack of training in computational methods, but another reason is also the very strong relationship that the historian has with the document, the archive. These two notions are disrupted with born and reborn digital sources.

Anat Ben-David: Reading the literature on web archives, one comes across the word "challenges" very often. Not only is the web a medium that is challenging to preserve, the solutions that have hitherto been proposed to archive it result in collections that do not lend themselves easily to computational research. As I previously mentioned, since the internet is a computational medium to begin with, it is rather tempting to try to apply computational analyses for studying its history.

But one finds out very quickly that even the simple computational methods that are used for studying the live web, or other digital data, cannot be applied to the archived web, for the following reasons. First, copyright and privacy constraints limit access to web archives, which is often restricted to viewing at the premises of national libraries. Second, current interfaces to web archives are primarily designed for viewing, or "surfing" archived snapshots (one page at a time), but not for their treatment as corpora. Third, archived web materials often lack sufficient context on the circumstances and techniques of the archiving; without such provenance information, it is difficult to determine which snapshots should be included or excluded from the analysis, or to explain temporal incoherence or "holes" in web archives. Finally, most infrastructures that are currently being used to host very large web archives are not designed to support computational processing.

Federico Nanni: I agree with the point made by Sophie on the fact that humanities/social scientists should contribute to the design of tools. However, it is often not easy for a humanities researcher to develop the computational skills and data science knowledge actually required for contributing and therefore moving out of a setting where they are simply "computer scientist customers", as Adam Crymble once put it (Crymble, 2015). Quite often Digital Humanities researchers spend their entire doctoral studies in building up such expertise, and they might never have the time/chance of actually using such tools in a substantive research.

William J. Turkel: But Crymble is an excellent example of someone who started developing computational skills as a graduate student, and continues to do so, and to share what he has learned.

Federico Nanni: As I mentioned before and as Anat has also remarked on, I believe that the number one issue is the prompt accessibility to web archive data. While this is due to understandable reasons, the lack of access for the broad academic community has limited, among other things, the development of tools specifically tailored for particular web archiving issues and, I would argue, also the perception of the challenges that web archivists are currently facing. For instance, information retrieval approaches that address the complexity of dealing with different temporal-layers of a web archive are often developed by research groups having direct access to a web archive (for instance through a research project or a collaboration with a web archive).

A tool that, at least in my opinion, seems to be highly needed by both web archivists and internet studies researchers is a method for building topic-specific collections from a web archive (e.g. by isolating only pages referring to a specific event); this would, therefore, produce a smaller and hopefully manageable sub-collection that the researcher could further study on its own. However such complex methodological challenge is currently not fully addressed by the broad information retrieval research community.[5]

Richard Rogers: Most histories of the internet have been written without computational techniques, just as most histories generally. Thus, the internet is not special in that regard. Moreover, many histories of the internet have been written without (citing) web archives, which could be considered a main source of historical material. These archives also could be the site for computational techniques and tools. To date, however, the computational study of web archives has been quite distinctive from internet and web historiography. This state of affairs may be changing, as there are examples of collaborations between digital methods researchers and internet historians as well as between web archivists and internet historians, though projects with the three parties could be developed.

Matthew Weber: One question that comes to mind is whether there is anything unique or remarkable about our ability to "replay" the internet? Is it enough to replay an image of a webpage, or do you need access to the underlying code? In other words, do you need to see the technology as it was constructed? I would argue that for the internet the code and technology are critically important.

William J. Turkel: A very interesting question. Since web page Mementos are reconstructed from components that were archived at various times (or not), the "fidelity" of the playback is limited and the reconstructed pages are at best an approximation of the past. That said, they are a valuable and widely accessible resource.

Matthew Weber: I believe there are many collections that are researcher-friendly. The Internet Archive's Wayback Machine is a wonderful interface for viewing the history of a webpage from a qualitative point of view. Their research services team has developed tools designed to improve access to a subset of data. In the academic space, the Web Science and Digital Libraries Research Group at Old Dominion has produced a great collection of computer science oriented tools for research and access. The Archives Unleashed team at the University of Waterloo has also developed tools that are much easier to use than what we have seen in prior years. At George Washington University, Social Feed Manager allows researchers to work with social media data, and to collect their own datasets. I believe we have a host of tools from different disciplines that have enabled access and opened up researcher access to large-scale data. These tools, however, often require technical skills in order to wrangle the tool to return the desired results. As is common with this type of computational work, I believe that interdisciplinary collaboration is a key to success.

William J. Turkel: I once read somewhere that the most successful interdisciplinary work happens when a single individual is trained in the techniques of multiple disciplines. While I agree with Matthew's point that interdisciplinary collaboration is a key to success in computational work, I also think that each of us needs to strive to be "a kind of import-export specialist between the disciplines" as James Clifford put it (Clifford, 2003, p. 55). More than once, I have seen historians or other humanists expect their technical collaborators to get up to speed on the literature of the topic, while resisting any engagement on their own part with the literature of the technical methods. Those kind of collaborations tend to fail.

Peter Webster: To reiterate a point made by other contributors, for me the biggest single challenge (of the many) is the fragmentation of a medium that only very loosely behaves in a "national" way into nationally conceived archives. As I've argued elsewhere, the pattern into which web archiving has fallen has its own history, and we have to be very thankful for non-print legal deposit since without it we would be even more reliant on the Internet Archive than we already are. But in order for us to effectively study the Web in a way that aligns with its fundamental nature, we need methods of transnational discovery and analysis, and if that necessitates government-level action to amend copyright legislation in different nations, then we should be lobbying for that. (We perhaps stand the best chance of success at the level of the European Union.)

Niels Brügger and Ian Milligan: How do you see the relation between subject-matter experts like historians and new media scholars and developers (from systems librarians to programmers)? Should internet historians learn to code, or conversely, is the onus on developers to learn about historical methods?

Sophie Gebeil: It depends on the research field. From a cultural history perspective, it does not seem essential to me to know how to code but it is necessary to have some knowledge of coding and HTML language in general. If the "programmer historian" (Le Roy Ladurie, 1973) exists, in my opinion, they will remain a minority. Above all, I believe that historians must develop a digital culture and computer skills in order to be the best possible interlocutors to participate in the design of computational analysis methods with developers. In return, I find it interesting to consider the fact that computer scientists also develop a culture in the human and social sciences even if I had never asked myself the question in this sense. In my research experience, I had to learn to use Navicrawler, Hyphe and Gephi on my own and therefore I use them in an approximate way. It seems to me that one of the challenges is precisely to succeed in cooperating all together (historians, engineers, archivists, programmers, etc.) to propose innovative methods but also easily usable tools that would democratise the use of natively digital sources in history.

Anat Ben-David: From my experience working with developers, information scientists and computer scientists, the interdisciplinary collaboration is successful when the research questions, or the object of study, are interesting enough – scientifically – to all involved. Computer scientists might not be interested in a historical question if they do not find the computational challenge interesting enough. Reversely, historians do not necessarily need to learn to code to conduct simple computational analyses, but they may benefit from knowing the types of available analyses that can be performed, and how to communicate to developers what they would like to achieve with computational analyses.

Federico Nanni: I agree with the opinions above, but I tend to have an even more pragmatic view on the topic, probably influenced by the fact that I have spent the last five years as the only (digital) historian in a data science research group. It is true that the research question needs to be perceived as "interesting" by the computer scientist and the computational aspect of the problem needs to be "challenging enough", but I think that this is often not the main issue.

The problem and the developed approach also need to be in line with the methodological interests of the computer science community of reference (in my case often the natural language processing community). This means that if an interesting and challenging problem could not – for instance – be successfully addressed with a deep learning architecture (e.g. due to the sparsity/lack of training data), but instead with a more traditional word frequency-based approach, such work will suddenly become way harder to be published in a Natural Language Publishing (NLP) venue. Subject-matter experts and computer scientists starting a collaboration should not underestimate the complexity of such settings, especially for what concerns the publication process; the two communities have very different practices, from pre-print publications to data-sharing up to established policies concerning author names on research articles.

At the beginning of my Ph.D., I was very much guided by the idea of becoming a "programming historian" able to conduct my research in a completely independent way, benefiting from the knowledge of the two communities. However, developing a proper data science profile is actually very challenging and it could bring you far away from the research question that you originally intended to address, often to a place where it is difficult to demonstrate the relevance of your research to either community, because it is at the same time not "novel" enough for an NLP audience and not "substantive" enough for a historical one. I still believe that we need a generation of programming (internet) historians, for critically addressing many of the new challenges of dealing with web archives while at the same time pursuing historical scholarships, but we especially need very well prepared interdisciplinary educators.

Richard Rogers: I am reminded of the critique of the computational turn in humanities that invites those learning a corpus to at once be trained in analytical software operation. As a rejoinder, "button-pressing" is defended in the history of the humanities these days as contiguous with the long tradition of pattern recognition that has developed alongside hermeneutics. Thus, there always have been humanities coders, albeit in relatively smaller numbers. Perhaps the question concerns how central computational culture should be (and how strident the response) in the development of curricula and the larger programmatic agenda, which these days is favouring such work in new funding, career and other schemes.

Matthew Weber: Anat and Federico both raise important points of the nature of interdisciplinary collaboration. And as Richard points out, there are always those within a discipline who are able to translate work across disciplinary boundaries – for example, understanding code such that the barriers to collaborating with programmers are minimised. In my experience, the research questions need to be compelling to all involved in a project, but what is ultimately compelling to one person will not be the same for all others. On a recent project examining the change in local news ecosystems, I was interested in the dynamic nature of interconnections between websites in the data my team collected. The computer scientists were glad to help with the problem of coding the way I tracked these evolving networks but found the computational work to be relatively simplistic. Rather, their interests were driven by a desire to use the corpus of text as a way to trace patterns of misinformation through a network of news. The dataset and project were both sufficiently large as to allow each member of the team to carve out his or her niche. In sum, I believe it is important that each team member find their own motivation. I don't expect that historians will automatically learn code, or that computer scientists will learn the nuances of digital humanities scholarship, but it is important to find a common language. Understanding in both directions will ultimately increase the success of the research.

William J. Turkel: Looking at the question slightly differently, I would argue that *all* undergraduates should be encouraged to try programming to see if they like it. Assuming that the vast majority of our students will never become practicing historians, it is great to have skills that pay the rent. Whenever someone asks me for career advice I encourage them to develop marketable skills that resonate with them. Learn another natural language; learn to program; take a course on linear algebra, statistics, accounting or finance; learn GIS or databases, etc.

Peter Webster: I think there are two distinct questions in play here, although they are related. The first concerns how research projects are conceived in terms of their staffing, which in turns depends on models of funding. If a project is led by historians, and it is in history or other humanities disciplines that the research interventions are to be made, then the relationship with developers will most likely be one of contractor and client. If the scholar is able to articulate their requirements clearly enough (though this is very often not the case), then the relationship is relatively easy to manage. If, on the other hand, the project is conceived as one which speaks to both questions in the humanities and in computer science or library and information studies, then the dynamics will necessarily be different, as in the cases that Federico and Matthew outline. So, whether the onus is on the development side depends on the kind of project.

More generally, the question "should historians learn to program" is a slightly unhelpful one. If we were instead to ask: "do we need there always to be *some* historians who are learning to program", then the answer is clearly a positive one. And this, as Richard rightly observes, has been the case for many years, as small communities of scholars find and experiment with new tools and approaches as they appear, and show to the rest of the discipline what might be possible. Those people will continue to select themselves by the route that William describes. But it is (I think) neither possible or desirable for all historians to be proficient programmers, since the diversity of what it means to be a developer is already very great, and likely to become greater.

Even before one generation of scholars has mastered one language (or even begun to get to grips with it) it will have changed, and alternatives sprung up to replace it. What scholars do however need, I think, is a grasp of basic principles of computer science, data management, archival science, project management and (in particular) of the characteristics of successful development projects.

Niels Brügger and Ian Milligan: The use of computational methods in historical study has a history of its own. What are the most defining moments in the history of computational methods?

Anat Ben-David: That's a tough question, especially considering that media (and science) histories are not necessarily linear, or defined by key moments. But if I must answer, then I would note the development of cloud computing that allowed scaling analyses beyond the constraints of physical memory, and the development of open source programming languages such as Python and R, that attracted a wide community of users.

Federico Nanni: It's always a matter of considering computational as a sort of synonym for quantitative methods or not, which could open a never-ending digital humanities discussion. Apart from the most famous turning points in the relations between the quantitative/computational and the historical (from the discussion around "Time on the Cross" to the Google Culturomics project), I consider defining moments for our discipline all the improvements in information retrieval systems, and their impact on our everyday life and our work as historians. From Karen Sparck Jones' inverse document frequency term weighting to PageRank up to the more recent "things not string", these are all technical innovations that have influenced (and often improved) our digital archival research and consequently our scholarships.

Richard Rogers: The debates these days around digital humanities remind me of controversies surrounding the introduction of cliometrics in the 1960s. Cliometrics put a name to the use of quantitative methods in historiography, applied especially in economic history (and also the history of technology). To me, the interesting aspect of cliometrics was less the introduction of stats and data to history and the debates around disruptions to fields and paradigms, but rather the style of the research questions. The more well-known work employed counterfactual historiography. What if the American civil war did not take place? What if the railways were not built? The latter question concerned whether the canal system could have led to similar levels of economic development as the railways and the second industrial revolution in the USA. The point was to question the "axiom of indispensability" of the railways to development. (Robert Fogel won the Nobel Prize for Economics with this and other work.) As it matured cliometrics was no longer a movement in "new economic history" and rather experienced a typical pioneer's regress, becoming again a branch rather than a trunk route in the larger field of historiography.

No one is asking whether digital humanities would suffer the same fate or enjoy the same prizes, but the introduction of the quantitative, statistical, computational and similar instrumentaria, together with their styles of inquiry, could lead to temporary novelty or pockets of innovation.

Matthew Weber: The continued growth of a robust community of researchers working with Python and R has been a key development for computational methods. The community of scholars working in this space is generous with their time, and work to share best practices and code. I think there are other technologies, as well, that are helping to lower barriers. Interactive what you see is what you get platforms, such as Python notebooks, allow you to see code and output together in a seamless interface. Beyond that, there has been a groundswell in workshops and tutorials at annual meetings, over the summer, and online, that has served to create a rich set of educational resources.

Niels Brügger and Ian Milligan: How do you see the future of using computational methods for historical studies of the internet? What are the biggest challenges? The biggest opportunities or most exciting projects today? Which type of methods and tools would you like to see developed?

Sophie Gebeil: There are several perspectives to which I am committed.

On the methods and tools side, I am currently working with Ina on data extraction from web archives. This is important to me because I believe that the creation of corpus analysis tools would facilitate the appropriation of web archives by researchers in the social sciences and humanities. In the future, I would like to see the development of methods related to visual studies that allow the identification of the path of visual content from pre-existing media archives (print media, television) to and in the archives of the Web. For example, we could then trace the video or fixed image of General De Gaulle pronouncing the famous "I understood you" on 4 June 1958 in Algiers and follow the circulation of the image, its diversion in the web archives of the BnF or the Ina, or in other web archives.

Another aspect that is close to me is the development of a reflection on the archiving of the Web in the Mediterranean, which to date is mainly the work of scattered and isolated groups. In a context of instability and major political changes, the collection, preservation and study of natively digital sources is a fundamental challenge for Mediterranean societies.

Anat Ben-David: As Niels Brügger noted, web archives are not exactly archives, since their organisation and structure lack archival principles such as appraisal and provenance. In that sense, future computational methods may be helpful in improving archival appraisal and in adding provenance and other contextual information that may significantly increase the utility of the archived web for historical research. Important computational work is currently being conducted by the Memento project at Old Dominion University and elsewhere, where researchers develop methods, tools and web services for understanding the archived web beyond the boundaries of a single collection or archiving institution; and by "The Archives Unleashed" project, led by researchers from the University of Waterloo, which develops toolkits that facilitate the analysis of large scale web archives for historical research. There are two areas that require developing new methods and tools: the first is the question of web archiving after social media, and how to facilitate research across different types of web archives and other datasets, and the second is the need to develop tools specifically designed for critiquing the archiving process, or web archives as institutions.

Federico Nanni: As I remarked before, I believe the core challenges for the future of computational methods in historical studies are twofold: on the one hand, the difficulties of accessing (and therefore experiencing) web archived collections and on the other hand, the lack of critical attitudes towards computational methods. For these reasons, hands-on activities such as the ones organised by the Big UK Domain Data for the Arts and Humanities (BUDDAH) project and the more recent Archives Unleashed series are absolutely essential. I took part in the first two editions of the Archives Unleashed and that was an incredibly formative experience, especially because I had the opportunity of facing for the first time many of the issues that I knew only from literature. Another challenge that I believe is necessary to address involves extending the use of computational methods and web archives to other disciplines, first of all to researchers in political science, which would largely benefit from obtaining a novel diachronic perspective on party politics, international relations and overall democratic processes.

Richard Rogers: National libraries, perhaps understandably, are treating the world wide web as a national web and archiving only their "home" webs. Social media platforms are not providing public archives and are not being publicly archived. The encrypted ephemerality of messaging apps provides another challenge. These days it's as if much of the content, however valuable, is out of reach of the archivist. I'm buoyed by the increased usage of web archives by scholars and students and would encourage developing and also compiling teaching units with web archives.

Matthew Weber: Continued advancements with regard to research at scale will allow for new questions to be asked. We do not fully know the scale of the internet and the web, because we have not yet been able to crawl and analyse the full extent of the web. In this way, we do not know the full extent of the web, nor the history of many aspects of society and interaction on the web. Simultaneously, the tools that allow us to navigate through collections and to extract subsets continue to be developed. This is a burgeoning area of research and as more scholars come into this space it is clear work will expand into new domains. As noted by Anat and Federico, I believe that the current push for educational resources is the fields greatest strength, as new scholars will continue to push the domains of computational methods and internet research.

William J. Turkel: For me, one of the more interesting research areas right now has to do with the adaptation and development of sublinear algorithms that allow us to analyse internet phenomena at scale and/or in real time. One excellent recent example of this kind of work is Ben Schmidt's analysis of the approximately 13.6 M books in the Hathi Trust collection using a general-purpose dimensionality reduction that is ultimately based on the Johnson-Lindenstrauss lemma (Achlioptas, 2003; Schmidt, 2018). Another interesting research area is the development of increasingly high-level languages that encapsulate tens or hundreds of thousands of pages of low-level code into "superfunctions". The Wolfram Language (aka *Mathematica*), for example, allows programmers to implement supervised and unsupervised machine learners with a line or two of code (Bernard, 2017).

Niels Brügger and Ian Milligan: We're seeing a good note of optimism here, as we talk about how tools and programming languages are improving, new research questions can be asked, albeit with some challenges. As this new field comes together, we wonder if we might close our round-doc by asking if you had any recommendations or thoughts for scholars entering this new field? Beyond whether they should learn to program or not, what advice would you give a new entrant to the field?

Matthew Weber: I believe most would agree that computational methods applied in research contexts related to the history of the internet, to digital humanities, or the social sciences, has the potential to open up new avenues of research. I'm optimistic that we are working in an era of academic innovation, and that as scholars working with computational methods we have the opportunity, on the one hand, to look at existing questions in new ways, and, on the other hand, to ask new questions and build new theory. In my current work on local news, my team has been able to look at large subsets of a media ecosystem than ever before, allowing us to analyse and theorise about broad patterns of change with a greater degree of accuracy. Prior work in this space has generally been limited to a single cross-section or a subset of media. While I am knee deep in data, I am energised by the way in which we are able to take a fresh look at questions scholars have been grappling with for decades.

William J. Turkel: I couldn't put it better than Jonas Salk (who was paraphrasing Socrates): "Do what makes your heart leap rather than simply follow some style or fashion" (Salk, 1991).

Federico Nanni: Get in touch with the research community as early as possible, by going to a conference (and RESAW might be the perfect choice) or taking part in an Archives Unleashed Datathon! For me, both have been incredibly enriching experiences during my Ph.D. research.

Sophie Gebeil: The first thing I will say is "you are not alone", there are dynamic research communities on internet studies, the history of the Web in relation to computational methods that are at the origin of an important historiography. Second, I think that neophytes also need to trust each other because innovation comes from taking risks, meeting people, but also sometimes from questions that seemed candid.

Anat Ben-David: It is exciting to learn new methods for historical research. But following William's quote, what "makes my heart leap" is the old-fashioned excitement of archival discovery, and finding the common thread between the computational analysis and the historical narrative.

Notes

1. https://web.archive.org/details/histoire-immigration.fr, consulted on 29 March 2019.
2. See, for instance, how Jockers (2011) described Macroanalysis.
3. https://dh.fbk.eu/technologies/kd
4. See, for instance, the pricing for using the Premium Twitter API, which gives you the possibility of searching the full archive: https://developer.twitter.com/en/pricing.html
5. This is because web archives are a very different type of collection compared to for instance a newspaper archive, upon which traditional topical filtering algorithms are usually tested by the information retrieval community.

Disclosure statement

No potential conflict of interest was reported by the authors.

References

Achlioptas, D. (2003). Database-friendly random projections: Johnson-Lindenstrauss with binary coins. *Journal of Computer and System Sciences*, *66*(4), 671–687. doi:10.1016/S0022-0000(03)00025-4

Ben-David, A., Amram, A., & Bekkerman, R. (2018). The colors of the national Web: Visual data analysis of the historical Yugoslav Web domain. *International Journal on Digital Libraries*, *19*(1), 95–106. doi:10.1007/s00799-016-0202-6

Bernard, E. (2017). Building the automated data scientist: The new classify and predict. Wolfram Blog (10 October 2017). Retrieved from https://blog.wolfram.com/2017/10/10/building-the-automated-data-scientist-the-new-classify-and-predict/

Clifford, J. (2003). *On the edges of anthropology: Interviews*. Chicago, IL: Prickly Paradigm Press.

Crymble, A. (2015). Historians are becoming computer science customers – Postscript. Digital History Seminar. Retrieved from https://ihrdighist.blogs.sas.ac.uk/2015/06/historians-are-becoming-computer-science-customers-postscript/

Eriksson, M., Vonderau, P., Snickars, P., & Fleischer, R. (2019). *Spotify teardown*. Cambridge MA: MIT Press.

Graham, S., Weingart, S., & Milligan, I. (2012). Getting started with topic modeling and MALLET. The Programming Historian. Retrieved from https://programminghistorian.org/en/lessons/topic-modeling-and-mallet

Jockers, M. (2011). On distant reading and macroanalysis. Retrieved from http://www.matthew-jockers.net/2011/07/01/on-distant-reading-and-macroanalysis/

Jockers, M. (2017). Introduction to the Syuzhet package. Retrieved from https://cran.r-project.org/web/packages/syuzhet/vignettes/syuzhet-vignette.html

Le Roy Ladurie, E. (1973). L'historien et l'ordinateur. Le Nouvel Observateur, 05/08/1968.

Lyotard, J.-F., & Chaput, T. (1985). Épreuves d'écriture. Paris: Éditions du Centre Georges Pompidou. Retrieved from https://monoskop.org/images/f/f9/Les_Immateriaux_Epreuves_d_ecriture.pdf

Moretti, G., Sprugnoli, R., & Tonelli, S. (2015). Digging in the dirt: Extracting key phrases from texts with KD. Proceedings of the 2nd Italian Conference on Computational Linguistics, 3-4 December 2015, Trento.

Musiani, F., Paloque-Bergès, C., Schafer, V., & Thierry, B.G. (2019). *Qu'est-ce qu'une archive du web?* Marseille: OpenEdition Press.

Nanni, F. (2017). Reconstructing a website's lost past: Methodological issues concerning the history of www.unibo.it. *Digital Humanities Quarterly*, *11*(2), 1.

Salk, J. (1991). Interview with Jonas Salk. Academy of Achievement. Retrieved from https://www.achievement.org/achiever/jonas-salk-m-d/#interview

Schmidt, B. (2018, October 3). Stable random projection: Lightweight, general-purpose dimensionality reduction for digitized libraries. *Journal of Cultural Analytics*. doi:10.31235/osf.io/36neu

Index

Note: Endnotes are indicated by the page number followed by 'n' and the endnote number e.g., 20n1 refers to endnote 1 on page 20.